Caroline Howard Gilman

Stories and Poems by Mother And Daughter

Caroline Howard Gilman

Stories and Poems by Mother And Daughter

ISBN/EAN: 9783744713597

Printed in Europe, USA, Canada, Australia, Japan

Cover: Foto ©Thomas Meinert / pixelio.de

More available books at **www.hansebooks.com**

WHO IS THIS BOY?—Page 32.

Stories and Poems
by Mother & Daughter.

LEE & SHEPARD
BOSTON

LEE, SHEPARD & DILLINGHAM — NEW-YORK.

STORIES AND POEMS,

BY

MOTHER AND DAUGHTER.

CAROLINE GILMAN,

AND

CAROLINE HOWARD JERVEY.

ILLUSTRATED.

BOSTON:
LEE & SHEPARD.

NEW YORK:
LEE, SHEPARD, & DILLINGHAM.
1872.

Entered, according to Act of Congress, in the year 1872,
By LEE & SHEPARD,
In the office of the Librarian of Congress, at Washington.

Electrotyped and Printed by ALFRED MUDGE & SON,
34 School Street, Boston, Mass.

CONTENTS.

POEMS FOR CHILDREN OF ALL AGES.
By Mrs. Caroline Gilman.

	PAGE
The Bird's Nest	11
Fanny	11
The Plea for the Mouse	12
The Kite	12
Who made the Flowers	12
The Infant's Grave	13
Talking Pertly	13
Call to Sunday School	14
The Sailor's Daughter	14
Annie in the Graveyard	14
The Schoolboy and his Eight Troubles	15
Evening Hymns	21
Home Lectures	21
Youth	21
Of Such is the Kingdom of Heaven	22
The Child's Wish in June	23
The American Boy	23
What Would *You* Choose?	24
The Dumb Lunatic	28
Jairus' Daughter	28

CONTENTS.

	PAGE
Invitation to a Bird	29
The Little Birds' Answer	29
New Year's Day	30
The Sleeping Baby	30
Father Takes Me Up	30
The Boat	30
Poor Willie	31
Invitation to the Ant	31
The Ant's Answer	31
Who is this Boy?	32
Nancy Ray	32
"Jesus Took Little Children in His Arms"	32
The Youngest One	33
To a Butterfly at Church	33
Mother, What is Death?	33
Wishes	34
Jephthah's Rash Vow	35
Thought on Zerlina Thorn	37
On the Christening of a Little Child	37
To ——	38
The Mysterious Chair	38
Flight of the Muskoyco Indian	40
Maiden and the Marine	41
The Child on the Ocean	42
Seventeen	42
Joshua's Courtship	43
Mary Ann Gibbs of Stored	43
The Sentinel	48
Thoughts on the Portrait of Stuart's Washington	48

STORIES AND TALES FOR THE YOUNG.
By Mrs. Caroline Gilman.

	PAGE
Holidays at the Plantation	51
The Boy Who Wished it would Rain Money	60
Punctuation	65
Master Dicky Bluff	67
A Little Girl that Bites her Nails	68
The New Scholar	69
Cinder Claws	71
St. Nicholas	73
The Masks	76
The Wagon Boy	85
A Sullivan's Island Story	87
The Young Mathematician	102
Tiny Tella	105
The May Day Wreath	107
The French Traveller	109
The Missionaries	115
Mr. Niblo, the Bashful Lecturer	128
The Young Conspirators	139
Good Night	152
The Lost Mail	153
Mr. Inklin	166

FAIRY LAND, AND OTHER TALES.
By Mrs. Caroline H. Jervey.

Fairy Land	177
Lost and Found	196
Thoughts About the Moon	197
What Becomes of Pins	199

	PAGE
The Rich Child and the Poor Child	208
The Mouse Who Went to See the World	209
Nice Habits	218
Bad Temper and its Cure	219
Lillian	237
"I Wish I Had"	239
Our Father Who Art in Heaven	249
Morning and Evening Prayer	249
The Wish Granted	250
The Little Garden	260
Ten Stops	261
The School-Girl's Quarrel	261
The Wind	264
The Bird that Flew in through the Window	265
The Broken Necklace	266
Turn Away	283
The Fall from the Swing	284
Whitfield	290
Day and Night	291

OUR WELCOME TO YOUNG READERS.

BY MRS. CAROLINE GILMAN.

WHAT children come with busy feet,
Our double offering now to greet?
Here's Eliza, here is Sue,
Here is bright-eyed Sarah, too!
Here are Mary and Maria,
Here are Peter and Sophia;
Here are Thomas and Amelia,
Here is Charles, and here Cornelia;
Isaac, with his laughing eye,
And pleasant Julius standing by.
Here is David, here is Arthur,
Here are Rosamond and Martha,
Here are Benjamin and James,
'T is hard to think of all their names.
Here are Joe and Henrietta,
Here are George and Violetta;
There Lois now extends her hands,
And Lilian for our welcome stands,
While Georgia turns her pretty head,
To find young Roland near her tread.
Matilda gently comes along,
While Philip, too, is in the throng.
Here are Catherine and Theresa,
Christiana and Louisa,
Esther and young Margaret,
Emeline and Harriet.
Frederic and Adeline,
Justina sweet, and Valentine.
Here are Nathan and Eugene,
While Archibald comes in between.
Here are Jane and Theodore,
Rosaline and Eleanor;
Here are Lucy and Pamelia,
With Alonzo and Cecelia;
Here is Henry close to Sam,
You can't think how confused I am.
Here comes Virginia and Stephen,
And Mary Ann to make it even.
Here is Charlotte, here is Ellen,
Here is Francis, here is Helen;
Here's Rebecca, next to Ruth,
The children puzzle me in truth!
Here is Clara with Susannah,
And Alexander following Hannah;
Here's Nathaniel come to meet me,
And Valeria runs to greet me,
Now Amanda trips before,
Daniel, and Emma, and some more;
Robert and Ephraim skipping too,

And Richard, with his "How d'ye do.
Octavius hastens full of fun, —
Here Caroline and Julia run.
See William and young Lydia meet,
And Abby close on Frances' feet.
See Laura, Horace, Isabel,
Edward and John, I know them well,
Eugenia, Edith, Maurice, too,
And Alfred all of them in view.
Augustus and Elizabeth, —
But stop and let me catch my breath;
Here are Louis and Floranthe;
Here are Agnes and Ianthe,
Here is blushing Adelaide,
And Clarissa, the pretty maid.
Joanna too, and Amy, see,
'T is fortunate they all agree.

But listen, listen, what a noise!
Here run another troop of boys;
Andrew and Edmund shouting loud,
And Christopher to swell the crowd.
Edwin and Gilbert following on,
Bertha, too, and Jonathan.
Lawrence, Alice, Jacob, too,
And after Louis, master Hugh,
Owen, and Patrick; — are these all?
Oh, no; here Walter comes with Paul,
And hand in hand with little Annie,
My darling neighbor, black-eyed Fanny.
Now children, dear, go read your book,
And on the pretty pictures look;
I hope you'll take as much delight in
Reading, as I have in writing.

POEMS

FOR CHILDREN OF ALL AGES,

BY

MRS. CAROLINE GILMAN.

FANNY.— Page 11.

POEMS FOR CHILDREN
OF ALL AGES.

THE BIRD'S NEST.

ON a bright and pleasant day,
  John and James went out to play:
As they stopp'd a while to rest,
On a tree they spied a nest,
Pretty eggs were lying there,
Pretty eggs all placed with care.

"Come," says Johnny, with a laugh,
"You and I will each take half;
And the rest we'll give to Ann."
So towards the tree they ran.

Just then, upon a branch they heard
The fluttering of the mother-bird,
And a note that seem'd to say,
"Will you take my eggs away,

"When I've made my nest with care,
And put them all so nicely there?
Oh, do not, pray, my nest destroy!
Have pity on me, little boy.

"When you in the cradle lay,
No one took you far away,
Safe you were, and smil'd and smil'd,
A little bright and happy child.

"And your mother loved you so,
Better than you e'er can know.
Then do not take my nest away,
Little boy, I beg and pray."

John and James said not a word,
And their little hearts were stirr'd;
They wip'd their eyes and went to play,
And felt quite happy all that day.

FANNY.

THERE'S not a little girl I meet,
  Not even Sue or Annie,
That seems to me more fair and sweet
  Than my young neighbor, Fanny.

'Tis not because her eyes are black,
  And look so bright and funny;
'Tis not because her breath is pure,
  As new-mown hay or honey.

'Tis not because at dancing-school
  Her step is light and airy,
Or that she skips about the house
  Just like a little fairy.

'Tis not because in *Worcester*
　She learns a "*monstrous*" column ;
Nor that she sits in company
　Sometimes quite still and solemn.

Nor is it that her little hands
　She waves about so gaily,
When telling every artless thought
　That fills her bosom daily.

It is because *good-nature* comes
　To light each limb and feature,
That Fanny always seems to me
　A charming little creature.

THE PLEA FOR THE MOUSE.

OH, ma, speak to my pussy and
　　kitty ;
　They are dragging all over the house,
Without any mercy or pity,
　A poor little **innocent mouse !**

I hate to see such wicked cunning,
　For pussy allows it to go,
And just as the mouse thinks **of** run-
　　ning,
　She catches and teases it so.

MOTHER.

My son, our old puss cannot reason,
　And, therefore, she is not a sinner ;
Perhaps this is not hungry season,
　And this teasing is cooking her
　　dinner.

But when *children*, **my** darling, are
　　cruel,
　And injure the brutes heaven made,
They sully the beautiful jewel,
　That with a kind heart is inlaid.

THE KITE.

OH look at my kite,
　In its airy flight ;
How **gaily it flies,**
Right **up to the skies,**
With **its white breast stirr'd,**
Just like a bird !

Pretty kite, pretty kite,
In your airy flight,
What do you spy,
In the bright blue sky ?

I wish I were you,
To be there, too,
Oh, then, how soon
I would peep at the **moon,**

And see the man **there,**
Who gives me **a stare,**
When I **look up** at night
At his beautiful light !

WHO MADE THE FLOWERS?

A LITTLE child, who loves to see
　The bright sun shining clear,
Is often asking, "Where is He
　Who placed the bright sun here ?"

She sees the moonlight's silver gleam,
　And stars with twinkling ray,
And says, "Who made that gentle
　　beam,
Almost more fair than day ?"

She gathers for her mother **dear**
　A blossom rich and fair,
And asks, "Who placed these colors
　　here,
　And mixed them with such care ?"

'Tis God, my child, who will impart
  More glorious objects still,
A temper mild, a feeling heart,
  And strength to do His will.

THE INFANT'S GRAVE.

Come, mother, will you go and see
  Where little brother lies?
"I cannot, love, for if I should,
  The tears would dim my eyes.

"Not yet, not yet — I cannot gaze
  Upon that chilly clod!
Better it is for me to think
  That he is with his God.

"A few short months, and grass will
    grow
  Over his little grave,
And then, perhaps, the churchyard
    flower
  Will spring and gently wave.

"Then will we go, and I will see
  Where my sweet baby lies;
For God will soothe my breaking heart,
  And dry my weeping eyes."

TALKING PERTLY.

Mamma, I've lost my thimble,
  And my spool has roll'd away;
My arms are aching dreadfully,
  And I want to go and play.

I've spent the livelong morning,
  Picking out this endless seam,
So many pieces in a shirt,
  Is quite a foolish scheme.

If I could set the fashion,
  I know what I would do;
I'd not be troubling people,
  And make them sit and sew.

I'd put some homespun on their necks,
  And sew it all around;
And make them look like cotton bags,
  Placed endwise on the ground.

I hate to make these button-holes,
  I do not love to stitch;
My threads keep breaking all the time,
  With just a little twitch.

There's Johnny playing marbles,
  And Susan skipping rope;
They have finished all their easy tasks,
  While I must sit and mope.

I think, mamma, 'tis very hard,
  That you should keep me here,
When the blue sky looks so temptingly,
  And the sun is shining clear.

Mamma! She's gone and left me,
  And closely shut the door;
Mamma, mamma, come back again!
  I will not grumble more.

Oh, dear, how foolish I have been! —
  From dinner I must stay;
Mamma, mamma, come back again!
  Forgive your child, I pray.

Alas, she's reached the balcony,
  And means not to return!
Oh, what a look she cast on me,
  So sad and yet so stern!

CALL TO SUNDAY SCHOOL.

WAKE, sister, wake, 'tis a holy day;
  We must not linger here;
The birds are up, and have soared away,
  And are singing their anthems clear.

Young flowers have open'd their lovely eyes,
  And their rich perfume have given;
And they fix their looks on the distant skies,
  As if they knew something of Heaven.

We will go to the house of praise and prayer,
  The altar of youthful love;
And Jesus in spirit will meet us there,
  And bear our off'ring above.

Then wake, sister, wake, 'tis a happy day;
  Perchance from his blessed throng
Some youthful seraph has winged his way,
  To join in our Sunday-song.

THE SAILOR'S DAUGHTER.

SAFE rolls the the ship at anchor now,
The sailor clears his anxious brow,
And with a deep, but silent vow
  Blesses his little daughter.

His duty far has bid him roam,
Amid the dash of ocean foam,
But welcome now the sailor's home,
  And she, his little daughter!

Her velvet arm is o'er him thrown,
Her words breathe forth a gladsome tone,
He feels that she is all his own,—
  The seaman's little daughter.

"Father you shall not quit your child,
And go upon the seas so wild,
For scarcely has my mother smiled
  Upon her little daughter.

"We care not for the coral gay,
Nor costly shells when you're away;
Dear father, with my mother stay,
  And love your little daughter.

We hear the fierce wind rushing by,
And then my mother heaves a sigh;
And when it storms we sit and cry—
  My mother and your daughter."

Her head upon his shoulder lay,
He smoothed her silken ringlets' play,—
She fell asleep in that sweet way,—
  The sailor's little daughter.

ANNIE IN THE GRAVEYARD.

SHE bounded o'er the graves
  With a buoyant step of mirth;
She bounded o'er the graves
Where the weeping willow waves,
  Like a creature not of earth.

Her hair was blown aside,
  And her eyes were glittering bright;
Her hair was blown aside,
And her little hands spread wide,
  With an innocent delight.

She spelt the lettered word
  That registers the dead,
She spelt the lettered word,
And her busy thoughts were stirred
  With pleasure as she read.

She stopped and culled a leaf
  Left fluttering on a rose,
She stopped and culled a leaf
Pure monument of grief,
  That in our churchyard grows.

She culled it with a smile,
  'Twas near her sister's mound;
She culled it with a smile,
And played with it awhile,
  Then scattered it around.

I did not chill her heart
  Nor turn its gush to tears;
I did not chill her heart;
Oh, bitter drops will start
  Full soon in coming years.

THE SCHOOLBOY AND HIS EIGHT TROUBLES.

THE BOY IS COLD.

I THINK I might get near the grate,
  My toes they grow colder and colder;
I am sure I wish, early and late,
  That I could be bigger and older.

There's grandma' stowed close by the fire,
  And she's managed to squeeze in my brother;
Aunt Polly has got her desire,
  And sits like a toast next to mother.

My teeth they all shake in my head,
  And my hands are like skimm'd milk so blue;
And my feet feel as if they were dead,
  And I'm sure I can't tell what to do.

I have tried once or twice to go near,
  And they cry out, "Oh, don't be a baby,
Run about and you'll warm yourself, dear;"
  They think I've no feeling then, may be.

I just wish that from now till to-morrow
  They and I could change fingers and toes,
And then they'd find out to their sorrow,
  How a fellow must feel when he's *froze*.

THE BOY'S COMPLAINT.

OH, mother, won't you speak to Kate?
  I have not had enough to eat:
And when she spreads a little bread
  She thinks she gives me such a treat.

I only wish I was a man,
  To have my butter an inch thick,

And not be talking all the time,
 How this and that will make me sick.

Poor little boys are sadly used,
 They cannot have the thing **they wish;**
 While grown-up people help themselves
 To what they like from every dish.

As soon **as** I become a man,
 I'll have a pie as tall as you,
 With door and windows like a house,
 And lin'd with plums all through and
 through.

And I'll go **in whene'er I choose,**
 And sit as snug as Jacky Horner;
 And even Katey, though she's cross,
 Shall sometimes come and at a cor-
 ner.

My windows **all** with jelly made,
 Like Boston glass shall glisten bright,
 And sugar candy for the frames,
 At every turn shall meet my sight.

My floors shall be of gingerbread,
 Because that's pretty hard, you **know,**
 Sanded all o'er with sugar plums,
 Rolling about where'er I go.

And mother, Kate, my cellaret
 Shall be all butter, shap'd with ice,
 And then we'll see if I must fret
 Because I want a little slice.

And mother,—oh, she's gone away!
 And Katey,—what,—you've left me,
 too?
 I won't stand talking to the walls,—
 But go and find some work to do.

THE DRUMSTICK.

IT seems very strange, and I can't
 make it out,
 Why the drumstick is given to me;
 I think I deserve a nice part of the fowl,
 Yet forever **the drumstick** I see.

I pass the white meat **to Miss Ander-**
 son's plate,
 And old Mr. Rich takes **the** thighs;
 The side-bones go off at a terrible rate,
 And the pinion to Sister Ann flies.

If I were **to count** all the drumsticks
 I've had
 Since the pap-spoon was taken away,
 And I've sitten **at table with women
 and men,**
 You would hardly believe what I say.

'T is said **that a part helps a part, and
 I'm sure,**
 If that is the state of the case,
 I think I can enter before very long
 With "Bonnets of Blue" for a race.

I'm sure I'm not greedy, but really, papa,
 If you give me the drumstick again,
 Your son, in the place of a leg **like**
 your own,
 Will exhibit the **shank of a crane.**

THE NEW BOOTS.

COME, mother, and look at these
 beautiful boots,
 Just hear what an elegant **creak!**
 I declare, there's no word so sweet in
 the world,
 As that which a new boot can speak!

Take care, sister Anna, don't come in
my way,
Run farther, you troublesome chit,—
You would look at my boots? Oh, very
well, dear,
Come and see how completely they fit.

Why, really, the child has a share of
good taste,
Just see her admiring gaze!
Come, come, sister Nanny, and sit in
my lap,
Little children have such pretty ways.

Pray, mamma, don't look anxiously
down at my toes,
I assure you they don't hurt at all;
They only *look* tight, as is often the
case,
I would not have bought them too
small.

Young Loring and I chose our boots
at one store, —
His foot is the size of my own;
But really, mamma, he bought his so
large,
That he looks like a clown overgrown.

Hark! Toney is coming, — now don't
say a word,
Just see how his white eyes will shine.
Hear, Toney, my boy, what an elegant
creak
Proceeds from these new boots of
mine!

Did you ever behold a fit more com-
plete?
Why turn your big eyes to the wall?

"He new, and he bright, Massa Johnny,
for true,
And *pride neber feel pain at all.*"

OH, mamma, I am mortified, hurt
and ashamed,
And scarce can look up in your face:
Young Loring, who never could beat
me before,
Has beat me to day in a race.

You laugh! I would thank you, ma',
never to laugh,
As you do when I speak in this style;
I think I would sometimes prefer to
be whipped
Than to see that half-comical smile.

Well, mamma, we were walking just
out of the town,
When Loring proposed we should
run;
You know what a fellow I am for a
race,
And I thought to have excellent fun.

So we started together, the boys look-
ing on,
My boots felt as tight as a vise;
I hobbled and stumbled, just ready to
fall,
While Loring was off in a trice.

The boys shouted, "New boots, run,
new boots, hurrah!"
Their ridicule went to my soul;
I hopped like a turkey, and was not
half way,
When Loring was safe at the goal.

My toes were all cramp'd and my ankles
    were sore,
    And I made such a shocking grimace,
That Loring, though he's such **a gen-
tleman**, ma',
    Could not help laughing out in my
    face.

And big Billy Blackford took out his
hair comb,
    And said, as he sat on the grass,
" Though your boots spoil your racing,
they'll serve a good turn,
    And answer right well for a glass."

Pray, hand me my old boots, dear **ma**,
if you please,
    And Toney, do stretch these a bit;
No grinning, you rogue, they're scarcely
too small,
    Just **stretch them; I *know* they will
fit.**

THE BOY IN TROUBLE.

NOW look at this hat! is it fit **to
be seen**,
    All battered and tattered and torn?
I can't go to King street to get an ice-
cream,—
    I declare, it is not to be *borne*.

Nay, mother, you need not be shaking
your head,
    And looking as much as **to say**,
That you think I am **careless, and all**
about that,
    In your solemn, but good-natur'd way.

I am sure that American hats are **not
strong**,
    Or they never would wear out so
    fast, —
And here I must worry till Christmas,
you say,—
    I do n't think **this old thing will last**.

To be sure, I have kicked **it about for**
a ball
    And stuff'd it with ginger cake, **too**;
And once I let it drop into Bennett's
mill pond
    While paddling in William's canoe.

And once, I remember, I felt very **dry**,
    And just fill'd it up at the pump;
And once I was hunting with Dinah for
eggs,
    And gave it **a *terrible* thump**.

I confess **the two** kittens *did* make it
their bed,
    But then they were white as the snow,
And puss laid them carefully into the
hat,
    So I could not refuse her, you know.

This dent on the top was an accident,
ma',
    And *that* **cut** on the edge was **an-
other**;
And *this* stain with the physic you gave
me one day,
    And *that* hole, I got playing **with**
brother.

Master Robert call'd yesterday, dress'd
quite in style,
    And asked me to go out to ride,

But I had to say no, for a terrible sight
  My old hat would have been by his
  side.

And Miss Emma came also, **that sweet**
  little **girl**,
  And I wanted to see her home so,
  With her little straw bonnet, all trimm'd
  up with blue,
  But how shabby **I look'd for a beau.**

Oh, dear! **I must wait as** I have done
  before,
  Since dollars appear very few,
  But I tell you when once I get rid of
  this hat,
  I mean to take care of the new.

NOT READY FOR SCHOOL.

PRAY, where is my hat? It is
  taken away,
  And my shoe-strings are all in a knot!
  I can't find a thing where it should be
  to-day,
  Though I've hunted in every spot.

My slate and my pencil nowhere can be
  found,
  Though I placed them as safe as can
  be ;
  While my books and my maps are all
  scattered around,
  And hop about just like a flea.

Do, Rachel, just look for my atlas up
  stairs,
  My Æsop is somewhere **there,** too ;

And, sister, just brush down these troub-
  lesome hairs,
  And, mother, just fasten my shoe.

And, sister, beg father to write **an**
  excuse ;
  But stop, he will only say " No " ;
  And go on with a smile, and keep **read-**
  ing the news,
  While everything bothers me so.

My satchel is heavy, and ready to fall,
  This old pop-gun is breaking my map ;
  I'll have nothing to do with the pop-
  gun or ball,
  There's no playing for such a poor
  chap.

**The town clock will strike in a minute,
  I fear,
  Then away** to the foot I must sink ;
  There, look at my Eaton has tumbled
  **down here,
  And my** Worcester's covered with ink.

I wish I'd not lingered at breakfast the
  last,
  Though the toast and the butter were
  fine ;
  I think that our Edward must eat pretty
  fast,
  To be off when I haven't done mine.

Now Edward **and Harry protest they**
  won't wait,
  And beat on the door with their
  sticks ;
  I suppose they will say *I was dressing
  too late ;*
  To-morrow, *I'll be up at six.*

IN TOO GREAT A HURRY.

NOW, mother, don't laugh, because
    I've returned
Without a new hat on my head;
I am sure I am weary as weary can be,
    And puzzled enough, as you said.

In the first place, I went to those big-
    looking stores,
    Where the caps all so splendidly
shine;
But **the caps** looked so stylish I could
not decide,
    If a hat or a cap should be **mine.**

An elegant blue cap delighted me first,
    Which I felt quite determined **to**
buy;
But just as I found that **it fitted my**
head,
    A brown one attracted my eye.

I put on the brown, and it set like a **T**,
    So I took out the money to pay;
When Johnny came in, said, "Don't **be**
in haste;
    You have not been to Smith's store
to-day."

I looked at the pretty brown cap as he
spoke.
    John urged, though I wanted to
linger;
"Why the **fashion at** Smith's is **as**
handsome again,"
    And he snapped at my brown with
his finger.

So, mother, I thought I would look **at**
his choice,
    For 'tis right to look out for the best;
And an elegant sight I confess was dis-
played;
    There were black, brown, and blue,
and the rest.

I first tried on one, and **then tried an-**
other;
    One was large, and the other **too**
small;
The clock then struck three, and I had
to come home
    Without bringing any at all.

I know I was stubborn, and said **I**
would go,
    But I've tried it enough **to my sor-**
row;
So I hope you'll **forgive me this time,**
mother **dear,**
    And I'll **take what you choose** me
to-morrow.

CANNOT WRITE POETRY.

MY paper is ruled very neat,
    Father's made me an *elegant*
pen;
I sit quite upright on my seat,
    And have everything ready; **what**
then?

I have scratched my head several times,
    And nothing comes out of it yet;
For my life I **can't** make **out the**
rhymes;
    Not a word can I think of but—*fret.*

Dear mother, do help me a bit,
  I'm puzzled, — no matter, — here goes, —
But how the right measure to hit, —
  I have a good subject, — I know-s.

There was once a widow in trouble,
  She was aged and old, and advanced;
Not a word can I think of but *bubble*,
  And it won't do to say that she danced.

A widow she was of great feeling,
  Of great feeling this widow was she;
'Twill be shocking to speak of her squealing,
  And how can I lug in a flea!

This widow to woe was a votary,
  Oh, mother! you laugh at her woes,
And say I had better quit poetry,
  Until I know how to write prose.

EVENING HYMN.

'TIS evening, and the skies
  With starry lights are spread;
How very fair the moonbeams rise,
  And silver radiance shed!

I will retire to rest,
  'Neath Heaven's o'er-arching sky,
And feel my nightly visions blest,
  For God is watching by.

And if the wing of death
  Should sweep o'er my repose,
Resign'd, I'll yield to Him my breath,
  And rise as Jesus rose.

HOME-SICKNESS.

THE morning sun shines brightly,
  But it shineth not for me;
The breeze is blowing lightly,
  But my spirit is not free.

There's many a hand to meet me,
  But mine is sadly given;
I thank the friends who greet me,
  But my heart is chilled and riven.

My former home was lowly,
  And this is rich and rare;
But to me 'tis melancholy,
  And that was bright and fair.

I know here is much smiling,
  And graceful, easy mirth,
And ways of kind beguiling,
  And words of gentle birth;

And I try to check my sadness,
  And look as bright as they,
And call a fitful gladness
  To wile the long, long day.

If I could but see my mother,
  And press her cheek to mine,
Or take my darling brother, —
  My arms about him twine.

If e'en my loving dog were here,
  To eat from out my hand,
I think I should not shed a tear
  Amid this stranger band.

YOUTH.

I SAW a streamlet flow,
  With sparkles bright and free,

Still dancing to and fro,
  To meet the rolling sea.

It heeded not the rock,
  Whose shadow frown'd about;
It heeded not the shock
  Of gnarl'd roots spreading out.

And **when** a careless hand
  Disturb'd its sparkling breast,
And loos'd its wavy band,
  It dimpled into rest.

On, **on the** streamlet went
  Beneath the burning noon;
And onward in content
  Beneath the midnight moon.

And thus in gay delight
  Does youth in beauty play
Through **visions of the** night,
  And **pastimes of** the day.

"OF SUCH IS THE KINGDOM OF HEAVEN."

O, WHY should children fear
  When sickness dims the eye,
To spread their spirits' wings
  And soar beyond the sky;
Since Jesus Christ his word has given,
That such as they shall enter Heaven?

Then weep not, parents dear,
  Because we go above;
We leave you here below
  To seek our Father's love;
For Jesus Christ his word has given,
That such as we shall enter Heaven.

Sigh **not o'er** our pale brows,
  Where **death** has set his seal;
Nor shrink at **those chill** hands
  That have **no power** to feel;
For Jesus Christ **his** word has given,
That such as *we* shall **enter Heaven.**

Muse often on our graves,
  But not in stern despair;
Celestial thoughts will spring
  And teach kind lessons there;
And ask if Christ his word has given,
That parted friends shall enter Heaven.

Let our young playmates come,
  And view the grassy mound,
And plant their early flowers,
  As if 'twere happy ground;
For Jesus Christ **his word has given,**
That such as **they shall enter Heaven.**

Let old men wander **here,**
  And with **a** natural sigh,
Think why we've reached our home
  When they are lingering by;
And ask if Christ his word has given,
That their gray hairs shall enter Heaven.

And let the wordly come,—
  Pause on their busy way,
And while a transient tear
  Drops for our lifeless clay,
Ask their own hearts if Christ has given
His word that they shall **enter Heaven.**

Let sinners come alone,
  And bow down o'er our dust,

And crush each wicked thought,
　And seek a better trust;
For Christ to them sweet hope has given,
That if repentant, theirs is Heaven.

We pray that all may come
　This solemn truth to see
If dust to dust, then soul to soul,
　Must be the great decree.

Where can so bless'd a spot be given
To learn of God and think of Heaven?

THE CHILD'S WISH IN JUNE.

MOTHER, mother, the winds are at play,
Prithee, let me be idle to-day.
Look, dear mother, the flowers all lie
Languidly under the bright blue sky.

See, how slowly the streamlet glides,
Look, how the violet roguishly hides;
Even the butterfly rests on the rose,
And scarcely sips the sweets as he goes.

Poor Tray is asleep in the noonday sun,
And the flies go about him one by one;
And pussy sits near with a sleepy grace,
Without ever thinking of washing her face.

There flies a bird to a neighboring tree,
But very lazily flieth he,
And he sits and twitters a gentle note,
That scarcely ruffles his little throat.

You bid me be busy; but, mother, hear
How the humdrum grasshopper sound-
　eth near,
And the soft west wind is so light in its
　play,
It scarcely moves a leaf on the spray.

I wish, oh, I wish I was yonder cloud,
That sails about with its misty shroud;
Books and work I no more would view,
And I'd come and float, dear mother,
　o'er you.

THE AMERICAN BOY.

LOOK up, my young American,
　Stand firmly on the earth,
Where noble deeds and mental power
　Yield titles over birth.

A hallowed land thou claim'st, my boy,
　By early struggles bought,
Heaped up with noble memories,
　And wide, — ay, wide as thought.

On the high Alleghany's range,
　Awake thy joyous song;
Then o'er our green savannas stray,
　And gentler notes prolong.

Awake it 'mid the rushing peal,
　Of old Niagara's voice,
Or by our ocean-rivers stand,
　And in their might rejoice.

What though we boast no ancient tow-
　ers,
　Where ivied streamers twine;
The laurel lives upon our shores;
　The laurel, boy, is thine.

What though no "minster lifts its
　cross,"
　Tinged by the sunset fire?

Freely religion's voices swell
  Round every village spire.

And who shall gaze on yon blue **sea**,
  If thou must turn away,
When young Columbia's **stripes and
  stars
Are floating in the day?**

Who thunders louder when the strife
  Of gathering war is heard?
Who ranges farther when the call
  Of commerce' voice is heard?

What though on Cressy's distant field
  Thy gaze may not be cast,
While through long centuries of blood
  Rise spectres of the past?

The *future* wakes thy dreamings high,
  And thou a note mayest claim

Aspiring, which in after times
  Shall swell the trump of fame.

Yet scenes *are* here for patriot thought:
  Here sleep **the good and brave**;
Here kneel, **my boy, and altars raise**
  Above the martyr's **grave.**

On Moultrie's isle, on Bunker**'s height,**
  On Monmouth's bloody line,
On Eutaw's field, on Yorktown's bank,
  Erect thy loyal shrine.

**And when thou art told of knighthood's
  shields,**
  And English battles won,
Look up, my boy, and **breath one
  word,—**
  The name of **WASHINGTON.**

WHAT WOULD *YOU* CHOOSE.

CHOICE OF COUNTRIES.

FATHER.

I WOULD cross the wide Atlantic,
  And the cliffs of England hail,
For there my country's fathers
  First set their western sail.
I would view its domes and palaces,
  And tread each learned hall,
And on the spot were Newton trod,
  My foot should proudly fall.
I would gaze upon its landscapes,
  The dell and sunny glade,
And tread with awe the cloistered aisles,
  Where Addison is laid.

LOUISA.

I would seek the Indian Ocean,
  Where the sea-shell loves to grow,
Where the tints upon its bosom
  In gorgeous beauty glow.
I would chase the parting billow
  For treasures new and rare,
And with wreaths of blushing **coral**
  Entwine my waving hair.

CAROLINE.

I would be a ship's commander,
  And find the northern pole,
While o'er untravelled oceans

My venturous bark should roll;
Or I'd seek untrodden islands,
  Amid Antarctic seas,
And the standard of my country
  Plant first before the breeze.

ELIZA.

Oh, give me Carolina,
  My dear, my native home!
From her fair and sheltering borders
  I ask not e'er to roam.
My school-mates here are playing,
  My parents dear I see;
Oh, give me Carolina,
  She is dear enough for me!

ANNA.

I do not know where England is,
  Or any other place,
But I love to frolic with my puss,
  And see her wash her face.
I'll keep close by my baby-house,
  And be very good all day,
If one I love will dress my dolls,
  And let me have my way.

MOTHER.

The whole broad earth is beautiful,
  To minds attuned aright,
And wheresoe'er my feet have turned,
  A smile has met my sight.
The city, with its bustling walk,
  Its splendor, wealth and power, —
A ramble by the river side,
  A passing summer flower;
The meadow green, the ocean's swell,
  The forest waving free,
Are gifts of God, and speak in tones
  Of kindliness to me.

And, oh! where'er my lot is cast,
  Where'er my footsteps roam,
If those I love are near to me,
  I feel that spot my home.

CHOICE OF HOURS.

FATHER.

I LOVE to walk at twilight
  When sunset nobly dies,
And see the parting splendor
  That lightens up the skies,
And call up old remembrances
  Deep, dim as evening gloom,
Or look to heaven's promises,
  Like starlight on a tomb.

LAURA.

I love the hour of darkness,
  When I give myself to sleep,
And I think that holy angels
  Their watch around me keep.
My dreams are light and happy,
  As I innocently lie,
For my mother's kiss is on my cheek,
  And my father's step is nigh.

MARY.

I love the social afternoon,
  When lessons all are said,
Geography is laid aside,
  And grammar put to bed;
Then a walk upon the battery
  With a friend is very sweet,
And some money for an ice cream
  To give that friend a treat.

MOTHER.

I love the Sabbath evening
  When my dear ones sit around,

And tell of all their feelings
  By hope and fancy crowned;
And though some plants are missing,
  In that sweetly thoughtful hour,
I will **not** call them back again
  To earth's decaying bower.

CHOICE OF PAINTINGS.

WILLIAM.

I CHOOSE the racked Ixion,
  With his fierce and **burning pain**;
I love to see the pencil's **touch**
  Such awful mastery gain.

LADY.

Yet let the thrilling punishment
  Its moral truth inspire,
And keep your spirit pure, my son,
  Untouched by base desire.

LITTLE ELIZA.

I'll take the watermelon,
  With seeds so black and nice,
And give my little playmates,
  All round, a famous slice.
But oh! 'tis but a picture,
  And **on** a summer's day,
If they would not let me eat it,
  I would wish it far away.

HENRY.

Give me the brave Napoleon,
  With his war steed thundering by,
Where the snowy Alps majestical,
  Look upward to the sky.

LADY.

Oh! **boy,** that conqueror leaped **o'er** *hearts,*
  With reckless cravings **too,**
While his own was cold and **tempest-stirred,**
  As the mountain scene you view.

LITTLE JOHN.

I choose the views **of Liliput,**
  Where the tiny **people play,**
Looking with great astonishment,
  At birds more large than they.

While two of them with all their might,
  Attempt an egg to roll;
And some are diving, quite alarmed,
  Within a little bowl.

GEORGE.

Oh! give me Ariadne,
  With her **soft and dewy eye,**
Her lip of glowing coral,
  And her forehead fair and high.
I feel th' Ægean breezes,
  As they fan her braided hair,
And **cool her** chastened beauties,
  Nor leave a dark tinge there.

MARIA.

I love the finished manliness,
  That dwells on Bacchus' brow—
Where Earth and Inspiration,
  Seem boldly mingling **now.**
The sunny hue of India
  Glows burning on his cheek,
And lights those lips so eloquent,
  That ask not words to speak.

LADY.

Yes! o'er the form that Guido limned
  Our eyes enraptured stray,
And thrill with sudden joyousness,
  As if 'twere new to-day.

Fine chain of soul-formed sympathy,
  Electrical and strong,
Which, touched with by-gone intellect,
  Through time is borne along.

I bless you, bright creations
  Of painting's magic art,
Where classic dreams of poetry
  In local beauty start.
Ye raise our cramped and earth-bound
    souls
  To his creative power,
Whose sacred touch omnipotent
  Gives genius its high power.

CHOICE OF OCCUPATIONS.

JOHN.

I MEAN to be a soldier,
  With uniform quite new;
I wish they'd let me have a drum,
  And be a captain too;
I would go amid the battle
  With my broadsword in my hand,
And hear the cannon rattle,
  And the music all so grand.

MOTHER.

My son, my son! what if that sword
  Should strike a noble heart,
And bid some loving father
  From his little ones depart!

LOUISA.

I mean to be a cottage girl,
  And sit beside a rill,
And morn and eve my pitcher there
  With purest water fill;
And I'll train a lovely woodbine
  Around my cottage door,
And welcome to my winter hearth
  The wandering and the poor.

MOTHER.

Louisa, dear, an humble mind
  'Tis beautiful to see,
And you shall never hear a word,
  To check that mind from me:
But ah! remember, pride may dwell
  Beneath the woodbine's shade;
And discontent, a sullen guest,
  The cottage hearth invade.

CAROLINE.

I will be gay and courtly,
  And dance away the hours;
Music, and sport, and joy shall dwell
  Beneath my fairy bowers;
No heart shall ache with sadness
  Within my laughing hall,
But the note of love and gladness
  Re-echo to my call.

MOTHER.

O, children, sad it makes my soul
  To hear your playful strain;
I cannot bear to chill your youth
  With images of pain.
Yet humbly take what God bestows,
  And like his own fair flowers,
Look up in sunshine with a smile,
  And gently bend in showers.

THE DUMB LUNATIC.

FROM amid the crowd what unhal-
    lowed tone, —
What voice in misery cried?
It seemed like nature's lamenting moan
    For reason's blessings denied.

Oh, behold that face with its pallid hue,
    Like snowflakes at twilight's chime;
And that eye so burning, yet rayless
    too,
Like the moon in her waning time!

And the youthful form that with early
    pain
    Has withered in boyhood's glow;
And the tongue with motion so quiet
    and vain,
    And restless look of woe.

In anguish beside him his father stands
    In a statelier mood of grief;
He is grasping closely those thin white
    hands,
    And eagerly asks relief.

The disciples of Jesus cannot bless;
    He turns in anguish away,
And a smile of dark, unbelieving dis-
    tress
Seems o'er his closed lips to stray.

But, behold! the Saviour of men ap-
    pears!
    A thrill to his chilled heart flies;
His faith contends with decaying fears,
    And the warm drops fill his eyes.

A few soothing words to a father's woe
    Are breathed by that voice of power;
Sweet as the flush of a mountain's flow,
    In the blaze of a noontide hour.

A higher address of command is heard!
    Oh, what has that accent done?
It has banished "the sickness of hope
    deferred,"
Has restored the maniac son.

JAIRUS' DAUGHTER.

THEY have watched her last and
    quivering breath,
. And the maiden's soul has flown;
They have wrapped her in the robes of
    death,
    And laid her dark and lone.

But the mother lingers still behind,
    And weeps for that fallen flower.
Nay, start not, — 'twas the passing
    wind, —
    Those limbs have lost their power.

And tremble not at that cheek of snow,
    Over which the faint light plays;
'Tis only the curtain's crimson glow
    Which thus deceives thy gaze.

Didst thou not close that expiring eye,
    And feel the slow pulse decay?
And did not thy lips receive the sigh
    That bore her soul away?

She lies on her couch all pale and
    hushed,
    And heeds not thy gentle tread;
But is still as the spring-flower by trav-
    eller crush'd,
    Which dies on its snowy bed.

Her mother has passed from that lonely
    room,
  And the maid is still and pale;
Her ivory hand is as cold as the tomb,
  Which soon her form shall veil.

Her mother retires with folded arms,
  No tear attempts to flow;
Her heart is shut to joys or harms,
  And her head is bent in woe.

But listen! what name salutes her ear?
  It comes to a heart of stone.
"Jesus," she cries, "has no power here,
  My daughter's soul has flown!"

He leads the way to that cold white
    couch,
  And bends o'er that senseless form;
She breathes! she breathes! at his hal-
    lowed touch
  The maiden's hand is warm.

And the fresh blood shines with its
    roseate hue,
  And life spreads quick through her
    frame;
Her head is raised and her step is true,
  And she murmurs her mother's name.

INVITATION TO A BIRD.

LITTLE bird, come,
  Quick to my home.
I'll give you to eat
Everything sweet;
Sugar and cake
I'll save for your sake;
Melon and plum
You shall have some.
A peach and a pear,
And everything rare;
Some straw for your nest,
And what you like best,
A nice little house,
As snug as a mouse.
Come away from the tree
And live here with me.
I will give you a brush
  To smooth down each feather.
And brother will hush
  While we sing together.
Come away from the tree,
And live here with me.

THE LITTLE BIRD'S ANSWER.

I THANK you, my dear,
  But I'd rather live here:
The skies they are fair
And I love the fresh air.
The trees they are green,
And I sit like a queen,
On a branch as it goes,
While the pleasant wind blows.
I've more on my table
To eat than I'm able,
For the very large field
My dessert does yield:
But come from your book,
With a good humor'd look,
When with care you have read,
And your lesson is said;
Sit under the tree,
With your sewing by me,
And this afternoon,
I'll sing you a tune.

NEW YEAR'S DAY.

WAKE and see the morning ray —
    This is happy New Year's day!
View your toys and presents gay,
This is happy New Year's day!
Brother, sister, come and play,
This is happy New Year's day!
Father, mother, hear me say,
A happy, happy, New Year's day!
Waiting maids and nurses gray,
To you a happy New Year's day!
Friends at home, and friends away,
May you enjoy your New Year's day!
And while I laugh, and skip, and play,
I'll thank God for the New Year's day.

THE SLEEPING BABY.

HUSH, **hush,** with your noise,
    What a talking you keep,
You rude **little boys,**
    Now the baby's asleep!
        Hushaby, **baby.**

Mamma has just told **me**
    To stay quiet here,
And, oh, she will scold me,
    If wakes baby dear.
        Hushaby, baby.

How soft its white arm,
    As it lies on its breast!
Little baby, no harm
    Shall come here while you rest.
        Hushaby, baby.

My task has been given,
    And I will be true,
And sister and Heaven
    Will **watch** over you.
        Hushaby, **baby.**

FATHER **TAKES ME UP.**

I LOVE my mother's **gentle kiss,**
    I love to **join my brother's play,**
I love to walk with **little sis,**
    And view the shops and pleasures gay.

I love my toys and books to see,
    I love god-mother's silver cup,
But the best thing of things to me,
    Is when *my father takes me up.*

Father, when I'm as tall as you,
    And you are small like little sis,
I'll lay you on my shoulder too,
    And let you feel how nice it is.

THE BOAT.

OH, see my **little** boat,
    How prettily it glides;
Like a bird it seems to float,
    Press'd forward by the tides —
        By the tides.

The sky **is shining brightly,**
    The fishes dart **below,**
While my little boat so lightly
    Leaps onward as I row —
        As I row.

I would like to be a boat,
    And live upon the sea;
So merrily I'd float,
    With nought to trouble me —
        Trouble me.

But should a storm come near,
And fill me with alarms,
I would row to mother, dear—
My boat should be her arms—
    Mother's arms.

POOR WILLY.

POOR Willy, in play,
    I am sorry to say,
His head did hit;
To his mother he ran,
Like a little man,
    Not minding it.
Then she rubb'd it well,
And a story did tell,
    And kiss'd him too;
Then back did he run,
To his little fun,
    And so must you.

INVITATION TO THE ANT.

COME here, little ant,
    For the pretty bird can't.
I want you to come,
And live at my home;

I know you will stay,
And help me to play.
Stop making that hill,
Little ant, and be still.

Come, creep to my feet,
Here is sugar to eat.
Say, are you not weary,
My poor little deary,

With bearing that load,
Across the wide road?

Leave your hill now, to me,
And then you shall see,

That by filling my hand,
I can pile up the sand,
And save you the pains,
Of bringing these grains.

THE ANT'S ANSWER.

STOP, stop, little miss,
    No such building as this
Will answer for me,
As you plainly can see.

I take very great pains,
And place all the grains
As if with a tool,
By a carpenter's rule.

You have thrown the coarse sand
All out of your hand,
And so fill'd up my door,
That I can't find it more.

My King and my Queen
Are choked up within;
My little ones too,
Oh, what shall I do?

You have smother'd them all,
With the sand you let fall.
I must borrow or beg,
Or look for an egg.*

---

* When an ant's nest is disturbed, there may be seen processions of ants bearing little white eggs, for more than a day. Ants are divided into workers, sentinels, etc., like bees, and they have their king and queen, also.

To keep under my eye,
For help by and by,
A new **house** I must **raise**,
In a very few days,

Nor stand here and pine,
Because you 've spoilt mine.
For when winter days come,
I shall mourn for my home;

So stand out of my way,
I have no time to play.

WHO IS THIS BOY?

I WILL write **a** little story
   About a little boy;
He **is** his father's comfort,
He **is** his mother's joy.

When we give **a little errand,**
He thinks of **what is said,**
Pulls down his little waistcoat,
And holds up his little head.

He holds his little **fork**
   By the handle, as he should,
And never spills his coffee,
   Nor drops about his food.

His face is very pleasant,
   What he says is always true;
Now, tell me, *youngest reader,*
   If this little boy is *you.*

NANCY RAY.

MY bird is dead,
   Said Nancy Ray;
My bird is dead,
   I cannot play.

He sang so sweetly
   Every day;
He sings no more,
   I cannot play.

Go put his cage
   Far, far away;
I do not love
   His cage to-day.

She wiped her eyes,
   Poor Nancy Ray!
And sat and sighed,
   But could not play.

"JESUS TOOK LITTLE CHILDREN IN HIS ARMS."

I WILL go to Jesus now,
   His arms are open still for youth,
He will hear my early vow,
   He will lead my heart to truth.

When I wake with morning light,
   I will seek His blessed voice,
And when fall the shades of night,
   He shall be my happy choice.

He will teach me how to pray,
   He will **teach me what to do;**
How to pass a holy day,
   How to keep my God in view.

When my heart is faint and weak,
   And some foolish fear alarms,
I my Saviour's word will seek,
   He will hold **me** in his arms.

When a sinful thought comes by,
   Or angry passions move my breast,

THE YOUNGEST ONE.—Page 33.

I will bid the tempter fly;
  In His arms again I'll rest.

Then happy will the moment prove,
  When God shall call me up to
    Heaven,
When Jesus folds me in his love,
  And faults repented are forgiven.

THE YOUNGEST ONE.

I SAW a mother with her child,
  And each with each appeared be-
    guil'd;
So tenderly they spake and smil'd,
  I knew it was her youngest one.

She lean'd upon her mother's knee,
With look half tender and half free,
And oh, by that sweet liberty,
  I knew it was her youngest one.

A whisper came with love o'erfraught,
Soon was returned the whispered
    thought,
As though in this wide world were
    nought
  But her and her dear youngest one.

"Mother," she said, "you must not go
And leave your little girl, you know,
Because no other loves you so,
  Like me, your darling youngest one."

I heard a promise and a kiss,
I saw a smile of trusting bliss,
Oh, nought can sever, after this,
  The mother and her youngest one.

TO A BUTTERFLY AT CHURCH.

BUTTERFLY, butterfly why come
  here?
  This is no bower for you;
Go sip the honeydrop sweet and clear,
  Or bathe in the morning dew.

This is the place to think of Heaven,
  This is the place to pray;
You have no sins to be forgiven, —
  Butterfly, go away.

I see God has touched you with beauti-
    ful dyes,
  And your motion is graceful and
    light,
But the *heart* is the thing open now to
    His eyes;
  The *heart* must be pure in His sight.

He has made us to love what is airy
    and gay,
  And I will not despise your bright
    wings;
But I must not be thinking about you
    to-day, —
  It was given for holier things.

MOTHER, WHAT IS DEATH?

MOTHER, how still the baby
  lies!
  I cannot hear his breath;
I cannot see his laughing eyes, —
  They tell me this is death.

"My little work I thought to bring,
  And sit down by his bed,
And pleasantly I tried to sing, —
  They hushed me, — he is dead.

"They say that he again will rise,
　More beautiful than now,—
That God will bless him in the skies,—
　Oh, mother, tell me how!"

"Daughter, do you remember dear,
　The cold dark thing you brought,
And laid upon the casement here,—
　A wither'd worm you thought?

"**I** told you that Almighty **power**
　Could break that wither'd shell,
And show you, in a future **hour,**
　Something would please you well.

"**Look at the** chrysalis, my love,—
　An empty shell it lies;
Now raise your wandering thoughts
　above,
To where yon insect flies!"

"Oh, yes, mamma, how very gay
　Its wings of starry gold,—
And see! it lightly flies away
　Beyond my gentle hold.

"Oh, mother, now **I know full well,**
　If God that worm can change,
And draw it from its broken cell,
　On golden wings to range;

"How beautiful will brother be,
　When God shall give him wings,
Above this dying world to **flee,**
　And live with heavenly things."

WISHES.

ANNA.

I WISH I was **a small bird,**
　Among the leaves to dwell,
To scale the sky in gladness,
　Or seek the lonely dell.
My matin song should wake amid
　The chorus **of** the earth,
And my **vesper hymn ring gladly**
　The trill of **careless mirth.**

ELLEN.

I wish I was a floweret,
　To blossom in the grove,
I'd spread my opening leaflets
　Among the plants I love.
No hand would roughly cull me,
　As I looked up to the sky;
I silently should ope to life,
　And quietly should die.

MARY.

I wish I was a goldfish,
　To seek the sunny wave,
To part the gentle ripple,
　And amid its coolness lave.
I would glide along delighted
　Amid the coral way,
And when night came on in softness
　Beneath the starbeam play.

MOTHER.

Hush, hush, romantic prattlers,
　You know not what you say,
When soul, the crown of mortals,
　You would lightly throw away.
What is the songster's warble,
　Or the floweret's blush refin'd
To the noble thought of Deity
　Within your **opening mind?**

JEPHTHAH'S RASH VOW.

JUDGES XI.

THE battle had ceased and the victory was won,
 The wild cry of horror was o'er —
Now rose in his glory the bright beaming sun,
 And with him his journey the war chief begun,
 With a soul breathing vengeance no more.

The foes of his country lay strewed on the plain,
 A tear stole its course to his eye,
But the warrior disdained every semblance of pain,
He thought of his child, of his country again,
 And suppressed, while 'twas forming, a sigh.

"Oh! Father of Light!" said the conquering chief,
 "The vow which I made, I renew;
'Twas thy powerful arm gave the welcome relief,
When I called on thy name in the fulness of grief,
 And my hopes were but cheerless and few.

"An offering of love will I pay at thy fane,
 An offering thou canst not despise;
The first being I meet, when I welcome again
 The land of my fathers I left not in vain,
 With the flames on thy altar shall rise."

Now hushed were his words, — through the far-spreading bands,
 Naught was heard but the foot-fall around,
Till his feet in glad tread press his own native lands,
And to heaven are uplifted his conquering hands;
 Not a voice breaks the silence profound.

Oh, listen! at distance, what harmonies sound,
 And at distance what maiden appears?
See, forward she comes with a light springing bound,
And casts her mild eye in fond ecstasy round,
 For her parent is seen through her tears!

Her harp's wildest chord gives a strain of delight;
 A moment — she springs to his arms!
"My daughter? Oh God!" — not the horrors of fight,
While legion on legion against him unite,
 Could bring to his soul such alarms.

In horror he starts, as a fiend had appeared,
 His eyes in mute agony close.

His sword o'er his age-frosted forehead is reared,
Which with scars from his many-fought battles is seared,—
Nor country nor daughter he knows.

But sudden conviction in quick flashes told,
That his daughter was destined to die;
No longer could nature the hard struggle hold,
His grief issued forth unrestrained, uncontrolled,
And glazed was his time-shrunken eye.

His daughter is kneeling, and clasping that form,
She ne'er touched but with transport before;
His daughter is watching the thundering storm,
Whose quick flashing lightnings so madly deform
A face beaming sunshine no more.

But how did that daughter, so gentle and fair,
Hear the sentence that doomed her to die?
For a moment was heard a shrill cry of despair—
For a moment her eye gave a heart-moving glare—
For a moment her bosom heaved high.

It was but a moment — the frenzy was past,
She trustingly rushed to his arms,
And there, as a flower when chilled by the blast,
Reclines on an oak while its fury may last,
On his bosom she hushed her alarms.

Not an eye saw the scene but was moistened in woe,
Not a voice could a sentence command;
Down the soldier's rough cheek tears of agony flow,
The sobs of the maiden rose mournful and low,
Sad pity wept over the band.

But fled was the hope in the fair maiden's breast,
From her father's fond bosom she rose;
Stern virtue appeared in a manner confessed,
She looked like a saint from the realms of the blessed,
Not a mortal encircled with woes.

She turned from the group, and can I declare
The hope and the fortitude given,
As she sunk on her knees with a soul-breathing prayer,
That her father might flourish of angels the care,
Till with glory he blossomed in Heaven?

Oh, comfort him, Heaven, when low in the dust
My limbs are inactively laid!

Oh, comfort him, Heaven, and let him
    then trust,
That free and immortal the souls of
    the just,
    Are in beauty and glory arrayed!"

The maiden arose, oh, I cannot portray
    The devotion that glowed in her eye;
Religion's sweet self in its light seemed
    to play,
With the mildness of night, with the
    glory of day—
    But 'twas pity that prompted her sigh.

"My father!" the chief raised his agonized head,
    With a gesture of settled despair—
"My father!"—the words she would
    utter had fled,
But the sobs that she heaved, and the
    tears that she shed,
    Told more than those words could
    declare.

That weakness past o'er, and the maiden could say,
    "My father for thee I can die."
The bands slowly moved on their sorrowful way,
But never again from that heart-breaking day,
Was a smile known to force its enlivening ray
    On the old chieftain's grief-stricken
    eye.

THOUGHTS ON ZERLINA THORN.

DROWNED AT TRENTON FALLS, 1836.

AND art thou gone, fair, graceful
    child?
I dreamed not 'mid this cataract wild
    Thy form would lie,
When, like a bright and budding flower,
I met thee in a summer bower,—
    Life in thine eye.

I saw thee in the airy dance,
With floating step and kindling glance,
    With happy brow.
A brother's arm around thee clung,
A parent's smile upon thee hung,—
    Where art thou now?

Oh, cold and dark must be thy grave,
Love-nurtured one!—the dashing wave
    Rocks thy death sleep;
And o'er thy glazed and unclosed eye,
The high-heaved cliffs all frowningly
    Their vigils keep.

But why repine, though summer dews
And flowers of soft and blended hues
    Deck not thy sod?
Thy spirit from the wave upsprings,
Scatters the white foam from its wings,
    And soars to God.

ON THE CHRISTENING OF A LITTLE CHILD.

THE man of God stood there,
    His spirit bowed in prayer
Above the child;

And she, with wondering eye,
Gazed on him earnestly,
  Then brightly smiled.

Oh, sweet, devoted **one**,
With journey just begun
  In life's rough day,
What path soe'er **thou see**,
May hovering prayer for **thee**
  Still light thy way.

TO ———.

ON life's eventful sea
  May thy light bark gently glide,
And the true wind blowing free,
  Swell on the prosperous tide.

But should wild storms arise,
  And waves in fury roll,
Look up **to** God's far skies.
Anchor on him thy soul.

THE MYSTERIOUS CHAIR;

OR, TWO O'CLOCK AT NIGHT.

[A Letter to a Friend.]

DEAR John, As you know all our
  household affairs,
From the cellar beneath to **the attic upstairs**,
I am anxious to write of a recent transaction,
Which you may resolve **to your own** satisfaction.

Last night, in the room where the silver **is kept**,
And wherein the old lady and gentle**man slept,**

They were **woke** on a sudden **by singular sounds**,
For which **they could fancy no plausible grounds**.

The noise **issued forth from the large** rocking-chair,—
Which, distinctly **and loudly, as tongue** can declare,
Roll'd backwards and forwards **full six** or eight times,
As St. Michael's resounded **the two-o'-clock chimes**.

The old gentleman rose and explored the whole room,
For a dim-twinkling light still pervaded the gloom;
He looked under the bed, 'and examined with care,
In a very particular manner, the chair.

But no **living being was anywhere** found,—
The doors **were** both **clos'd,**—silence brooded around.
The mysterious chair was as quiet as *hush!*
And the window was up but the height of **a brush.**

You may say 'twas **by fancy** this whole thing was done,
And so should *I* think, were it heard but by *one;*
Yet, as *two* were awoke by, and *two* heard that rocking,
It is not a subject for doubt, sir, or mocking.

From that moment till daybreak, the honored old pair
Were absorb'd in conjectures about this affair;
Not a wink of sweet slumber could visit their eyes,
And they rose half an hour ere they usually rise.

At breakfast we saw something weighed on their minds, —
For, when dear ones are troubled, how quickly love finds?
They were silent and pensive, and heaved a few sighs,
Till we searched out the source, and drew forth their replies.

When the matter was known, all of course felt amazed,
Our coffee was slighted, our eyes were upraised,
Neglected, the spoons in our hominy stood,
And the waffles remained like unpopular food.

But at length, when our silent astonishment ceased,
Speculation, and talking, and guessing increased;
Every tongue in the group had a reason to spare
For the wonderful feat of the rocking arm-chair.

Louisa presumed that an earthquake had passed,
And had caused it to vibrate so loud and so fast.

But how could that happen, when nothing fell down
In the rest of the house, or the rest of the town?

Miss Carry was certain it must be a thief,
Who had come for the silver, and vanished so brief;
But the doors and the chimney-board all remained tight,
And no *man* could escape through that window by flight.

Little Nannie was sure 'twas a ghost, for her nurse
Had often informed her of such things and worse;
But we asked how a shade, without body or weight,
Such material rockings and noise could create.

Eliza believed that the chair, *of itself*,
Fell to moving without either spirit or elf:
But, if so, Dame Nature has altered her laws,
And effects must take place without impulse or cause.

Old Nan, who stood solemnly brushing the flies,
Being asked her opinion, slow raised her black eyes;
She could not guess the cause, but full sartin was she
That old massa or missis some sorrow must see.

At last the whole family turned to **your** friend,
And begged **I** would try their **dilemma** to end;
I had heard all their reasons; **I had,** too, **my** own,
Which with proper humility thus **I** made known.

To me it appeared that the source **of** dismay
Must **have** been a large **cat, who was prowling** for prey;
In the half-open window with ease she might pass,
Without forcing the sash, or disturbing the glass.

I presumed she had velvety entered the house,
And had searched round the room for a rat or a mouse ;
Sprung **up** on the table, leaped **down** on the chair,
Which of course began rocking with violent air.

Puss, probably frightened, at least much surprised,
Darted quick through the window, for so I surmised,
Stole along the piazza, jumped off on the ground,
Then forgot what had passed, and went still prowling around.

As I ceased from explaining, **I saw** every eye
Grow brighter with smiles, and the dismals lay by;
Our sensitive appetites quickened **once** more,
And justice was done to the tables' rich store.

Thus we all think **the problem resolved** by a cat,
And persuaded we feel, **if the cause** were not that,
The invisible agent who haunted **that** room,
Must never be known till the bursting of doom.
SAMUEL GILMAN,
Charleston, S. C., Sept., 1837.

FLIGHT OF THE MUSKOGEE INDIAN.

ON the shore of **Carolina an Indian** warrior stood,
A captive of the Shawnees, and reddened with their blood;
Strange arts of varied torture his conquerors tried in vain,
Like a rock that stands the billows, he dashed them off again.

He shouted, and the echo shrill returned the lengthened shriek,
I have rent you as the eagle rends the dove within his beak,
And ye give me women's tortures; see, I lightly cast them by,
As the spirit of the storm-cloud throws the vapor from the sky.

"Ye are women!" the wild echo came
  wilder on the air—
"*I* will show a worthy trial for a Mus-
  kogee to bear;
Let me grasp a heated gun in this raw
  and bloody hand,
And ye shall not see an eyelash move
  to shame my father-land."

They gave the glowing steel. He took
  it with a smile,
And held it as a plaything;—they stood
  in awe the while;
Then, springing like an antelope, he
  brandished it around,
And toward the beetling eminence* up-
  started with a bound.

One leap, and he is o'er! fierce dashing
  through the stream,
And his massy form lies floating 'neath
  the clear and sunny beam;
A hundred arrows sped at once, but
  missed that warrior bold,
And his mangled arms, ere set of sun,
  his little ones enfold.

MAIDEN AND THE MARINER.

THE toilet task was o'er;
  The satin slipper clasped the
  modelled foot,
The white glove rested on the snowy
  arm,
While Ella's heart beat lightly; light
  her tread

As down the steps with airy grace she
  sprang
To greet the neighboring ball-room's
  fairy scene,
Then bounded towards her carriage—
  and her laugh
Went ringing like a happy waterfall
  Bursting from summer hills.

  She nears the blaze
Of the saloon where sylph-like move-
  ments wait
On music, as an echo on its sound,
Where eyes like midnight stars shine
  joyously
From out the firmament of heart and
  mind.
The carriage stops. Hark, a low plain-
  tive voice!—
"Pity," it said, "the shipwrecked mar-
  iner,
Who has no friend, no country, and no
  home."
"Back, fellow," one exclaimed, "away,
  away!"
The vagrant was thrust off. With flow-
  ing robes
White as the garb a new-made spirit
  wears,
Fair Ella glided by. Again that voice!
She paused. A shade came o'er her
  sunny brow,
Soft as moon's vapor on a silver stream.
"That voice of woe will haunt my
  thoughts," she said,
"Will mingle with the dance discord-
  antly,

---

* A bluff near Augusta, ninety feet high.

Should I still coldly turn mine ear
    away;
And our dear William is a sailor, too!
What if *he* need a pitying stranger's aid,
Yon rebel from our hearth? God bless
    the boy!"
And here she heaved a sister's natural
    sigh,
And turning to the mariner, she asked,
"Stranger, what wouldst thou? Can I
    aid thy need?"
Bright fell the light upon the seaman's
    coarse
And tattered garments. Brightly, too,
    it shone
On Ella's flower-wreathed brow and
    graceful form.
He paused. Ripe for the witcheries of
    the dance,
E'en though her heart was touched with
    sympathy,
The maiden's slippered foot kept eager
    time
To the loud gush of harmony that filled
The new saloon, while her slight ivory
    fan
Tapped on her open palm impatiently.
Nearer the seaworn veteran pressed,
    and crossed
His hands upon his threadbare cloak
    and bowed.
A moment. Back he throws the rag-
    ged robe,
And lo, a manly form in youth's fresh
    glow,
And laughing eyes beneath the cluster-
    ing curls

That hang in ripened fulness o'er his
    brow.
'Tis William, the gay wanderer! and
    he clasps
The youthful Ella to his brother heart.

THE CHILD ON THE OCEAN.

"MOTHER, how small a thing
    am I,
Rocked on the restless sea!
I ask, when gazing on the sky,
    Can God remember me?
How solemnly the stars appear
    Upon the broad blue deep!
Their mighty songs I seem to hear
    As they their vigils keep.

"How beautiful the moon to see
    Walk proudly through the night,
Unshadowed by a single tree
    To mar her queenly light!
How brilliant is the track we mark,
    As leaps our vessel on,—
A rival light that cheers the dark
    When stars and moon are gone!
Mother, I am a feeble thing,
    'Mid scenes so vast and bold."
"My child, your thoughts can o'er them
    spring,
    Your *mind* they cannot hold."

SEVENTEEN.

IN childhood, when my girlish view,
    Glanced over life's unfading green,
Thoughts undefined, and bright and
    new,
    Would blend with thee, sweet Sev-
    enteen.

Restrained at twelve by matron care,
  My walks prescribed, my movements seen,
How bright the sun, how free the air,
  Seemed circling round fair seventeen!

Thirteen arrived; but still my book,
  My dress, were watched with aspect keen,
Scarce on a novel might I look,
  And balls — must wait for seventeen.

Fourteen allowed the evening walk,
  Where friendship's eye illumed the scene;
The long, romantic bosom talk, —
  That talk which glanced at seventeen.

The next revolving circle brought
  A quicker pulse, yet graver mien;
I read and practised, studied, thought,—
  For what? To stop at seventeen.

Sixteen arrived; that witching year
  When youthful hearts like buds are seen,
Ready to ope when first appear
  The genial rays of seventeen.

They came; have passed; think not, fair maids,
  My hand shall draw that magic screen;
But this I urge, — fill well your *heads*,
  And guard your *hearts*, for seventeen.

JOSHUA'S COURTSHIP.

A NEW-ENGLAND BALLAD.

STOUT Joshua was a farmer's son,
  And a pondering he sat
One night, when the faggots crackling burned,
  And purr'd the tabby cat.

Joshua was a well-grown youth,
  As one might plainly see
By the sleeves that vainly tried to reach
  His hands upon his knee.

His splay-feet stood all parrot-toed
  In cowhide shoes array'd;
And his hair seem'd cut across his brow
  By rule and plummet laid.

And what was Joshua pondering on,
  With his widely-staring eyes,
And his nostrils opening sensibly
  To ease his frequent sighs?

Not often will a lover's lips
  The tender secret tell,
But out he spoke, before he thought,
  "My gracious! Nancy Bell!"

His mother at her spinning-wheel,
  Good woman, stood and spun,
"And what," says she, "'s come over you?
  Is't *airnest*, or is't fun?"

Then Joshua gave a cunning look,
  Half bashful and half sporting;
"Now, what did father do," says he,
  "When first he came a courting?"

"Why, Josh, the first thing that he did,"
  With a knowing wink, says she,
"Was to come dressed up of a Sunday night,
  And *cast sheep's eyes* * at me."

* Tender glances.

Josh said no more, but straight went
    out,
  And sought a butcher's pen,
Where twelve fat sheep, for market
    bound,
  Had lately slaughtered been.

He bargained with a lover's zeal,
  Obtained the wished-for prize,
And filled his pockets fore and aft
  With twice twelve bloody eyes.

The next night was the happy time
  When all New-England sparks,
Drest in their best go out to court
  As spruce and gay as larks.

When floors are nicely sanded o'er,
  When tins and pewter shine,
And milk-pans by the kitchen wall
  Display their dainty line;

While the new ribbon decks the waist
  Of many a waiting lass,
Who steals a conscious look of pride
  Towards her answering glass.

In pensive mood sat Nancy Bell;
  Of Joshua thought not she,
But of a hearty sailor lad
  Across the distant sea.

Her arm upon the table rests,
  Her hand supports her head,
When Joshua enters with a scrape,
  And somewhat bashful tread.

No word he spake, but down he sat
  And heav'd a doleful sigh;
Then at the table took his aim
  And roll'd a glassy eye.

Another and another flew
  With quick and strong rebound,
They tumbled in poor Nancy's lap,
  They fell upon the ground.

While Joshua smirk'd, and sigh'd, and
    smirk'd
  Between each tender aim,
And still the cold and bloody balls
  In frightful quickness came.

Until poor Nancy flew with screams
  To shun the amorous sport,
And Joshua found to *cast sheep*'s *eyes*
  Was not the way to court.

MARY ANNA GIBBES, of STONO,
  Saved a boy's life during the Revolutionary
  War. He was Col. Fenwick, afterwards
  distinguished in the war of 1812.

STONO, on thy still banks
    The roar of war is heard;
  its thunders swell
And shake yon mansion, where domes-
    tic love
Till now breathed simple kindness to
    the heart;
Where white-armed childhood twined
    the neck of age,
Where hospitable cares lit up the
    hearth,
Cheering the lonely traveller on his way.

  A foe inhabits there, and they
    depart,
The infirm old man and his fair house-
    hold too,
Seeking another home. Home! who
    can tell

The touching power of that most sacred word,
Save he who feels and weeps that he has none?

    Among that group of midnight exiles fled
Young Mary Anna, on whose youthful cheek
But thirteen years had kindled up the rose.
A laughing creature breathing heart and love,
Yet timid as the fawn in Southern wilds.
E'en the night reptile on the dewy grass
Startled the maiden, and the silent stars
Troubled her mind. No time was there for gauds
And toilette art in this quick flight of fear.
Her glossy hair, damped by the midnight winds,
Lay on her neck dishevelled; gathered round
Her form in hurried folds clung her few garments.
Now a quick thrilling sob, half grief, half dread,
Came bursting from her heart, — and now her eyes
Glared forth as pealed the cannon; then beneath
Their drooping lids sad tears redundant flowed.

    But sudden, mid the group, a cry arose —
"Fenwick! where is he?" None returned reply,
But a sharp piercing glance went out, around,
Keen as a mother's towards her infant child
When sudden danger lowers, and then a shriek
From one, from all, burst forth, — "He is not here" —
Poor boy! he slept; nor crash of hurrying guns
Nor impious curses, nor the warrior's shout
Awoke his balmy rest! He dreamed such dreams
As float round childhood's couch of angel faces
Peering through clouds, of sunny rivulets
Where the fresh stream flows rippling on, to waft
A tiny sail — and of his rabbits white,
With eyes of ruby, and his tender fawn's
Long delicate limbs, light tread and graceful neck,
He slept unconscious. — "Who shall wake that sleep?"
All shrink, for now th' artillery louder roars; —
The frightened slaves crouch at their master's side,
And he, infirm and feeble, scarce sustains
His sinking weight.
            There was a pause, a hush
So deep, that one could hear the forest leaves

Flutter and drop between the war gun's
  peal.
Then forward stood that girl, young
  Mary Anna,
The tear dried up upon her cheek, the
  sob
Crushed down, and in that high and
  lofty tone
Which sometimes breathes the woman
  in the child,
She said, "*He shall not die*," and turned
  alone,
Alone? oh, gentle girlhood, not alone
Art thou if ONE watching above will
  guard
Thee on thy way. Clouds shrouded up
  the stars;
On, on, she sped, the gun's broad glare
  her beacon.

The wolf-growl sounded near, — on, on-
  ward still;
The forest trees like warning spirits
  moaned.
She pressed her hands against her
  throbbing heart,
But faltered not; the whizzing shot
  went by,
Scarce heeded went; passed is a weary
  mile
With the light step a master spirit gives
On duty's road. But she has reached
  her home.
Her home? Is this her home at whose
  fair gate
Stern foes in silence stand to bar her way?
That gate, which, from her infant child-
  hood, leaped

On its wide hinges, glad at her return?
Before the sentinels she trembling
  stood,
And, with a voice whose low and ten-
  der tones
Rose like the ringdove's in midsummer
  storms,
She said, —
"Please let me pass and seek a child
Who in my father's mansion has been
  left
Sleeping, unconscious of the danger
  near."
While thus she spake, a smile incredu-
  lous
Stole o'er the face of one; the other
  cursed
And barred her from the way.
"O, sirs," she cried, —
While from her upraised eyes the tears
  streamed down,
And her small hands were clasped in
  agony, —
"Drive me not hence, I pray! Until
  to-night
I dared not stray beyond my nurse's
  side
In the dim twilight; yet I now have come
Alone, unguarded, this far, dreary mile.
By darkness unappalled; a simple worm
Would often fright my heart and bid it
  flutter;
But now I've heard the wild wolf's hun-
  gry growl
With soul undaunted, — till to-night
  I've shrunk
From men; and soldiers! scarcely dared
  I look

Upon their glittering arms; but here I come
And sue to *you*, — men, warriors; drive me not
Away. He whom I seek is yet a child,
A prattling boy, and must he, **must he die**?
Oh, if you love your children, let me pass!
You will not? Then my strength and hope are gone,
And I shall perish ere I reach my friends."
And then she pressed her brow, as if those hands
So soft and small could still her throbbing pulse.
The sentinels looked calmly on, like men
Whose blades had toyed with sorrow, and made sport
Of woe. One step the maiden backward took,
Lingering in thought, then hope, like a soft flush
Of struggling twilight, kindled in her eyes;
She knelt before them and re-urged her plea.
"Perchance you have a sister, sir, or you, —
A poor young thing like me; if she were here,
Kneeling like me before *my* countrymen,
They would not spurn her thus!"
"Go, girl, pass on,"
The softened voice of one replied; nor was

She checked, nor waited she to hear repulse,
But darted through the avenue, attained
The hall, and, springing up the well-known stairs,
With such a flight as the young eagle takes
To gain its nest, she reached the quiet couch,
Where in bright dreams the unconscious sleeper lay.
Slight covering o'er the rescued boy she threw,
And caught him in her arms. He knew that cheek,
Kissed it half waking, then around her neck
His hands entwined, and dropped to sleep again.
She bore him onward, dreading now for him
The shot that whizzed along and tore the earth
In fragments by her side. She reached the guards,
Who silent ope'd the gate, then hurried on;
But, as she passed them, from her heart burst forth,
"God bless you, gentlemen!" then urged her way;
Those arms, whose heaviest load and task had been
To poise her doll, and wield her childhood's toys,
Bearing the boy along the dangerous road.

Voices at length she hears, — her
friends are near;
They meet, and, yielding up her pre-
cious charge,
She sinks upon her father's breast, in
doubt,
'Twixt smiles and tears.

THE SENTINEL.

SEE the sentinel! When others
sleep, he watches, that no one may
disturb them.

When the night is dark, and the
winds are abroad, he walks alone.
When all the city sleeps, the sentinel
wakes and walks alone.

Perhaps he thinks of his children and
his home; their eyes are closed in quiet
rest, but he walks alone.

The moon shines brightly on him,
the stars are his company.

Who guards the sentinel? God
guards him.

MATTHEW 2: 6.

WHEREIN, O, Bethlehem! doth
thy greatness lie?
In warlike host, proud tower, or palace
high?
No! a sweet babe's first slumber I
have seen,
And hence the cities own me as their
queen.   S. G.

MATTHEW 2: 18.

IN Rama there was heard a wail of
grief,—
Rachel refusing solace or relief;

But *Christian* lands can show a sight
more rare, —
A mourner comforted by thought and
prayer.
SAMUEL GILMAN.

THOUGHTS ON THE PORTRAIT OF STUART'S WASHINGTON.

SEE, they advance and press around
Columbia's son!
I joy to hear the murmured sound,
'Tis he, 'tis Washington!

Come on, fair boy, and thy young eye
Shall catch a ray,
Will teach thee how to act, or die,
In danger's way.

Maiden, with feelings pure and warm,
Gaze on yon field;
He fought to throw on woman's form
A soldier's shield.

Approach, old man! reflected light
Shall beam on thee,
For thou wert with him in the fight,
And shouted, " Victory!"

Yet, is't his martial bearing high
That charms us now?
Is it the statesman's thoughtful eye
And manly brow?

Not these alone, — his moral worth
The spell imparts,
And make his noble throne on earth
His people's hearts.

STORIES AND TALES

FOR THE YOUNG.

BY

MRS. CAROLINE GILMAN.

HOLIDAYS AT THE PLANTATION. — Page 51.

HOLIDAYS AT THE PLANTATION.

A SOUTHERN STORY OF BYGONE TIMES.

CHAPTER I.

THE Spring holidays had arrived, and George and Clara were wild with joy at the idea of going into the country. They raced about the house, caught their old black *maumer* around the neck, and exclaimed, —

"Good-by, old city; good-by, books!"

Clara was a careful girl, and laid her basket of books away neatly and safely. She fancied that they were her children, and that she was putting them to bed, and said, —

"Hush! lie still, Spelling Book; be a good child, Geography, and sleep beside Table Book, and do not wake him up. Look," said she, as she saw that the cover of her Grammar was ragged, "you have torn your frock, naughty Grammar. Here is my Bible; shall that go to sleep, too? Oh, no, Bible dear, I must have you in the country, too."

George and Clara bade the town servants good-by. George mounted his pony, calling his dog *Fido* to follow him, and Clara sprang into the carriage with her parents, thinking she could ride forever without being tired.

It was a bright April morning; the sun shone, the birds sang, and the flowers smelt sweetly. Clara was delighted for ten miles, and then she grew weary. Her mother said, —

"Sing some hymns and songs, Clara."

So Clara sang, and George cantered his little pony up to the side of the carriage and sang too. While they were singing —

> "Where do children love to go,
> When the wintry tempests blow?
> What is it attracts them so?
>   'Tis the Sabbath school,"

they saw the woods on fire. The flames ran like snakes up the dry trees and on the grass. Clara said to her father, —

"May we cry fire?"

"Yes," said her father, "as loud as you please."

"May Ben cry fire, too?" said George.

When his father said **"Yes,"** George and Clara and little Ben, who was behind the carriage, cried "fire! fire! fire!" as loud as they could roar; and what with the cries and the laughter, the woods rang again.

At one o'clock they all stopped to rest the horses and themselves and dine. This is called a *maroon*. The servants spread a small carpet on the grass, under a large oak, hung all about with green vines and gray moss-like fringe. The children assisted in taking the cold ham and fowl from the basket. Oh! how nice every mouthful tasted! Fido jumped about merrily, and sometimes they threw him a bone, for they were not fearful of greasing the grass.

"Mamma," said Clara, "I think this is as pretty as our dining-room. The oak branches are our curtains, the sky is our ceiling, the birds are our musicians, and they sing as prettily as sister Kate at the piano-forte."

"Hush!" said George; see that rabbit crossing the road. Quick,

Jack, with my gun. Look! the fellow is on the fence; now he is on that gum-tree!"

The gun was brought; George fired and missed his aim, and the merry party laughed at him.

"Never mind," said George; "you shall see what I will do when I get to Oak Hall. A fellow's hand shakes a little after riding."

When the servants had dined, they all set off quite refreshed. Clara was almost asleep when they entered the avenue at twilight, but was soon aroused by the bright glare of the *bush-lights* kindled about the negro houses, which threw a cheerful light upon Oak Hall.

No wonder that Clara's sleepy eyes were opened by the bush-lights, for they are brighter than a drawing-room lamp. The way they are arranged, is this: A carpenter drives a stake into the ground quite deep; he then nails boards together, like an open box, and fastens them on top of the stake, which is about a yard from the ground; then he fills the box with earth. When night comes on, one of the negroes lays a small heap of dry pine sticks on the earth in the box, and sets fire to them, adding others as these are burnt out.

"Here we are!" shouted Clara; "look, George, there is the tree where you shot the pretty blue-bird. Don't shoot any more pretty birds."

Clara did not say any more, for a turn in the road brought them near to Oak Hall. A large number of negroes were awaiting their arrival, and the little ones came leaping and skipping about the bush-lights.

George and Clara found their aunt in the house, ready to welcome them, and were delighted to see the sweet roses that their cousin Eliza had laid upon their pillows. After supper they assembled at prayers, and the servants who wished joined them. Clara took her Bible to her room to read, and remembered that the same God watched over her in the country as in the town.

A light shower fell in the night, and when the children arose in the morning, the trees, bushes, and flowers looked bright as their smiles.

After prayers, Clara kissed her parents and then ran into the garden. The seeds were all up in her own bed, and the roses were in full bloom. There was her seat beneath the cedar, and she fancied the very same mocking-bird of the last season was singing in its branches.

George and his cousin James called Clara to help them get ready to go out gunning. Clara stitched up two odd looking things, which she called hunting caps to save their city hats, and James put on his jacket wrong side out, because his sleeve was torn at the elbow. When they were equipped, they looked like Robinson Crusoe and his man Friday.

They came home in three hours, with one solitary Kingfisher. Clara mourned over its bright crest and glossy feathers, a little while; but when the boys asked her and Eliza to go to the fields with them and cook it, she forgot to be sorry.

Ben carried salt and rice, and a sauce-pan to cook it in, and Clara, with her sun-bonnet crushed all on one side, attended the boys, while Fido capered by their side. When they reached the field, they found a large oak tree, quite hollow in the trunk, though it was green and beautiful above. There were ashes inside, where the field negroes had been cooking. Ben struck a light, and gathered some dry brush for kindling. George picked the bird. Clara examined the rice, and James arranged the sauce-pan. Great was the labor for that meal. They forgot water, and had to run to the spring; they forgot a spoon, and were obliged to whittle a stick to eat with. A gust of wind blew the dust and ashes into their eyes, and many other troubles had they; but they turned them all into fun, and after a while the bird and rice were cooked, and they all declared it was remarkably nice. It did not seem to take away their appetites, though, for when the **dinner horn** blew, they all raced home, and **ate** as much as if they had never cooked the little Kingfisher.

Clara was very fond of seeing her mother give out fish, tobacco, sugar, etc., from the store-room, **and she followed her** there after dinner.

"When you are sixteen years old, you may help me," said her mamma.

"Oh, mamma," said Clara, "I shall never live such a *heap* of years!"

While Clara's mother was giving the fish, tobacco, and other things that she thought proper, many **of the negroes came with** eggs, groundnuts, poultry, and sweet potatoes, **of their own raising,** and she gave them more articles in **return.**

"Mamma," said Clara, "**these people put me in mind of the** parable of the talents; they all get their reward."

Clara then asked her mother if she might give the little negroes **a** treat. Her mother said "Yes," and gave her biscuits and sugar, and told her to go to the dairy-woman for milk. After Clara had made all her arrangements, she went **to** the piazza and **called out,**—

"Dick, La Fayette, **Pompey, Cuff,** Daphne, Dido and Moll, go and tell all your broder and titter come, cause. I been have something good for 'em."

Away they scampered, and came back with the rest, with their wooden piggins.

Clara then told them to sit **on the grass in a circle, while she stood** in the midst of them, giving most to those **who had** little infants **in their arms.** They were **all** beginning to eat, when she said, "Stop!" They obeyed her like **so** many soldiers.

"**Get up,**" said she, "Make curchy." They understood her better than some readers of this story, for the girls all made courtesies, and the boys all scraped **their** right foot, or kissed their hands, while some of **them** said,—

"Tank you, my young missis."

Then Clara said, "Eat,"—and they began without delay, their iron spoons clattering against the piggins.

George and Clara loved to go to the burial-ground where their little baby sister lay. They could see the moss-covered brick wall from the piazza, and the old cedar tree that stood in the centre. They were not sad when they walked to the graveyard, but gathered flowers, and chatted like birds. When they opened the gate, there seemed some solemn feeling to come over them; they went to a white slab that was under the cedar and read the name, "JANE"; then they pulled up some weeds that grew near the tombstone, and Clara said,—

"I am not afraid of snakes here, brother. Look, George, our lily is in bloom!"

And, sure enough, there were two white blossoms beneath the old cedar, and George said,—

"It may be that our little sister is blooming just so in Heaven."

Then Clara stooped and pulled up another weed; then they went out and shut the gate softly.

The sun was sinking in the west when George and Clara returned to the house, and they stood in the piazza with their father, seeing how beautifully the trees looked as the light bade them good night.

Then the living creatures all about came to rest. First the horses galloped up the avenue, as the little negroes clapped their hands and shouted to make them go fast; then the cows came to their pens.

Then came the geese walking along quite solemnly; then followed the sheep, and George threw them some corn; then the ducks flew across the green, *quacking;* then the little birds went to their nests, and the crows to the high trees.

On a cluster of huge oaks, near the house, ran an immense grape-vine. It twined up the limbs of one tree, then dropped down from a vast height near to the ground, and then threw up its tendrils to another. This was the children's favorite swing, and here came George and Clara, with their cousins and a troop of little negroes.

After the little family had swung, they gave the little negroes a turn; and it was droll to see how the black babies, in their little nurses' arms, tried not to be scared. They rolled up their eyes, and all who were old enough to have teeth, showed them.

George was a rogue, and wished to swing them high and frighten them; but Clara and Eliza would not let him. They caught hold of the swing and said, —

"For shame, George! You shall not frighten them! See, little Toney is crying! He has as much feeling as you. Come here, Toney, and we will protect you."

So Toney *sidled* up to the girls for protection, and wiped his nose on his jacket sleeve, and did not cry any more; and George consented to put the rest in the swing gently, and be kind to them; and it was a pretty sight to see them standing in a circle, waiting patiently for their turn to come, and to hear the shouts when any of them went high, and the still louder shouts when they tumbled out on the soft earth.

When the setting sun cast again a soft, yellow look over everything about Oak Hall; when the shadows of the last negroes who had lingered over their tasks looked long as they came home to their families, the children asked leave to go to the Frog Pond.

"Must you carry all these little negroes?" said the father, looking around on about twenty that stood waiting.

"O, yes!" they exclaimed, giving various reasons. "Pompey must go, because he has a good bass voice for the bull-frog, and Moll squeaked the best, and Dick was to take George's fishing-tackle, etc., etc., etc.; and, as for all the rest, they must go wid dem broder and titter."

So forth they all went to the Frog Pond, and George undertook to marshal the party.

"You, mamma, and Clara, and cousin Eliza," said he, "must stand together with these little negro girls, for treble, and squeak like one pig. Father and cousin James, you must stand with the boys, for bass. Pompey first, because he is used to it. There, that is right. Now, mamma, and all the girls, call out, as loud as you can, Fried bacon, fried bacon; and father, we must say on our side of the pond, as gruffly as we can, Tea-table, tea-table."

For some time the frogs were silent, and would not utter a sound. Perhaps they were frightened at the shouts of laughter that mixed in with "Fried bacon," and "Tea-table"; but after a while they became more sociable. A great bull-frog began, but his note was greeted with such a roar of fun, that he could not get courage to go on.

"Now, father," said George, "you and the boys must grunt out, Who marry my wife when I dead? and mother and the girls must say, Not me, not me, not me. Who take my fader when I dead? (Answer.) Not me, not me, not me. Who take my chillun when I dead? (Answer.) Not me, not me, not me. Who take my money when I dead? (Answer.) Me, me, me, me, me — "

The frogs, not caring much for grammar, liked this very well, and as the darkness increased, what with the noise of the frogs and the children, George's mother had to stop her ears.

The stars now came out, and the merry party started homeward, but through the walk, as Pompey now and then roared out, "Who take my money when I dead?" the children squeaked, "Me, me, me, me."

NEGRO HYMNS.

The children loved to collect the little negroes and hear them sing. The place they chose for the choir was beneath an orange tree, near the piazza, where the bush-lights were brightly shining.

Children's concerts are very sweet as they sit dressed finely, in grand halls, or fine churches; but so is a negro concert under a waving tree.

There was a whispering among them for a few moments, after Clara bade them sing, and then they began with a shout, —

"Master Jesus is my Captain,
He is my all in all,
He give me grace to conquer,
And take me home to rest!
I'm walking on to Jesus,
Hallelujah!
I'm walking on to Jesus,
Hallelujah!

George and Clara and their cousins grew drowsy, and the infants fell asleep in their little nurses' arms. As the singers separated, each to their own hut, they sang, —

"Don't you hear the gospel trumpet
Sound Jubilee?"

The children often went with their parents to visit the sick, and Clara saved many a fourpence from sugar-plums to give her old favorite, Maum Nelly.

Maum Nelly had been the nurse on the plantation, but was now too infirm for that office. Her manners were soft and grave, and her low courtesy almost graceful. She had always a present of eggs for the children when they came from town.

She was now very feeble; but as Clara entered her house, she dusted the bench with her apron, and begged her to sit down. After Clara was seated, Nelly paused a little, and then said, —

"My journey most done, my little missis. De Lord ben very kind to me. When Miss Clara come back again to Oak Hall, Maum Nelly bones will lie yonder under de pine, but her soul will gone to God Almighty. Me poor, weak creature, but de Lord Jesus bery merciful, — praise Him."

Clara walked slowly back to the house, and thought much that day of her old friend.

The day came for the children to return to school. It seemed a sad thing to leave the beautiful country, with its wide fields and green trees, the riding and fishing, for the dusty city.

All the people that were not at work came to bid them good-by. They stood in a row, to let the carriage pass, and Clara saw Maum Nelly standing at her door, with her apron to her eyes; then Clara remembered what she had said about lying beneath the pine-trees, and she wanted to cry; but the coachman cracked his whip, the carriage rolled on, and she began to think of the city.

THE BOY WHO WISHED IT WOULD RAIN MONEY.

A FAIRY TALE.

"I wish it would rain money," said Harry Merdon to his father.

"Why so?" said Mr. Merdon. "You have clothes and food, and a nice house to live in; what more do you wish for?"

"Oh, a thousand things!" answered Harry. "A rocking-horse, and a gold watch, and a library, and plenty of sugar things, and —".

"Stop!" said his father; "that is enough for the present. You are as restless as a great king the books tell about, who made himself master of all the countries about him, and then wept because he had no more to conquer. Silly boy! You have all your proper wants gratified, and yet you are dissatisfied"; and as Mr. Merdon said this, he went into his office, and Harry walked on.

"I don't care," said Harry, "about the old king, Alexander, I believe they call him. I wish it would rain money."

It was a pleasant afternoon, and Harry, having permission to walk, strolled out of the city. He was not contented with seeing the pretty, fresh-looking grass spread out like a carpet, nor the setting sun sailing like a balloon down the sky, nor with the fresh breeze, as if unseen hands were fanning him, nor with the river lying like a glass, showing the beautiful clouds over again; no, no, Master Harry cared for none of these things that God has given to his children so kindly, but he went on saying, "Oh, dear, if it would only rain money!"

While he was walking along, thinking about it, he saw a dark cloud rising from the north. It moved so fast he could not help watching it. At length it stopped over his head, and came down slowly, and while he looked with his face upward, he felt something fall on his forehead, and saw it drop on the earth. He stopped to see what it was. He could hardly believe it to be true when he found it was a sixpence, as bright and new as if it had just been made in the mint. He clapped his hands, and skipped for joy.

"I will go straight home and show it to father and mother," said he, "and then buy something nice, and divide with the children."

So he set off to go home. As he passed the market, he saw the old woman sitting there with molasses candy and fresh cakes.

"I should like one of those cakes," said Harry to himself; but he walked on, thinking he would tell his parents first how he came by the money; but at the corner of the street he saw another black woman selling cakes.

He stopped. "I can buy a cake and carry a part of it home," thought he, "and then tell the family about it."

So he bought it, and began to eat his share, and it was very nice and sweet; and alas! before he reached home, he ate all the cake.

"I am ashamed to tell them about it," thought Harry, "because I have been so selfish. Perhaps, if I walk out to-morrow, I shall see some more money drop out of the cloud, and then I am sure I shall carry it home and divide it."

Harry went home, but his thoughts were so full of his cloud-money, that he was careless and disobedient, missed his lesson at school the next day, and was very unhappy.

As Harry was preparing to take his walk the next afternoon, it began to rain so violently that he could not go. The foolish boy became angry, and almost cried for vexation. His sister asked him to play chess with her, and he began, but lost his patience, and of course lost the game; and when she said, "Checkmate," he rudely told her that she cheated.

"What is the matter with you, Harry?" said Sue. "I never saw you so cross before."

Harry would not answer, but piled up the chess-men, and then knocked them down.

Sue did not know that he had a "secret fault," or she could have told what made him unhappy. We are never very unhappy when we can tell our troubles to some kind friend; but Harry was ashamed to tell his, even to his dear sister.

The clouds passed away, and the sun shone in time for Harry to walk out.

"Where are you going?" said Sue. Harry would not answer, but hurried away. Again he visited the same spot, and again he forgot the brightness and beauty of the grass and the trees after the shower. He looked only at the north where his money-cloud had arisen before.

At length it came and rose slowly, and then faster and faster on the blue sky, and hovered over him.

I hope it will not drop a foolish sixpence this time, thought Harry. I should like a twelve and a half cent piece.

As he spoke, the cloud came slowly down, and the very thing he asked for dropped out of it — a bright, new shilling.

Harry did not jump and dance, and give thanks as before; he looked very serious, and thought what he should do with the money.

"Of course," said he to himself, "I must carry it home."

On the green he saw some boys playing marbles. They were bigger than he was, and he did not know them, but he just stopped to see the play. He was very much astonished when he found they played for money, and when one of the boys took a quarter of a dollar from another, he knew it was wrong. Alas, poor Harry, if you had only then walked away and told your kind parents all that had happened to you, you would have saved them many tears; but no, Harry stood *looking at the game*. At length one of the big boys saw the shilling shining in his hand, and he began to talk with Harry, and urged him to play. At first Harry said no, that it was wicked gambling, and that his parents would be angry. The bad boys laughed, and told him that his parents would not know anything about it, and they coaxed, and urged, and he said *he would play*.

He did play, and the big boys won his shilling, then laughed at him, and went away.

By this time, it was dark, and a sad walk had Harry, and he wept as he went along; but Harry's tears were not half so sad as those of a parent who has a bad son.

Even now all might have been well had he gone home and told his father and mother, and begged their pardon, and prayed to God to be made better; they would have put their arms about his neck, and said, "My son we forgive you," and he would have laid his head down on his pillow and slept in peace; "But how can I say it?" he told them a *lie*, and said he had been to see a friend.

They kissed him and bade him good night, but the kiss did not comfort him. He sobbed upon his pillow alone, and said, "I am wicked! I am wicked!" and he fell asleep, dreaming that a dark cloud was bearing him away from his dear home.

I pity the child who dares not go to his mother when he rises from his bed, and offer her a kiss. It is a sweet half hour when coming down from the bed-rooms, with glossy hair and sparkling eyes a circle of children gather round their parents wishing them a kind good morning, telling all their thoughts, and looking as bright as the sunshine.

But where is Harry Merdon? Why is not his merry voice heard among his brothers and sisters? He sits in one corner of the room sad and lonely, and when they speak **to him** he answers angrily. He will not play battledore with Henry, nor look over the new book of prints with Jane, and when his little sister Julia, **of whom** he has **always been so** fond, comes near him, he pushes her roughly away. **So will children always** do when they have been artful **and done** those things which they ought not to have done, and they **will never be** happy until they feel sorry and say so, and have been forgiven.

In the afternoon Harry was permitted to walk abroad. He went with an eager step. "I will not ask for those small pieces of money again," said he to himself. "Nothing **less** than dollars shall satisfy me. Those good-for-nothing sixpences **are not worth** talking about. I will buy a pony to begin with. Jack **Stedman's father** wants **to** sell his, but his saddle is not good enough for **a person** who can **get** money **as I** can for wishing. I will **have another suit of clothes,** too, and see if I cannot cut a little figure at the races next winter."

Harry **went on** talking to **himself until his spirits** were quite **raised, and he forgot that he had told a lie.** At length **he came to** the spot where the cloud money always dropped.

"Now," he exclaimed, "I hope it will rain dollars"; and no sooner had he wished, than down came the dollars. One hit him on the **eye** and hurt him so that he could not see; another came tumbling down on his nose and set **it a** bleeding; **as** he was going to **pick up some from** the ground there came such a shower of them **on** his knuckles that they almost put his fingers out of joint, and he could not handle them at all. His head began **to** ache with the thumps; and at last he roared out with pain. He was a sight to behold; the blood was streaming from his nose, his eyes were blood-shot, and his **hands** were held up over his head to keep the dollars from killing him. **He** could stand it no longer, but kicking up his heels he ran as fast as his feet could **carry him.**

The people who saw him thought he was crazy, and some boys who were playing called out "stop thief" as he went racing by, for nobody could believe he was a gentleman's son. The cry was raised among the people in the street, who followed him screaming "stop thief."

Poor Harry was terribly frightened, and glad he was when he came to his own house. He rushed in at the door, and fell down with fear and fatigue. His mother went to him and laid him on a bed, and bathed his face, and was surprised at his strange situation; then Harry confessed all and wept tears of real sorrow, and his mother forgave and comforted him, and told him that God knows best what is good for us, and that we ought not to seek for those things which he refuses, and she said,

"Be cheerful, Harry, and contented, and you will not wish for those things that will injure you."

Then Harry became a wise boy, and never concealed anything from his parents again.

PUNCTUATION.

COMMA — COUNT ONE.

,

WHAT is that little dot with a tail to it? and what is it for? I see it in all my books.

It is put there to make you read slowly, Louisa. Its name is a comma, and when you see a comma in your book, you must stop long enough to count one. Louisa will never read well, unless she looks at the commas. Big men and women look at the commas, and stop long enough to **count one.**

How many commas are there in this piece? Count them. Now bring your slate and pencil, and make commas until you are weary.

PERIOD — FULL STOP.

●

I HAVE counted the commas, ma'am, and Alfred has come to see me, and we wish you to tell us what the little round dot is without a tail.

Sit down, Alfred. Sit down, Louisa, and open a book. Look at this (.) It is a period. If you do not stop and breathe when you see periods, your reading will never please your father. You must stop long enough to count four, or six. All the lawyers and ministers have to stop and breathe when they see a period. They dare not pass it by without doing so. What does a period look like, Alfred?

Like a black pin's head broken off, ma'am.

How many periods are there in this piece? Now take your slates and see which can make the neatest period. Good-by.

SEMICOLON — COUNT TWO.   COLON — COUNT THREE.

COME here, Thomas, and read these names. **Colon: semicolon.** What does a colon (:) look like?

A colon (:) looks like two periods.

You must *stop* long enough at a colon to count three. It is not often used.

What does a semicolon (;) look like?

It looks like a comma with a hat on.

Very well, Thomas. Mind that you pay great respect to your semicolons. Semi means half.

Here is some poetry for you.

> Whene'er I meet a comma (,) I'll think of saying *one*,
> And *two* at semicolons (;) will be very pleasant fun;
> The colon (:) till I've counted *three*, my little mind will fix —
> At periods (.) I'll make a pause, and think of *four* or *six*.

THIS IS A NOTE OF INTERROGATION — COUNT FOUR OR SIX.

WHAT a long word! Spell it, John. In-ter-ro-ga-tion.

We use the note of interrogation when we write a question. How are you, John? Do you love to play ball?

There are two notes of interrogation. I will make six. ? ? ? ? ? ? What do they look like, John?

They look like soldiers marching backwards, ma'am.

That is a nice boy. Now tell me how long you mean to stop at a note of interrogation.

I will stop long enough to count four.

Good-by, Johnny. Go, make some on your slate.

MASTER DICKY BLUFF.

HE never takes off his hat in the house without being told.

When you are speaking he either interrupts you, or turns on his heel and walks off.

He has been taught to use an oath.

He fancies that he looks very manly when he stands **outside the** church door at prayers.

He takes the best place at table, and sits down before any one else.

He helps himself plentifully from the rarest **dish.**

He takes the wall from ladies and gentlemen when **he meets them** in the street.

When on horseback he goes full gallop.

He was once seen with a cigar in his mouth.

He **thinks it manly to talk loud** at public places.

Who seizes on the eatables at a party before any one can be helped? Dicky Bluff.

Who follows the waiter and empties it? Dicky Bluff.

Who thinks it very manly to **kick and shuffle in dancing?** Dicky Bluff.

Who likes to make a noise in the street? Dicky Bluff.

Who **amuses** himself writing on fences? Dicky Bluff.

Who **breaks** windows and pulls down **blinds, lamps,** and signs? Dicky Bluff.

A LITTLE GIRL THAT BITES HER NAILS.

WHAT are you eating, little Miss? Nuts?

No, ma'am.

Cake?

No, ma'am.

Sugar plums?

No, ma'am.

Let me see your hands. Oh, for shame, you are eating your nails! Bring some bread for the little girl. Nails were not made to be eaten. Next week we will see if **the** little girl has pretty nails on her nice little fingers.

THE NEW SCHOLAR.—Page 69.

THE NEW SCHOLAR.

The first Monday of January, 1820, Master Richard Homespun, under the direction of his mamma, made the usual preparations for entering an academy in a southern city of our Union. Richard was fourteen years old, and well grown,—a fact particularly perceptible, as his tight sleeves only came to his wrist, and left his purple hands fully exposed to anatomical observation. Nature had been singularly bountiful to Richard in a thick, bushy head; but, like most overgrown populations, "each particular hair" could not have its due attention, and the whole mass stuck up in turbulent strength.

Richard's mamma had given him various directions on his journey, with regard to his deportment.

"Dicky, my dear," said she, "you must be careful when you go into school to hold up your head, and make your manners, or the boys will laugh at you."

Richard was a good son, and promised to bow, little thinking of the tremendous difference there is between the dodge of a country boy, and the sweeping curve of a city obeisance.

"And mind, Dicky, dear," said his mamma, "keep your new hat safe, and don't get any dog-ears in your books; and when you open them, do it softly, and don't break the covers; read so, my dear"; and Mrs. Homespun inserted her nose between the blue covers of a spelling book.

Richard was a smart boy, and had been one of the best students and kite-players at a country school; but he felt in great trepidation at the idea of encountering so many strangers, besides having had hints of pumping and other school tricks. His mother kept him so long on Monday arranging his collar, picking the threads off his jacket, and smoothing his new hat, that the exercises of the school had commenced before he entered.

As soon as a face, accompanied by the insignia of a satchel, appeared at the door, the school hum ceased, and every eye was fixed upon him. He took off his hat, and, holding it straight before him, gave an agitated jerk with his head, and scraped his foot with a fling up backwards.

A smile, to say the least, spread over the young assembly. The principal, who saw the gathering commotion, advanced to his country catechumen, and seated him where he would not be exposed to the observation of the scholars.

There are few scenes where a good heart and regulated understanding are more conspicuous than in the ranks of a school on the introduction of a new pupil. Whatever may be his appearance, a perfectly well-bred boy will welcome a schoolmate to his new duties with politeness. Who does not remember the moment when he first entered the dreaded school-room; how anxiously he cast a glance around to see if there were any who meant to respect and love him in that strange circle?

The principal of the seminary, to which Richard was introduced, was generous and kind. He saw by the boy's bright eyes that he was intelligent, though awkward. After the exercises of the morning were over, he called on the class in which Richard had entered to remain.

"Young gentlemen," said he, "allow me to introduce to you a new schoolmate. He is a stranger, and will depend on you in some measure for happiness, now that he is away from his home. I hope that by your kindness you will make him feel that he is among friends."

The boys looked a little disconcerted, for they had been planning a hoax; but better feelings prevailed. He was received, not as a butt, but as an equal, and they learned that kindness was better than fun.

Some of these very boys are now voting for Mr. Homespun as member to Congress.

CINDERCLAWS.

ANOTHER CHRISTMAS DREAM.

SUSAN EGGLESTON'S fair cheek rested on her pillow, a few curls strayed from her night-cap, and her breathing was like the motion of a lily leaf on the smooth waters, when her mother went on tiptoe into her room, opened her stocking and placed something within it; then casting a look of satisfied fondness on the little sleeper, she touched her cheek with the lightest of kisses, and departed with a mother's prayer of love.

Susan dreamed that something descended slowly down the chimney, covered with a sooty blanket, from which proceeded a female voice, singing sweetly. When it had reached the hearth, she observed four hooks let down by cords to the four corners of the blanket, which carefully drew it up the chimney again, without scattering a cinder.

Under this singular canopy sat a small airy figure, in a glass barouche drawn by eight peacocks, surrounded by numerous little attendants.

"It would be very strange," thought Susan, "if this pretty creature should be Cinderclaws."

The little lady in the barouche was holding with some difficulty a large wax doll, and as she fondly caressed it, her soft voice sang,—

> "Hush thee, my darling,
> Thy journey was drear,
> But I bring you to Susan,
> And why should you fear?"

There was a short consultation among the attendants, when a little footman in scarlet livery, let down the steps like a flash, and taking the lead of twenty others, bore with some difficulty and much wiping of brows, the doll to the stocking. Finding it impossible to get her in, they laid her on the toilet-table, and returned to the barouche with a flourish of little trumpets.

Another consultation followed, and the little people, darting about like fire-flies, began to display the contents of the barouche. Swan, fish, turkey and cat pincushions, thread-cases of all forms and colors, implements of industry, from the silver-eyed needle to the gold in-laid work-box, were successively unfolded, and, among other things, Susan distinguished a nice box of French sugar-plums. As the breath of Cinderclaws passed over them, everything looked fresher and fairer.

Another whispering took place, and Susan heard the words,

"A dessert for Susan's dinner-party."

Quick as thought was arranged a small polished table, with plates for twelve. A taper, colored with rain-bow hues, suddenly shot up in the centre, by the side of an iced pyramid, on which was a waving flag, with the inscription —

"*A Merry Christmas and Happy New Year.*"

Fruits of every description, from the bead-like currant of the North, to the beautiful pomegranate of the South, were deposited in glass and silver dishes on the festive board.

"What are you placing there?" said Cinderclaws suddenly, as the waiters were busily arranging little decanters at the corners, and a tiny little cordial stand at the head of the table.

"A little French cordial," answered one, consequentially.

A frown rose to the little brow of the fairy, like a thundercloud on the blue sky. She rose suddenly, and stamping her small foot until the barouche rang again, exclaimed, —

"How dare you do this? If men turn brutes with stimulants, leave at least temperance to the young. Bring here the poison," she continued, her small voice rising in worthy indignation, "bring it here, and away!"

With both hands she grasped the bottles, and dashing them on the hearth, shivered them to pieces, while the blushing liquid flowed around.

The awe-struck attendants looked down in shame. A low whistle sounded; the blanket slowly descended, enveloping the barouche; the peacocks spread their wings, and Susan heard departing voices chanting as the fairy ascended.

> "Wake! wake! bonny birds,
> 'Tis the dawning of day;
> We must flee from the city,—
> Mount, mount, and away."

. . . .

"Papa," said Susan, as she caressed a beautiful doll he had given her before breakfast, "I dreamed last night that Cinderclaws belonged to the Temperance Society."

"I hope it is true," said her father.

ST. NICHOLAS.

A CHRISTMAS DREAM.

One Christmas Eve, John Eggleston hung his stockings carefully by the chimney corner, and after saying his prayers, fell asleep.

John dreamed that he was in bed, peeping at his stocking over the bed clothes, when he saw a very pleasant-looking old gentleman come down the chimney on a nice little pony, precisely like one named Lightfoot, that his uncle Ben had promised to give him. It was funny, indeed, to see the pony slide down feet foremost, and John laughed out in his sleep; but he laughed still louder when he examined old Nicholas, the rider.

His hair was made of squibs, and as he came nearer and nearer to the lamp that stood on the hearth, pop went off one of the crackers, and then another. St. Nick was not a bit frightened, — he only rubbed his ears with his coat sleeve, patted the pony to keep him quiet, and laughed till he showed the concave of his great mouth full of sugar-plums.

John was excessively amused, and shouted so loud that his mother thought he had the nightmare. He watched the old gentleman closely, and then looked at his stocking. It hung very conveniently.

"He can't put the pony in it," said he to himself, "and that is a pity."

The old gentleman's pockets stuck out prodigiously, and he panted and puffed as if he had been cudgelling an alligator.

"Well," said he, wiping the perspiration off his face, although it was cold December, "if this is not hard work! Sixty-five youngsters have I called on the last hour. Hark! the clock sounds down the chimney, one, two; I shall have a tough job to pop down all the chimneys in the town before daylight. I wonder what this chap would like for a Christmas present," continued he, eyeing the stocking; then putting his arms akimbo, he began to consider.

John's heart beat.

"Good Mr Nicholas," said he to himself, "if you could only give me that pony."

But he kept quite still; for he saw the old man thrust his hands into his tremendous pockets.

"Let me see," says old Nicholas; "here is a jack-knife that I was to have given to Tom Butler if he had not quarrelled with his sisters. *Hocus pocus!*" At this the stocking opened, and in went the jack-knife.

It was the very thing John wanted.

Then the old man pulled from his pockets twine, tops, marbles, dissected maps, books, sugar-plums, and divers other notions, all the while talking to himself.

"This lignumvitæ top," said he, "is for Tim Barnwell, a clever chap, who never tells lies. This line and fish-hook Master Troup must have for his kind care of his father when he had the gout. This annual was for William Wiley, but the lad kicked his brother and called him a wicked name, so we will lay it by for Tom Trout."

John thought he could stay forever to see the old gentleman take out his knick-knacks, and tell whom they were for; but he began to be a little frightened for his own stocking, when he recollected that he had been remiss in his Latin the last quarter.

"I hope the old gentleman don't understand the classics," said John to himself; but he stopped short, for this queer visitor held the stocking up to his nose, saying,—

"I think this lad loves gunpowder, by the smell."

He then took hold of his hair, and pulling out squibs by the dozen, tied them up in parcels, and threw them into the stocking. As fast as he pulled them off, new squibs appeared, and hung down over his ears and forehead.

"This accounts for the noise* we hear on Christmas," thought John. "I never knew before how squibs were made"; and he had to hold his sides for laughing, the old gentleman looked so droll.

As St. Nicholas was stooping over the light to put a new supply into the stocking, a great number exploded, and the little pony giving a start, disappeared up the chimney.

John awoke; it was just daybreak. He sprang out of bed, roused all the family with his "Merry Christmas," ran to the stable, and what should he see but uncle Ben's pony, with a bridle on his neck, on which was pinned a piece of paper written,—

"*A Merry Christmas, with the pony, Lightfoot, for my nephew, John.*"

---

* In all of the Southern States, fire-crackers and squibs are sent off at Christmas time, as well as on the Fourth of July.

THE MASKS.

LUCILLA ARMORY, in her sixteenth year, was a lovely-looking creature, flushed with youth and beauty, just between the woman and the child. All hearts were taken by her at a glance, she was so frank, witty, and sparkling. She led the enjoyments of the young, and enlivened the gravity of the old; was the prime leader of games, and could guess conundrums like a sibyl; was apt at everything; sang the last new songs, chatted phrases at French stores, was admired, sought, and yet, alas! dreaded, — for Lucilla was a *liar!* I know it is a hard word to digest, but call it by what name you will, whether white lying or black lying, — disguise it in the "*not at home*" of the busy housewife, or lounging novel reader, cover it up with all the shades that Mrs. Opie can devise, still, like her, we feel that lying is lying.

Lucilla's mother had imbibed loose notions on this subject. If her daughter's wit set a circle in a roar of laughter, or her prettiness fascinated them, it was enough for her. Sometimes the idea of her want of veracity startled her; but she comforted herself by saying, "Oh, Lucilla is so young! what can be expected of a girl of fifteen!"

Lucilla was always in extremes. It was either the coldest or the warmest day she ever felt in her whole life; a party was delightful or it was horrible; a young gentleman was either exquisitely charming or a stupid thing; a young lady was a beauty or a fright.

This spirit of exaggeration, as it is apt to do with females, extended to numbers. Everything increased on her lips like Falstaff's sixteen men in buckram; tens were hundreds, and hundreds thousands.

Helen Mortimer called on her one day.

"Why were you not at the Bancrofts' party last night?" said Lucilla.

"I was not invited," replied Helen.

"Oh, what a pity," said Lucilla; "we had a divine evening. I danced every time, and was invited six sets beforehand."

"Indeed!" said Helen. "I understood there was but one set danced on account of the heat of the evening."

"Good heavens! Helen," said Lucilla, "there were at least half a dozen. I wish you had been there to have seen Miss Triptoe, from New York. You know how vulgar it is to take steps; well, this belle cut such capers and leaped so high, that I bowed and nodded to Miss Dwindle under her feet while she was up in the air."

Helen cried out, "Oh, Lucilla!"

"It is a fact," said Lucilla; "you may ask any of the girls. Oh, by the way, have you seen Mary Donald's comb? It beats the South American ladies out and out. I declare to gracious, it is as high as grandmother's mahogany-backed chair, that was made before the old war. Don't shake your head, Helen. It was *so* high (measuring from the floor with her hand). They say Mary Donald's mother calls her children together and flogs them every morning before breakfast, to keep them in order."

Helen colored deeply, — "Mrs. Donald is a relation of ours, Lucilla," said she, "and we think her a most estimable woman. It is true that she assembles her family every morning, but it is to give them an opportunity of attending religious worship."

"Good powers!" exclaimed Lucilla, "who would have thought that you were related! It must have been Mrs. — "

"Stop," said Helen, "I will not listen to any more calumny. You know that you are slandering, and that such remarks often fix a stain on any individual which only time can wipe away."

Lucilla trotted her foot in some excitement, and took her turn to blush. As Helen rose to go, she asked if she had seen her bell-ropes.

"No, they are beautiful indeed," said Helen; "how ingeniously you have shaded them."

"I am glad you like them," said Lucilla; "see how my finger is marked with the needle."

At that moment her mother entered.

"What, Miss Helen," said she, "admiring my worsted work? I tried to persuade this lazy child to help me, but she would not."

Helen immediately took her leave.

Lucilla was passing her last quarter at a school, and her fine mind was rapidly opening under all the advantages of education.

By some unwarrantable calumny, she had caused the disgrace of a schoolmate, and the indignation of her class was so great she was glad to return home. Towards twilight her parents were absent, and as it was a sultry evening, she seated herself in the piazza.

Absorbed in a kind of reverie, she was startled by the tread of many feet, and lifting her eyes, she saw a procession of figures slowly enter the porch, and arrange themselves against the balustrade, with their faces towards her. A strange and horrible variety appeared in their countenances. Some looked dark and sullen, others distorted and malicious; some turned half aside with a glance of triumph, and others leered with gestures of disgusting familiarity. The line extended to the extremity of the building, gradually softening from ferocity to beauty, and as her eyes recoiling from the nearer bent to the most distant objects, distinguished a majestic form holding a torch, whose clear beautiful eyes seemed to penetrate her thoughts.

A restless silence pervaded her followers, while the figure with the torch, approaching Lucilla with a firm and measured tread, addressed her thus,—

"I am Truth. Alas! that I should be a stranger to one so young and fair. These are my attendants, and though forbidding in aspect they perform my will. All the shades of falsehood are represented on these faces, from the first exaggerated word to the crime of slander. They will follow you unseen; for slight offences the least deformed will become visible, but should you injure any one, expect to see their avenging eyes peering into yours in the domestic circle and the sparkling ball-room."

As she said these words, some of the vilest faces turned eagerly towards her as if already claiming her as their own.

"Before we part," said Truth, "let me warn you that your very exclamations are deceitful. Whom do you address when you say, 'My Heavens! Great Goodness! Good Gracious!' Do you invoke the Deity? You shudder, and say no. Beware, then, how you take His name in vain, for such language belongs only to Him."

"Lucilla," continued she, "these are masks which terrify you. When you conform to truth, you will know her followers and see them as you do me."

Lucilla looked eagerly at her. Resplendent indeed was Truth. Her torch, whose clear and steady beam was colored with variegated rays, threw a glory over her form, and seemed to light the way through her serene eyes to her very soul. A veil was thrown over her graceful limbs, revealing with modesty their fine proportions. Not an ornament was on her person, but there she stood glorious in simple beauty.

> "Authority, with grace
> Of awfulness, was in her face."

Intently gazing on Lucilla, she remained awhile silent, then turning to the fantastic procession, she said, —

"Ye know my signals. Calumnia, I wave my torch thrice and again for thee; Deceptia, thrice for thee; Exaggeratia, twice for thee; Flatterania, one flash for thee; disappear."

A momentary rush was heard, and Lucilla sat alone.

Lucilla retired to rest that night with a disturbed conscience;

there was a dread at her heart that made her cling to her young sister, who slept with her for companionship.

"I will be very careful of my words and conduct," thought she; but she did not pray nor look to the "Rock of Ages" for aid.

She slept and forgot her resolutions; forgot the God who never sleeps. The sun rose bright and lovely, but no beam of thankfulness dwelt in her heart; her form moved in strength and beauty, but no gratitude breathed from her lips. Sleep was to her like night on a flower; it tinged her cheek, enlivened her eye, but nothing more. Oh, how dreadful is the sleep of the soul! The bird may spring aloft with its matin song thoughtless of its powers; the leaf may lie open to the sun unconscious who colors it with emerald beauty; the stream may glide in soft meanderings ignorant of Him who bids it rise in the mountains and rush to the sea; but shall they, whose young *minds* are fresh from the Creator, whose first leaf of sin is almost unwritten, whose souls are capable of celestial sympathy, — shall *they* rise from sleep untouched by the thought of a protecting Deity?

Lucilla repaired as usual to the academy, and by her application gained the praise of her teachers. When the young ladies retired at the customary hour of recess, she was attracted by a bead bag which one of her schoolmates was embroidering. It was a libel on taste; the sheep were as tall as the men, a waterfall stood as still as if the earth's attraction was suspended, and a shepherdess held something which might have been called a stick as well as a crook.

"My dear Sarah," said Lucilla, "what a pretty idea! where did you get that pattern? Do draw it for me. I declare I shall not rest until — "

Before she could conclude her sentence a flash of light startled her, and on recovering from the glare she saw the face of Flatterania over Sarah's shoulder. Her head was fantastically ornamented with feathers. She held a fan with a simper to her lips and nodded and beckoned to Lucilla with an air of familiarity.

Lucilla felt faint at this recognition and suddenly returning to her desk pursued her studies in silence.

Lucilla was entertaining her friends one afternoon with an account of her father's sumptuous style of living.

"We always have three courses, and invariably ice-cream," said she, and busily talking, perceived not two flashes of light that played through the apartment. "What allowance of spending money do you have, Arabella?" continued she to one of the girls.

"Twelve and a half cents a week," was the answer.

"Mercy! how little," said Lucilla; "my father gives me a dollar."

Two soft flashes of light crossed her eyes and revealed a figure which she knew to be Exaggeratia. She held in her hand a magnifying glass, and as she glided with rapid steps past Lucilla, the frightened girl saw her own features enlarged to an immense size. She was hushed in a moment and the figure disappeared.

A few days passed without a visit from her visionary rebukers, until one evening Lucilla was desirous of wearing a ribbon-belt to a party, to which her mother had objected. She dressed herself according to her mother's wishes, but after bidding her good-by, ran up-stairs softly to her drawer and taking the forbidden belt hastily fastened it around her waist. Three flashes of light illuminated the room, and a female figure appeared in whose countenance two faces seemed joined together.

The two mouths spoke together, "Deception, Miss, at your service. Have you any commands?"

Lucilla threw down the belt in terror and wore the sash directed by her mother.

Several articles had from time to time been missed from Mr. Armory's premises, and suspicion fell on the house-servant, Amos, who was familiar with the establishment.

The apprehensions of the family were again excited by the loss of some silver spoons. Lucilla's lively imagination fixed at once on

Amos as the thief, and from talking about it unhesitatingly, she began to believe that it was actually the case. Her assertions were so positive, that Amos was regarded with distrust and aversion.

Her father questioned her on the subject, and said seriously, —

"Lucilla, have you reason to believe that Amos **is a thief?**"

"Certainly, sir. Do you not remember the umbrella, the walking-stick?" and she went on enumerating other abstracted articles.

"**But that is not to** the point, my dear," said he; "**have you ever seen** Amos take what does not belong to him?"

Oh, why did not Calumnia appear at this fatal moment?

Lucilla hesitated, but **her foolish** and wicked love of excitement was too strong, and she replied, —

"Yes, father, very often; but I did **not like to tell you about it.**"

Amos was instantly summoned and committed to the work-house.

Lucilla had not calculated on this, for **her feelings** were tender and she could not bear to have any one suffer. She burst into tears and pleaded for the release of **Amos with all the eloquence in her power.** She even suggested **the idea of his innocence;** but Mr. **Armory,** knowing her habit **of** prevarication, thought she spoke only from impulse and would not **heed her.**

The grandmother of Amos had been a nurse in the family **of Mr.** Armory for many years, until her intellect became disordered in her old age; but though her usefulness was gone, the strong **ties of** child's nurse united her to the family.

Hagar was nearly seventy years old; tall, erect, with **eyes full of** that strange light that beams out from a disordered intellect like phosphorescence from animal decay. Sometimes she closed the shutters of her apartment and addressed "the spirits" through small crevices where the light entered. Sometimes she sat for hours on a bench in the sun, with her hands clasped, reeling to and fro, singing psalms. But Hagar's delight was her church. A nice wrapper, a white handkerchief crossed over her bosom, and an apron **pinned** on without injuring one of its starched folds, with a check turban carefully tied over her gray hairs, formed her Sunday toilet. Slighting the seats in the gallery, her favorite one was in the porch of the broad aisle, where, sitting a little forward on a bench in the rear of the first pew, she could see the preacher. When a hymn was commenced, she rose, clasped her hands and inclined her body forward; at the end of every verse she courtesied, bending lower and lower until the close. Sometimes, particularly at the dismissal hymn, she advanced with a measured step up the aisle, gently waving her clasped hands, and courtesying, until led back by an observing friend.

Lucilla was a favorite of Hagar's, and possessed more control over her than any other person. For some time after being informed of her grandson's disgrace, her passions were unusually roused and Lucilla was sent for to soothe her. The wretched girl herself needed consolation, for conscience began to be busy. She went, however, to Hagar's room one day and found her in the attitude of listening.

"Hush!" said she, "don't you hear my boy?"

Lucilla wept bitterly.

"Are you so sorry," said Hagar, "for a thief?"

"Amos ain't sorry for the old woman's gray hairs"; and pushing aside her cap, she showed the crisp, white curls that edged her forehead.

At this moment Amos entered after his punishment. He threw himself on a bench with his head on his knees and groaned bitterly.

"Thief! thief!" screamed the old woman.

"I swear to heaven I'm not a thief, grandma," said the poor fellow.

A servant suddenly rushed in and informed them that the real culprit had been discovered and that Amos was innocent.

A wild scream of joy burst from Hagar at this intelligence and, aiming to spring towards her grandson with extended arms, she fell. The chords of life were broken, — old Hagar was dead.

Four vivid flashes of light illuminated her stiffened form, and Calumnia, with a shout of triumph, stood beside her. In her shrivelled right hand she held a poisoned arrow and in the other a bleeding heart.

Wild with terror, Lucilla flew from the scene and weeping in her father's arms confessed the crime of slander.

. . . . . .

Months elapsed and Lucilla's character had changed from idle trifling to thoughtful truth. She was sitting one evening in **the** piazza reflecting on the **past and** seeking aid for the future, when the masked figures of her former vision appeared before her.

"Lucilla," said Truth with a gentle tone, "I need not now **tell** you who I am. You know me. Has my lesson been too severe? You will not think so if you are wholly mine."

She approached nearer to the now really **lovely girl,** — **lovely with** the beauty **of** soul, — and gazed into her eyes. **Lucilla shrank not;** Truth **laid her cool, firm** hand against Lucilla's heart. **It fluttered not.**

"You are mine," said Truth; and, saying this, she breathed a breath as odorous as infancy's upon an adamantine seal and touched it to Lucilla's coral lips, and then passed her hand with a slow and gentle pressure on Lucilla's eyes. They opened on the visionary train whose falling masks were revealing sweet, unclouded faces, reflected in polished mirrors. There was no deformity now; with chaste and gentle motion they glided on and the smiling **welcome they gave her** shone from mirror to mirror, until **the** beautiful **vision passed** away.

It was gone and the stars of evening looked pleasantly down **on** Lucilla's placid soul.

THE WAGON BOY.

ONE clear wintry Saturday, Richard Edwards accompanied his father on a hunting excursion. They were unsuccessful, but comforted themselves with the jokes which good-natured sportsmen make on each other when they return from the chase empty-handed. They were a mile from any habitation, and had taken a short cut through the woods, when Richard called —

"Stop, father; I hear sounds of distress."

Mr. Edwards reined in his horse and listened.

"I perceive nothing," said he, "but the forest birds that gather at night-fall. But hark! so, Fido, down boy," continued he to a hound which was leaping up at his side.

A wild, but child-like sob of agony burst distinctly on their ears.

"We must look into this, Richard," said his father; and starting in the direction of the sound, he was followed by his son.

As they rode over the uncleared space, they heard at intervals the same cry, and they were soon near enough to perceive the object of their search. In one of the *turnouts* made through the woods by wagoners, they perceived a country team; and near it, extended on the sand, lay a man with the cold, stern countenance of death, while a youth of fifteen, kneeling on one side with his head resting on the silent breast, sobbed as if his heart would break, and a dog looked wistfully, as if he knew the helplessness of his master and the anguish of the boy.

At the sound of footsteps, the youth sprang up.

"Sir," he cried, "can you save my father? Save him, save him!"

Mr. Edwards alighted from his horse and approached the body. It had all the marks of death, — the cold and shrunk countenance, the appalling repose of mortality bereft of soul. The eyes of the youth brightened with eager hope as Mr. Edwards felt the pulse and breast of the deceased. There was no answering sympathy in his look; he shook his head mournfully, and said, "My poor fellow!"

The wagon boy threw himself on the body of his father, and gave that cry of deep and wailing sorrow that God allows to the crowded heart to keep it from breaking. The cold wind swept by with a wintry gust and seemed faintly to echo his subsiding moan.

Richard took his hand.

"We will try to comfort you, my poor lad," said he.

"Father, shall he go home with us?"

"What, leave *him?*" said the wagon boy, clinging to his father, while a deep shuddering shook his frame.

"No," said Mr. Edwards gently, "you shall not leave him; but would it not relieve your mind to see him laid in a decent grave?"

Mr. Edwards had touched a string that finds an answering chord in every heart.

The wagon boy silently rose, passed his arm across his eyes, from which the large tears still rolled, and, assisted by Mr. Edwards, placed the body on the wagon.

The sad procession moved along and reached the ferry-boat in time to pass to town.

Mr. Edwards was rich and generous. He clothed the wagon boy in appropriate garments the following day, and walked with Richard as mourner to the grave. The faithful dog mutely followed, and when the wagon boy returned from the mournful ceremony, he laid himself down by the side of the poor brute, and throwing his arms around the animal, hid his swollen eyes upon his neck, as if he only could understand his feelings.

For many days they tried to comfort him in vain, for religious emotions were new to him; but when Mr. Edwards explained to him the resurrection and the life, and Richard read to him those sublime and touching portions of Scripture which tell us that afflictions are not of the dust, and that whom the Lord loveth he chasteneth, the wagon boy was comforted. He returned to his home sad but resigned; and Richard, too, was taught a reliance on Providence, that was often renewed when he rode by the spot where the cry of the wagon boy first pierced his ear.

A SULLIVAN'S ISLAND STORY.

"FATHER says he will take us all to the island this afternoon," said Edward Marion, with a shout that reached his sisters in the third story of their residence.

None but those who have passed a languid August morning in Charleston, S. C., can tell what an effort it costs to prepare a large family for the four-o'clock steamer. But Mrs. Marion was a good manager, and they were all in the carriage in season, with the loss only of Sophia's mit, and Charlotte's basket for shells. John, who was thinker-general for all the group, foreseeing this difficulty, had provided a basket large enough for both, which was in the hands of a bright-looking little colored boy, who, being just from the country, wished to see "dem big boat what trow up fire."

When on board the steamer, Charlotte drew near her father and whispered, "You promised you would tell us something about the revolutionary war when we should go to the island."

"Yes, my dear," said her father, "and I will gladly keep my word. You must first imagine all those large buildings on the wharves removed, and fortifications placed along from South bay to Cooper river."

"Did they pull down the stores, father?" said Sophia.

"Yes, my daughter," answered Mr. Marion. "It is necessary to place fortifications between the buildings of a city and the enemy. You know the Charlestonians, in 1776, expected the British frigates would come up to town. But stay,— who is this old gentleman coming on board? Is it possible! Captain Cowpens, I am most happy to see you!" and Mr. Marion shook hands cordially with the old gentleman, whose bronzed face and suit of blue homespun indicated an up-country farmer.

"Thank you, Mr. Marion," said the captain. "You see my eyes are not so bad, but that I can recognize an old friend. I thought to have ended my days at the High Hills; but your steamboats and your railroads have tempted me to come and take a look at what is going on hereabouts. Ah, if General Lee could have had a steamer, when he went from town to take a peep at Moultrie, in the fight of '76, he would have been a happy fellow!"

"My dear children," said Mr. Marion, introducing them, "Captain Cowpens is the very man to gratify you with anecdotes of the Revolution. He has had real fighting, while I have only

'Shouldered my cane, and told how fields were won.'"

"We should be delighted if he would tell us all about the war," they exclaimed.

The old captain said, "Happy to gratify the young people. Inquiring minds, hey? Well, you must know there were lying off the island several British vessels, full of Red Coats; reg'lars,— knowing ones. Let me see," said he, counting on his fingers; "there was the Bristol, fifty guns; the Experiment, fifty guns; the Active, twenty-eight guns; the Solebay, twenty-eight guns; the Syren, twenty-eight guns; the Acteon, twenty-eight guns; the Sphinx, twenty-eight guns; the Friendship, twenty-six guns; the Rangers' sloop and Thunder Bomb, each eight guns. But what did we care for them? General Moultrie was not a man to start at—" (Here the steam was raised with its usual noise.) The captain, quite frightened, exclaimed, "Hey! what's that? (Whizz, bizz, sizz!) Smoke and thunder! what's the matter?"

Charlotte, whispering to John, said,—

"Captain Cowpens does not stand fire so well as he did in '76."

Captain Cowpens was too experienced a veteran to be long agitated by noise and smoke. He gazed composedly on the dense column, that rose like a living thing on the air, and floated off in gentle circles on the distant sky, and then, nodding his head, as much as to say, "this beats everything," sat down, with both hands resting on his hickory cane.

After meditating a moment, he took a long pinch of snuff. The children wondered that any man could make a good-looking nose such a receptacle.

"He was in the old war," said Edward, "and we must forgive him everything."

"I suppose, boys," said Captain Cowpens, after he had diffused, rather than removed the snuff on his face, and scattered it so freely that black Billy who stood behind him began to sneeze: "I suppose we must talk about '76. Do the young folks know anything about General Lee?"

"Yes, sir," said Edward, promptly. "He was born in North Wales, in Great Britain, and became an officer at the age of eleven. He came to New York in 1773, to fight for the Americans. He was made commander of the Southern forces, and inspired the people with great confidence."

Captain Cowpens clapped him on the shoulder, saying, "Very well, my boy; I like to see a lad with his wits about him. To be sure his presence did put us in great spirits. Colonel Moultrie said it was equal to a reinforcement of a thousand men. He was here, there, and everywhere; and though he was mighty quick-tempered, we soon got used to that. I remember him well. He was a tall man, and his face was not agreeable. When he chose, he could be gentlemanly; but he was often coarse, and in his latter years, was very slovenly in his dress. He said sharp things, and made enemies, though those who are judges of such things called him a bright scholar. He was a great lover of dogs, and often annoyed the ladies with them. He had a poor opinion of Sullivan's Island, — said there was no way to retreat, and called it a — "

"Oh! I remember," said Sophia; "he called it 'a slaughter pen.'"

"So he did, miss," continued the captain. He would have given up the post if — "

"What does giving up the post mean?" asked Sophia. "What do they do with posts in war?"

"You little simpleton," said Captain Cowpens. "Do you not know what a post is?"

"Certainly, sir;" said Sophia, pertly, "I do. It is a long stick that you drive into the ground."

"You little goose," said the captain. "You know, Miss Charlotte, don't you?"

"Yes, sir," said Charlotte; "a military station, where soldiers stay."

"Yes; that is it, my dear," said the captain. "A post to drive in the ground — eh?" chucking Sophia under the chin, who looked rather offended. "Let me see, — we were talking about General Lee. Rutledge, President of the General Assembly of South Carolina, would not let him give up the Island. Then General Lee ordered a bridge to be made of empty hogsheads, after the manner of buoys, over to Haddrel's Point, where there was a good stand of men. After the hogsheads were steadied, the workmen put planks across them, the whole way. Colonel Clark set out from Haddrel's with 200 men, and before they were half on, the hogsheads began to sink lower and lower, and back they huddled, as fast as if the enemy had been at their heels.

"Colonel Moultrie was as easy as possible, — joked about the bridge, and considered himself able to defend his *post*, — eh, Miss

Sophy? General Lee was very uneasy about the Island, and doubted Colonel Moultrie's prudence. Even during the action on the 28th, when the British were firing like vengeance, he came down from town, and pointed two or three guns himself. But from that moment he seemed to feel confidence, and said, 'Colonel, I see you are doing very well here; you have no occasion for me; I will go up to town again.' He left us, then, in the midst of a heavy fire. When he was observed to be coming, Colonel Moultrie and several other officers were smoking their pipes as they were giving orders; but when General Lee came into the post, they thought best to lay them down.

"After the 28th, Colonel Moultrie said that he and Lee were bosom friends."

"Father," said John, "Edward told us that General Lee was made an officer at eleven years of age. How can that be?"

"Persons of wealth and influence," replied his father, "secure commissions and titles for their children, that they may enter the service as soon as their education is completed."

"Can you tell us any thing more of General Lee," said Charlotte to her father.

"My children," replied Mr. Marion; "General Lee gained great fame by his wisdom and bravery in conducting the southern campaign; but he has not left behind him a reputation to be envied. How much superior is true goodness to bravery, though a good man will generally be brave. General Lee was disgraced in the United States army for disobedience of orders, misbehavior before the enemy and disrespect to General Washington. He retired to an estate in Virginia, lived secluded in a small hovel and died in obscurity. The part he took in securing our independence claims a sigh at the thought of his lonely and distant grave. His last words were, 'Stand by me, my brave grenadiers!' How much more affecting, at that solemn moment, would have been an appeal to his God, and an expression of trust in his Redeemer."

There was silence in the little group as they reflected on Mr. Marion's words, which was broken by John's exclaiming, "Castle Pinckney, father! how soon we are abreast of it!"

"Heigh! what is this?" said Captain Cowpens. "That tight piece of brick and mortar was not here in '76. Ah! friend Marion, these changes make us feel old."

Mr. Marion looked a little nervous at the word *us*, and rubbed his hair, as if, like a blind man, he could feel colors.

Captain Cowpens could not take his eyes from Castle Pinckney; and a beautiful object it is, sitting like an ocean bird amid the noisy solitude of dashing waters.

"I should love to live there," said Charlotte, whispering to her mother, "and hear the music of the winds and waves."

"I remember," said the captain, after musing a little while, "they used to say that there lived on that spot, before the year 1752, an old man and his daughter, who kept a tea-house where parties of pleasure resorted from Charleston to spend the evening and drink tea; that the house was washed away by the gale of 1752, and the old man certainly was drowned, and probably his daughter also."

"Its history since that period," said Mr. Marion, "is soon told. It remained unoccupied from 1752 to 1780, when Charleston was besieged by the British forces under the command of Sir Henry Clinton, and they erected a battery under the supervision of Colonel Moncrieff, engineer, and called it Mud Fort. This fort, of course, was held by the British as long as they held Charleston. After the revolutionary war, in 1798, and during the administration of Mr. Adams, in anticipation of a war in France, our government erected a fort or castle and denominated it Castle Pinckney, in compliment to Charles Cotesworth Pinckney, ambassador to France, who just about that time returned home. Charles Pinckney was at the same time governor of South Carolina, but the compliment was paid to the ambassador. This fort had not been built upon a stable foundation, for it was some time afterwards washed away. The present fort, or castle, **was built**, in the year 1811, by Mr. John Gordon, a resident of Charleston, and was erected in anticipation of a war with Great Britain, which **was** declared the year after."

While he spoke, the good steamer darted on her way, and in a few moments the boys thought of nothing else but their fishing tackle, and the girls their prospect of picking up shells.

It was a languid afternoon in August when the Marions and Captain Cowpens visited the island. Edward's thermometer, a prize from **his** teacher, stood **at** eighty-seven in the entry, although the piazza **was** shaded by a spreading fig-tree.

All who had energy to move in the city were enjoying their summer recreations. **Nurses** were loitering, and children playing, in the city square; throngs crowding to the battery; elderly ladies taking quiet drives beyond the lines; younger ones partaking ice-creams, sitting tête-à-tête in the arbors, or sipping the grateful refreshments with unbonneted heads in their carriages; schoolboys were rushing from five-o'clock labors to their ponies, and our fair Di Vernons arranging their round straw hats, or waving plumes, for their equestrian exercises.

The steamboat afforded **its** customary motley groups, — **reclining invalids, with their eyes shooting a sudden brilliancy as the sea**-breeze swept over their languid brows; **the** sickly infant seizing the first relished morsel; the happy and healthy, who come to add another tinge to a bright cheek or preserve one already glowing; the mechanic, generously recreating his industrious family; the **professional** man, escaping from the stifling court-room, the chamber **of** disease, or the secluded study, to feel the Atlantic breeze untainted with human breathing, **and** gaze on the clear sky and unfettered sea, — all were there. It is not for us to enter on this innocent catalogue those whose motives are gross and impure, — the sensualist and the gambler, who dare to sojourn where God's mercies pass by in purifying love, and whose stagnant souls are untouched with sensibility by the wave or the breeze.

Captain Cowpens glanced from Fort Johnson to Haddrell's Point, then to Sullivan's Island, and there his eyes rested with an American gaze of delight on the beautiful flag waving from the citadel.

When he landed at the Cove, he said nothing, but with an energetic stamp, thrust his cane into the sand as if to assure himself that he stood again on that sacred spot.

The girls were disappointed in gathering shells as they strolled on the beach. For several years they have been becoming more and more infrequent, though occasionally an eye sharpened by conchological skill, may detect a valuable one in the hollows on the beach, at the back or eastern part of the island.

Charlotte picked up a buccinum, with the living animal in it; but when she recollected its slight value and the torture it would endure, she laid it down on the beach again and with a generous pleasure watched its uncouth motions on the smooth sand, until a friendly wave with dancing steps came and bore it into the sea.

Captain Cowpens was overcome by the emotions that crowded on his mind. He was trying to realize that the spot he now saw was the "wilderness he remembered covered with live oak, myrtle and palmetto trees."

Mr. Marion took him gently by the arm, led him within the fort and introduced him to the commanding officer. There, in the commodious and not inelegant dwelling, the old gentleman sat down, and as he wiped his forehead, Sophia perceived that he passed his handkerchief across his eyes to conceal a gathering tear.

The children were gratified with the military display at the fort, and after satiating their curiosity returned to the beach. Mrs. Marion once shook her head at John, as he stood behind a sentinel, imitating his stiff attitude and shouldering her parasol like a gun.

The boys and girls shouted in the fulness of freedom as they regained the beach. Black Billy put his feet carefully into the water at the suggestion of the children, then a little farther and a little farther, until finding it quite safe and feeling the ground firm beneath his feet, he rolled up his pantaloons and dashed in, singing and dancing like a Merry Andrew.

How happy were they all! True, there were no hills rising up to meet the blue sky, no sloping fields winding gracefully to the shore, no rocks stationed like guardians around our coasts, but oh! how much there was that was beautiful and glorious!

Generous and warm-hearted youths, as you tread these level sands, do you experience a blank for memory or a pause for hope? Gentle and light-hearted girls, are there not pleasures enough in the stirring air and rushing wave? Go, then, in your innocent joy; gather rough shells and throw them in the dark waters; greet your conscious dog as he comes dripping with his prize from the surge; write sweet names on the sand; run and shout with careless laughter against the breeze, or muse on those thoughts which come even to children from the bounding sea!

Some planks that had been washed up by the waves formed a pleasant seat for our little party, after they were joined on the beach by Captain Cowpens and their parents.

"This is a nice time," said John, "for you to tell us some anecdotes, Captain Cowpens. I do not mean dates and such things, those are bad enough in school."

"If I could hobble about the island," said the captain, "I should like to see the spot where they tell me Captain Tufts used to live."

"Who was he?" asked Sophia.

"A faithful old Massachusetts seaman," replied the captain, "who, previous to the battle of Fort Moultrie, was sent in command of a gunboat to attend to the sinking of some vessels in Hog-Island channel, to prevent the British from using that pass to attack Charleston.

"The first night that Tufts took his station for this service, the British sent one of their fleet, which anchored within gunshot and kept up a smart fire on him. No particular damage was done, except on an old hog, being the only *soul* wounded on board. This was the commencement of hostilities with the British.

"On many occasions after, Tufts was serviceable throughout the war. We borrowed two hundred pounds of powder during the action of the 28th from his schooner lying behind the fort."

"At the end of the war," said Mr. Marion, "he was rewarded by our State's allowing him the entire sovereignty of Sullivan's Island, where, except the small garrison at the fort, he was for some time the only resident. He made some money from his large flock of goats, selling them to captains of vessels. He was called *Governor* Tufts, — a title of which the old gentleman was very proud. I have often, when a boy, seen Governor Tufts in his hut looking like Robinson Crusoe. By carrying with you some wine and sugar, you might be sure of procuring from his excellency a fresh syllabub."

"Father," said Charlotte, "was he buried here? I should like to find his grave."

"I have heard," said Edward, "that he lies among the Myrtles.* Why, in the present fashion for monuments, cannot the youth of South Carolina erect one to this old man? General Moultrie was elevated in society, and the name of the fort and island are his monuments; but poor Captain Tufts, who brunted the first blow of the enemy, the wild winds must blow over his solitary remains, and no patriotic voice question where they lie!"

"Right, boy, right," said Captain Cowpens, grasping his hands. "You deserve to be a general."

"I think it was about here I stood," said the old officer, in the course of their afternoon drive, "when the British frigate Acteon,

---

* A wild, unoccupied piece of ground, where the dead are deposited on the island.

which had run aground on the 28th during her attempt to take the right flank of the fort, was burnt and forsaken by her crew."

Captain Cowpens put himself in an oratorical position, and nearly knocked off Mrs. Marion's bonnet with his cane, while he recited,—

> "Acteon thus, as ancient fables tell,
> By his own hounds pursued, expired and fell."

"While she was in flames," continued he more quietly, "Captain Jacob Milligan boarded her and coolly fired off three of her guns at Sir Peter Parker's vessel; then brought off the ship's bell and a few other articles, and had scarcely left her, when she blew up. Colonel Moultrie said, as a grand pillar of smoke issued from the explosion and expanded itself at the top, 'that it formed the figure of a palmetto tree.' Anyhow, it was a grand sight,—not only then, but when the smoke burst in a great blaze which burnt down to the water's edge.

"In the defence of Sullivan's Island there was but one instance of cowardice, though there were but three hundred and fifty troops, all newly raised, and not one of them regularly educated for service except Colonel Motte. The case was that of a soldier, whose nerves would not allow him to stand on the platform during the severe cannonading and bombardment of the fort. By the articles of war, this poor fellow should have been shot, but the officers were rendered too good-natured by their success to resort to that extremity, and changed, perhaps, to a severer punishment. They gave him up to his comrades to do whatever they pleased with him. The soldiers dressed him up in women's clothes, and after worrying him nearly to death, drummed him out of the fort."

"I am glad of it," said John.

"One would think," said Mrs. Marion, with a smile, "that the costume worn by Mrs. Motte, Mrs. Heyward, Mrs. Edwards, Mrs. Brewton, Mrs. Elliot, Mrs. Pinckney, Mrs. Holmes, Mrs. Shubrick, Mrs. Izard, etc., would not be *very* disgraceful."

Captain Cowpens received this rebuke with a respectful bow to the lady and continued: "Poor M'Donald, one of our sergeants, was mortally wounded. Did he flinch even then? No! he died exhorting his comrades to continue steady in the cause of their country."

"Your dog Cæsar, John," said the captain, after alighting from the carriage, "reminds me of one which amused some of us even in the fight, by running after the cannon balls on the beach, as they rebounded from the brick work of the lower part of the fort."

Sophia patted Cæsar, saying, "He wags his tail as if he understood you, sir."

"The most trying moment to our friends in town during the battle," continued the captain, "was that in which our flag was shot away. They gave up all as lost; but Sergeant Jasper, in the hottest of the British fire, jumped on the beach, took up the flag, secured it to the stump of the sponge-staff, gave three cheers while on the ramparts, and amidst a shower of balls returned to his duty on the platform."

"My children," said Mrs. Marion, "while you admire this act of heroism, let me tell you of an instance of Jasper's *good sense*, a quality more desirable in our peaceful times. Governor Rutledge presented him a sword, and offered him a commission. The first he gratefully accepted, but declined the last, saying, 'Were I made an officer, my comrades would be blushing for my ignorance.'"

"Mamma," said Charlotte, "are you not glad that Sullivan's Island is called Moultrieville?"

"Yes," replied her mother; "but I should have preferred Moultrie's Isle."

Captain Cowpens was so much invigorated by the air and interested by the sight of the Islands, that he decided to remain for the season. A convenient house on the front beach was selected for his accommodation and Mr. Marion promised to visit him frequently.

SATURDAY AFTERNOON.—Page 99.

The children passed every Saturday with their old friend, who entered into their amusements and was as eager as themselves for the holiday. His fishing-boat was always cleaned with extra care, and the boys' guns placed behind the door ready for their ramble to the curlew-ground. Charlotte invariably protested against their firing a single gun. She wondered they could have the heart to disturb the flight of the birds, as she watched their airy processions against the sky, now mingling as if for consultation, now extending in a pencilled line, lengthening and lengthening until lost in the viewless air.

As the season advanced, the visits of the Marions were limited to the day-time, as a change of night-air is considered dangerous in southern climates in the autumnal months.

One September morning, Mrs. Marion and the children prepared for their Saturday excursion, their father being prevented by business from accompanying them. The steamboat had stopped running, and with gay spirits they stepped on board a packet, delighted with the change.

They found their old friend well and happy. He had been ornamenting the fishing-boat — even her oars were painted a bright green, and she danced on the waves as if expecting her lively crew.

Nor had the young people been unmindful of him. Charlotte and Sophia affectionately threw around his neck a watch-guard, the result of their joint industry, on which was wrought, in glittering letters, "28th June, 1776." Edward had superintended the repairing of his spectacles and John came drumming his fingers on a tortoise-shell box, containing a present of best rappee.

They all entered the fishing-boat. Nature was as bright as their feelings. A few large pillowy clouds rested beneath the heavens, softening, but not obscuring the autumnal sun. The city, with its spires, rose in the distance. The light-house, beautiful emblem of hope and safety, towered on one side, and on the other the main, with its level verdure, seemed like a fringe of green on the azure horizon. Pleasure-boats were darting from the cove; the rocking skiff of the fisherman lay easily on the waves and the majestic merchantman passed through the channel with its freighted store.

Some there were, on that day, who with a prescient fear looked round and fancied signs of evil, and the accustomed ear could detect the roar of a distant swell upon the ocean. It blew freshly; but who, after the panting fervors of the heated south wind, would not welcome that cooling breeze?

The wind gradually, but not alarmingly, increased. The Marions ate their late dinner with true Island *goût*, and not one want was felt or expressed but that one so full of love in the domestic scene, "Oh! if father were only here!"

As they sat at table passing innocent jokes on their fishing skill, a sudden gust shook the slight tenement, and a drizzling rain began to fall. They instantly prepared to return to town, but every moment the wind rose and the sky became darker. They hurried, chilled and alarmed, to the cove. There was evident anxiety among the mariners; a gale was apprehended and they declined the responsibility of female passengers in their slight packets.

The disappointed party returned to the house in silence, for now the rain began to pour in torrents and the building rocked like an infant's cradle.

At the approach of night, Sophia was dreadfully alarmed, and as each gust came with its roaring accompaniments of angry waves, she screamed with terror. Mrs. Marion tried to soothe and reason with her. It was in vain. Now her cheek was pale as death, and her eyes seemed starting from their sockets; and now the blood rushed to her forehead, and she covered her eyes with her hands to shut out the scene before her.

"Sophia," said her mother, sternly, "I will not suffer this violent emotion. Conquer your feelings immediately, or you must leave me.

Your unchristian violence is worse than the storm. God is with us. Let us be prepared for his will, while deliberating on the best means of safety."

Sophia, with a strong effort, conquered her feelings and only once, but with what different emotions, cried out, "If father were but here!"

How rapidly night came on! They had hoped the storm would lull at twilight; but it rose and rose, and at length the waves, like some living monster, lifted the piazza beneath them. Moving masses of ruins were seen floating on the white foam, while their voices could scarcely be heard through the din and roar of the elements. An able and faithful servant was summoned to accompany them to the fort. He took Sophia in his arms, who lay there like a blighted flower. Charlotte and John held to the skirts of his coat; Captain Cowpens, Mrs. Marion, and Edward with the remaining servants, following closely behind. The darkness was intense and their way lay through rising waves.

For a short time, a shout, a word of encouragement, even a jest to attempt to conceal their alarm and to assure themselves of each other's presence, were heard; but this was soon hushed. At this crisis there was an awful pause in the elements; it seemed that Nature was preparing a nervous heave, and clinging to each other, they thought to die together. It came, — the gale rushed thundering on, roaring and raging over bursting waves.

That loving band were parted; only Sophia and John reached the fort in safety.

Bitter was that night! — sad the morning. Oh, thou bright and glorious sun! how could'st thou return smilingly on such a scene of desolation?

Mrs. Marion and Edward had regained each other, after that fearful shock, and succeeding in reaching the piazza of a building, which though but a wreck withstood the waves. Charlotte was protected by a fisherman. His boat, that had been washed far up on the sands, he turned and made good shelter, though a rough one, for the delicate and bewildered girl.

Their venerable friend, however, was nowhere to be found. Alas! amid the sad discoveries of that day, with tearful eyes they recognized his well-known form. Grasping his hickory cane, his gray hairs wet with surf, and his eyes fixed in death, lay the veteran on the beach.

As the soldiers raised him to bear him to the fort, the gold beads of the watch-guard sparkled in the sun, and the date of "1776" came to the eyes of the girls, through their blinding tears.

A mournful and respectful train was that which, with its military escort, wound its way by the curlew-ground to the Myrtles where the Island dead repose. The muffled drum, mingling with the sounds of air and sea, and the minute guns, with sad precision, told the tread of death. Fit was the burial. Let the worldling be laid amid the city's hum; let the babe and the maiden rest beneath the green tree, and flowers blossom over their graves; but the hero of the South, where can he find a better monument than those sands, or a holier dirge than that which comes sweeping over the ocean, bringing echoes of his fame?

THE YOUNG MATHEMATICIAN.

LAURA SINCLAIR was an intelligent girl, studiously devoted to all her lessons except arithmetic.

"O, mother!" she would exclaim, "this is arithmetic day. How I hate it."

"My daughter, do not make use of such expressions," said her mother. "Nothing is wanting but attention and perseverance to make that study as agreeable as any other. If you pass over a rule carelessly and say you understand it for want of energy to learn it, you will continue ignorant of important principles. I speak with feeling on this subject, for when I went to school a fine arithmetician shared the same desk with me, and whenever I was perplexed by a difficult sum, instead of applying to my teacher for an explanation, I asked Amelia to do it for me. The consequence is, that even now, I am obliged to refer to others in the most trifling calculations. I expect much assistance from your perseverance, dear Laura," continued she, affectionately taking her hand.

Laura's eyes looked a good resolution and she commenced the next day putting it in practice. Instead of being angry because she could not understand her figures, she tried to clear her brow to understand them better, and her tutor was surprised to find her mind rapidly opening to comprehend the most difficult rules. She now felt the pleasure of self-conquest, beside the enjoyment of her mother's approbation, and for many years steadily gave herself up to the several branches of mathematics.

Laura was the eldest of three children, who had been born to the luxuries of wealth. Mr. Sinclair was a merchant of great respectability, but in the height of his supposed riches, one of those failures took place which often occur in commercial transactions, and his affairs became suddenly involved. A nervous temperament and a delicate constitution were soon sadly wrought on by this misfortune. Mr. Sinclair's mind, perplexed and harassed, seemed sinking under the weight of anxiety. Laura was at this period sixteen years of age; her mind was clear and vigorous, and seemed ready like a young fawn for its first bound.

One cold autumnal evening, the children with their wild gambols were playing around the room, while Mr. Sinclair sat leaning his head upon his hand over a table covered with papers. Mrs. Sinclair was busily employed in sewing, and Laura, with her fingers between the pages of a book, sat gazing at her father.

"Those children distract me," said Mr. Sinclair, in a sharp accent.

"Hush, Robert; come here, Margaret," said Mrs. Sinclair gently, and she took one on her lap and the other by her knee, and whispering to them a little story calmed them to sleepiness and then put them to bed.

When Mrs. Sinclair had left the room, Laura laid down her book and stood by her father.

"Don't disturb me, child," said he roughly: "my head aches." Then recollecting himself, he took her hand and continued, "Do not feel hurt, my dear; my mind is perplexed by these complicated accounts."

"Father," said Laura with a smile, "I think I can help you if you will let me try."

"You! my love," exclaimed her father; "why these papers would puzzle a wiser head than yours."

"I do not wish to boast, father," said Laura modestly, "but my teacher said to-day — " Laura hesitated.

"Well, what did he say?" asked Mr. Sinclair encouragingly.

"He said," answered Laura blushing deeply, "that I was a quicker accountant than most men of business; and I do believe, father," continued she, earnestly, "that if you were to explain your papers to me, I could help you."

Mr. Sinclair smiled incredulously; but, unwilling to check his daughter's wish for usefulness, he made some remarks and opened his leger. Insensibly he found himself entering with her into the labyrinth of numbers. Mrs. Sinclair came in on tip-toe and seated herself softly at the table to sew. The accounts became more and more complicated; but Mr. Sinclair seemed to gain energy under the clear quick eye of his child; her unexpected sympathy inspired him with new powers. Hour after hour passed away, and his spirits rose at every chime of the clock.

"Wife," said he, suddenly, "if this girl gives me aid like this, I shall be in a new world to-morrow."

"My beloved child," said Mrs. Sinclair, pressing Laura's fresh cheek to her own.

Twelve o'clock struck before Laura left her father, when she commended herself to God and slept profoundly. The next morning, after seeking His blessing, she repaired to Mr. Sinclair and sat by him day after day, until his books were faithfully balanced.

"Father," said she, "you have tried me and find me worth something; let me keep your books until you can afford a responsible clerk, and give me a little salary to buy shells for my cabinet."

Mr. Sinclair accepted the proposition. Laura's cabinet increased in beauty, and the finished female handwriting in his books and papers was a subject of interest and curiosity to his mercantile friends.

TINYTELLA.

A FAIRY TALE.

ALICE SOMERS was an interesting girl, beloved by watchful and affectionate parents. She was perfectly obedient and very useful. No one was more just than Alice in distributing from the store-room, or more adroit in the mysteries of the pantry. The servants knew they could gain nothing by coaxing, though their young mistress was ready to aid and advise them of her own free will.

Already, with ingenuity beyond her years, she could cut clothes for her dolls, and her needle was a welcome sight among her young acquaintances. She had but one fault; that, alas! was a great one. She could not look cheerful unless she had her own way. It is true she performed her duties faithfully; but her bright eyes were often clouded, and not a smile hovered on her lips.

One day, when Alice was gaily talking over a plate of nuts, her mother requested her assistance in sewing. She of **course complied,** but a frown gathered on her **brow.** She took her work in **one corner** of the room, and commenced **sewing as if life** depended **on every** stitch. Mrs. Somers began to converse; Alice **was silent**; she related a laughable anecdote, not a smile illuminated **her daughter's** countenance; she asked her questions, monosyllables **were the only reply.** Tired of this **uncivil** intercourse, Mrs. Somers withdrew **to** another apartment. **Alice** sewed **on** with **a face** elongated **beyond all** prettiness; in other words, she was *sulky.*

Sitting in this uncomfortable state of mind, she **felt** gradually **a** singular sensation on **her chin, and on** passing her hand **over it, it** appeared longer than usual. **She** resumed her work, trying **to** look unhappy, but her chin attracted her attention **for it was** certainly lengthening. She dropped her work and **felt it with both** hands,— it pushed itself between them; she tried to **rise —it was** impossible; she attempted **to call** her mother,— her **voice seemed** chained; her chin increased every moment, until **at length she** *saw* it. What **a moment of** horror, **a horror increased by the idea that this was a** punishment for ill-nature! In **dreadful alarm and perplexity she** gazed wildly around.

Suddenly she heard a soft fluttering, with delicate tinklings like **musical** wings, and, gliding on a sunbeam, appeared a minute female figure, which floated before her. Her form was chaste and **symmetrical as the** column of a seashell, her drapery was woven from humming-birds' plumage and dazzled the eyes of Alice, until **they rested** on her tiny face, fair **as a** clematis's blossom peeping from its robe of green. At every motion of **her** wings, a thousand **little bells,** musically tuned, rang out a sweet melody, while her feet, white and noiseless as the falling petal of a bay-flower, kept time in graceful transitions to their soft harmony.

The music ceased, and a voice still sweeter, though piercing as the cicada at summer's noon, addressed poor Alice:

"I am Tinytella," it said, "the friend of youth. I know your misfortune and its cause. There is but one cure, — the feeling and smile of *good-humor*."

Her bright blue eyes looked full in Alice's face, her little mouth dimpling like the water in a rose-vase when it receives flowers. Alice *smiled*. Instantly the frightful deformity disappeared, and she heard the bells of Tinytella tinkling on the distant air.

THE MAY-DAY WREATH.

ELVIRA ALLEN, a girl of extreme beauty, was receiving her education at a boarding-school, where every possible attention was paid to her moral and religious as well as intellectual habits. But though intelligent and industrious, nothing could conquer her devotion to her own personal attractions. The good sense of her teachers had assisted in part to correct this fault of her character; but, like all efforts that are not founded on religious principle, it sprang up at the spell of temptation.

A May-day celebration was to take place, and the school-girls were all in a glow of expectation. The day arrived, and a queen was to be chosen. Who should it be?

"It must be Ellen," said one. "How amiable and generous she is! Do you remember her assisting that old negro woman we met on the road yesterday, and giving her all her cake, while we ate ours?"

"Ah, but Jane must be queen," said Susan Harrison. "She is so lively that she will amuse us every moment while she is on her throne; and then she looks so grave all the time, and prims up her mouth while we are aching with laughter. Oh, I should love such a funny queen."

"I know she is very droll," said another, "but she is not a perfect scholar. Elizabeth Glen never missed a **lesson.** She ought to be queen."

"Oh, Elizabeth is too grave," **said one.** "I like Lucy Manson. She is very religious, but always cheerful, and trying to make others happy."

The argument ran quite high as each contended for her **favorite, until** Alice Matthews clapped her hands and exclaimed, —

"I know who will **be a** splendid queen, — Elvira Allen. How superbly she **will look,** sitting on her grassy throne with **a wreath** on **her** white forehead."

The children, like other mortals, were fascinated by appearances, and Elvira was proclaimed **queen** by acclamation. She retired **to her** toilet, and the girls, after **a** little consultation, flocked to **their** teacher.

"Have the goodness," they exclaimed, "to **loan us the wreath** you were shewing Mrs. Lewis the other day. **We wish Elvira to** wear it for her crown."

The consent was **readily given. They** rushed to Mrs. Warren's **dressing** room, but the **flowers were not** there. Looking with dis-. appointment at each other, **they returned** to their teacher **with** exclamations of regret. The girls, preceded by Mrs. Warren, hastened to Elvira's room, to inform her of their intention and its failure, **and** consult on **a** substitute for the May-day crown.

They **entered** abruptly, and found Elvira resplendent **in** conscious beauty ; **her** eyes had the color of Heaven and **its** brightness ; her **form was** graceful **as** the fringe tree, and her **dress,** arranged with a view to contrast and effect, **was** rich as a catalpa blossom. And what was that mantling glow upon her cheeks, deep as the last look the sun casts upon **an** evening sky? Envy her not, ye lovers of personal beauty. That glow was *guilt;* for twined among the ringlets **of** her glossy hair, was the wreath sought for by her young companions.

The withering truth fell at the same moment on every mind. At length Mrs. Warren, advancing to the culprit beauty, said, in a cold, stern voice, —

"This wreath, Miss Allen, was to have been yours. Your playmates, proud of your personal attractions, thought that innocent blossoms would grace your lovely face. My heart is sick, Elvira; sick and sorrowful." A large tear slowly rolled over her cheek as she spoke, and the girls sobbed aloud.

"Keep the wreath, unhappy child," she continued, as Elvira tore it from her hair, "it may be a warning to you."

The May-day was passed in sadness and tears.

THE FRENCH TRAVELLER.

Louisa and Cecilia Rutledge once loitered through the avenue of their father's plantation. The morning was such an one as April only knows at the South, where vegetation is almost seen to grow under one's eye. Rich white clouds, kindly gathering over the softened but not hidden sun, allowed them to gaze on the varied hues which the spring, struggling with winter, was throwing through sunshine and cloud, dew, shower, and breeze, over shrub and tree. So picturesque was nature, that the fair girls who gazed on it were only lovelier from the souls that looked through their eyes.

Yet beautiful they were, when, in the energy of some sudden thought, they stopped under the oaks, which, far as the eye could reach, formed an arch of almost architectural fitness above them, whose regularity was disturbed only by the gray moss floating in garlands on the breeze; and to an eye of love, — a mother's eye, — that watched their receding forms, as in the security of solitude they gave way to frolicsome spirits, they were indeed more fascinating than inanimate nature.

The mansion from which they were wandering was a fit residence for such fair inmates. The hand of *taste* was in every department. Wealth may heap up its luxuries, and the eye be sated and unallured; but let such an hand arrange but a flower, and it speaks a language wealth can never learn.

A branch from a rose-bush was trained at each window, whose blossoms, without excluding the breeze, looked within on lips and cheeks bright as their petals. Small vases of flowers were scattered around, several fine old pictures covered the walls, and the boast of modern art was not wanting.

A guitar, that delicious country friend, stood ready to beguile a weary or hasten a happy hour, while its hostess, the presiding genius of the scene, moved and looked like one whose aim was first a pure intercourse with Heaven, and then a study of the happiness of others.

One window of the sitting room was devoted to birds; not to caged birds, whose notes, however gay they may seem, carry to the ear of the sentimentalist those of Sterne's starling, "I can't get out." There was no imprisonment here; a little ledge projected from this window, where Cecilia spread rough rice every morning to attract the feathered visitors. There the beautiful red-bird came fearlessly, and others cautiously, and poised themselves on the stem of a shrub that entered within the casement, and hulled the yellow rice-grains with dexterous art, or listened with inclined head and peering eyes to the soft tones of the guitar.

The sisters, Louisa and Cecilia, paused in their rambling talk beneath a tree in the avenue, attracted by the notes of a mocking-bird, which seemed pouring out its little soul in melody, and after listening awhile resumed their conversation.

"I always told you, Louisa," said her sister, "that it would be of no use to spoil your sweet eyes with writing French, and your pure English in speaking it. With whom can you converse in French, after having twisted your mouth and ideas with the idioms for so many years? The only French beau you are likely to see, is old Cato, and his St. Domingo *patois* has not all the purity of l'Acadamie Française, and if you talk to the trees they will only make you a Parisian bow."

"I feel no regret," answered Louisa, "for the time I have bestowed on French, for I have conquered myself. I used to shrink, you well know, from the effort of conversation, and I have often felt my cheeks burn at the apprehension of a mistake; but I never learned anything that has not been of use to me."

"Oh, you are always reasoning," said Cecilia; "you began when very young to get the start of me in the race of mind, though thanks to brother Edward's teaching and these (putting forth her pretty feet), I can beat you in the avenue."

So saying, she pointed to a distant tree as a goal, and off they flew like the nymphs of Diana. Cecilia had, as usual, the advantage, when, with glowing cheeks and fluttering hair, her sister reached the appointed bound.

"I have run so fast, I am weary," said Louisa; "ah, here is Edward with the barouche!"

Edward was hailed, and she took her seat beside him, leaving Cecilia to enjoy a botanical ramble. Allured by her fascinating study, she wandered some distance on the main road, and was about returning, when she heard a violent crash among the bushes, and saw a pair of horses approaching at full gallop, drawing the shattered remains of a travelling carriage, to which the driver still clung. It immediately occurred to her that there must be sufferers by the accident, perhaps in that vicinity, and she resumed her walk in the direction from which the carriage came, until her attention was arrested by groans. A few steps brought her to a female lying in the road, whose dress indicated her to be a foreigner. Through the agonized expression of her face, Cecilia immediately discerned the cast of refinement which distinguishes the educated and the intellectual. In her efforts to rise, her travelling turban had fallen from her head, and her long dark hair was loosened from the comb that confined it. By the difficulty of her movements, Cecilia soon comprehended that one of her limbs was fractured, and she hastened to assist her; but with an impatient motion, the lady pointed to the forest, and in the French dialect seemed entreating aid for another.

All that Cecilia could comprehend was, that some one was missing. She entered the woods, while the lady gazed after her with prayerful eyes. Cecilia could find no one, and returned to the sufferer. The unfortunate woman burst into tears, attempted to rise, then poured forth pleadings of most impassioned and eloquent sorrow, clasping Cecilia's hand in hers, and vainly attempting to make her comprehend the cause of her agony.

What would Cecilia have given at this moment for the knowledge of the language she had despised? With tearful eyes she attempted to tell the stranger that she was going for assistance. A thousand emotions distracted her, — to leave the unhappy lady seemed the only alternative, and she turned toward the avenue.

The agony of the traveller amounted to frenzy at seeing this, and uttering every expression of entreaty of which the French language is susceptible, she still pointed to the opposite woods. Cecilia almost flew towards the house, not daring to look back, and at every turn of the avenue, the wild entreaties of the traveller burst on her ear, and rent her heart. On reaching the house, she found the barouche at the door, and as well as her agitation would permit, related the accident. Her brother and sister sprang into the carriage with her, and Edward drove at full speed.

"O, Louisa," said Cecilia, the tears streaming from her eyes, "had I understoood her language, I might have saved this unfortunate lady; now, perhaps, we may be too late!"

When they reached the sufferer, she had fainted, and her face, on which the lines of distress were still visible, was pale as marble. Edward took her gently in his arms, and lifted her to the barouche. She was roused by her pain, and struggled to disengage herself.

"Do not take me away," she cried in French; "Eugene is in the forest; I will die with him!"

Louisa took her hand, and in a low voice said to her in the same language,—

"Dear madam, what distresses you? We are friends."

A smile of hope illuminated the face of the stranger at these familiar accents.

"Thank God!" she exclaimed, pressing Louisa's hand to her heart, "you will find my child. Our horses were terrified by a deer crossing the road,—the carriage was upset, and Eugene and I thrown at some distance from each other. I was so much injured as to be incapable of raising myself. I called to him, he turned, smiling roguishly, but went farther. I saw his little feet tottering through the bushes until he disappeared."

Louisa translated her words to Cecilia, who darted, quick as thought, to the wood, while the lady was conveyed home, soothed by Louisa's gentle and familiar language.

Cecilia entered the forest with a beating heart, and was nearly discouraged, when, after searching fruitlessly for some time, she saw white garments by the roadside. She approached, but almost started at the sweet apparition. A beautiful child slept there; one hand was thrown up amid his clustering hair, and the other was gently moved by the motion of his beating breast, while near him a coiled snake seemed preparing for a spring.

Though almost breathless with terror, Cecilia preserved her self-command. She seized a dry branch, and thrashing the neighboring bushes, alarmed the reptile, which rapidly glided away.

The noise awoke the child; he raised his head, and brushing the curls from his dark eyes, called,—

"*Maman, chère maman!*"

Cecilia softly advanced towards him.

He moved his little lip in grief at the countenance of the stranger. "Do not be afraid of me," said Cecilia; "I will carry you to your mamma."

The child gazed at her with increasing alarm, and hiding his face, began to weep bitterly. Cecilia, perplexed and agitated, wept, too, as the boy pushed her from him.

Louisa having committed the stranger to her mother's care, returned with Edward in the barouche, to assist in the discovery of the child. Her sister called them as she heard the approaching wheels, and they were soon at her side. The boy still hiding his face against a tree, refused to move. Louisa whispered to him; the child sprang to her arms with a laugh of joy.

During the slow recovery of the invalid, while Cecilia sat in silence ready to perform the kind offices which require no words, the stranger rewarded her with a languid smile; but when Louisa, though even sometimes inaccurately, spoke to her in her native tongue, her eyes were lit up with joy and sympathy.

"What book is that you are studying so intently?" said Louisa one day to her sister.

"A new phrase book," replied Cecilia, blushing; "I am determined to get one of those real smiles that *Madame* bestows on you"; and turning to Eugene, she said, "*Baisez moi, mon petit.*"

The French boy did not wait a second bidding; he caught her round the neck and imprinted a hearty kiss on the lips of the smiling American.

THE MISSIONARIES.

A TALE OF SANIPIE.

ONE summer twilight, two girls yet in the opening bloom of life, were resting on a rural seat by the borders of a Southern river. The fingers of one rested between the closed leaves of a book, while the glow of a communicated thought from its pages dwelt on her abstracted countenance, and the other was pointing out the softening glories of the western sky. An artist might have lingered near that lovely spot. Above and around were spread the branches of an oak from which the gray moss hung quietly in the hush of nature, sweeping the greensward below. A garden rich in flowers lay near in front of the white walls of the family mansion; an amphitheatre of woods enclosed the planted fields, forming a green curve in the distance, stopping where the river, beautifully clear, came in with its graceful flow at the foot of the oak in which one huge branch could admire it sown glossy leaves and gray drapery. A warmly-tinted sky broke in bright flickerings through the leaves and tinged the stream, while the birds flitted to their nests with farewell strains. The only other sounds that interrupted the stillness, were the flash of an oar and the distant horn and chorus of the negroes.

"Look up, Isabel," said the speaking girl, "from that book to this glorious sunset. It is worth a thousand volumes!"

Isabel shook her head gravely, her downcast eyes bent upon the turf at her feet. At length she sighed and said,—

"Cousin Ellen, a solemn duty is pending over me which makes me blind and deaf, even to these great natural manifestations of Deity. I begin to feel a thrilling consciousness that I have no right to linger over these scenes of my earthly joys. This book describes the wants of the heathen, the poor heathen, who, when *they* look at nature, acknowledge no creating hand, and if they possess a friend, dear to me as you are, Ellen, know nothing of that world where such friendship shall be made brighter and unbroken through eternal years."

A soft and solemn depth was in the tones of the speaker and her full, dark lids were wet with tears.

"And can you be willing to think for a moment of leaving your home duties, your father and mother and little Rosalie, for an uncertain sphere among the heathen?" said Ellen, earnestly.

"There is nothing uncertain in the missionary's path," exclaimed the enthusiast, as she rose and clasped her hands with an onward gesture. "Every step he takes is heavenward; every sorrow he endures adds a gem to his immortal crown. Yes, dear garden, where my childhood's foot has trod, skies that have so long looked down upon me, birds that have sung to me from year to year, father, mother, sister, farewell! I must go."

"With which of these handsome students are you about to partake the crown of martyrdom?" said Ellen, archly trying to suppress a smile upon her lips.

"With Henry Clayborne, as his wedded wife," said Isabel with dignity, scarce a blush tinging the delicate hue of her cheek.

Ellen turned a rosy hue; a rush as of sudden winds sounded through her brain; but recovering instantly, she stooped to caress a tame fawn that was browsing at her side, for the name was not the one she feared to hear.

We will not penetrate the secrets of that young heart; like many others, it must feed itself in silent happiness and bide its time of joy.

Isabel, absorbed in the contemplation of her own lofty purposes, did not observe the agitation of her cousin. These almost masculine purposes belonged to a young and fragile being; but it is wonderful how feminine enthusiasm will bear up the frail and delicate where seemingly stronger spirits fail. One who looked into her soft eyes, and noted Isabel's slight figure, would never dream that she could leave the feathered nest of her childhood for the dangers of the ocean and the hardships of an Indian exile. But such have not studied the promptings of human will, coupled with strong religious enthusiasm.

That evening Henry Clayborne came to hear his final sentence. He felt what it would be, for Isabel's touching welcome told more than words. It was not the downcast blush of common acceptance, but the frank determined glow of a holy resolution.

"This kindness augurs well for me," he said, fondly, as he held her confiding hand; "but I have come resolved not to take advantage of it. Better, dearest, is it for me to brave this wild path alone. I leave neither father, mother, nor sister; besides, I am a man who can tread through dangers where your softer spirit will droop. I could not bear to see this white brow sink beneath those sultry skies, nor those tender feet fail in the wilderness; but be my bride, and with that claim upon you, I shall depart braced for danger. . But I must go alone."

"You have been tempted, Henry," said the brave girl. "God has withdrawn his countenance from you, or you would not talk so. My parents will feel a pride in their missionary girl as friend after friend gathers round in religious sympathy. Besides, Henry, who should think of such ties when God calls? We must tread the waves at the voice of Jesus. His voice is near; I hear it now. Help, Lord, or we perish," she exclaimed, as her face glowed like an angel's as she sank on her knees with clasped hands and prayerful eyes. "Shall we sink while he is by? Look on thy servants in this hour of need; the storm of temptation is near; the billows rage; put forth thy hand to save."

Henry knelt beside her; he caught the enthusiasm of his promised bride; his voice was not heard, but his lips moved. In those moments of stillness a sublime self-dedication had been made. They both rose. "We go *together*," he whispered, and folded her to his heart.

There were busy preparations for the bridal and voyage. Religion, love, and friendship were active, as they heard the story of the self-immolation of the young and beautiful girl. When friends came to give their parting kiss, Rosalie's pretty eyes filled with tears, but the gifts and novelty of preparation soon dried them up again. A doubting cast of care was on the father's brow, but he bade God-speed, and blessed his child. Ellen went through her duties, and if she were sadder and paler than her wont, was it not for Isabel, her dear friend and cousin, and would not her life soon beam with love also? And how fared it with the mother of the young exile? She busied herself, for she dared not be idle. She checked the struggling sigh and wiped the gathering tears, and her short prayer for patience and submission went up when none could hear.

Time sped; how soon he flies with moments counted by parting friends! and the bridal was to take place on the morrow, and the departure on the succeeding day. One by one the family retired, the mother last, for a troubled and restless emotion made her wakeful. As she sat alone the ticking of the clock seemed almost shrill to her excited ear. She recalled the childish joy of Isabel when she used to clap her hands at the revolving moon of the old timepiece. There was the little chair in which Isabel had sought in vain to rest her dimpled feet upon the floor. That room could almost tell her history. There was the framed and faded sampler, the more elaborate decorations of the pencil, the beloved piano-forte which had soothed and brightened her various hours. Was it possible that those dear hands might never touch its chords again? There was her work-box, the quiet, precious instrument over which a woman's heart pours out its home emotions in most unconscious freedom. She opened it with a trembling hand. How tasteful! how judicious! Character was seen in all its combinations. It spoke of economy, just arrangement and fancy, while little touches of the affections peeped forth from its many compartments. As she gazed on these things, her tears gushed forth, and she did not hear Isabel's footsteps, until her arms were thrown around her.

"I would that you had not witnessed these emotions," said her mother, almost coldly. "You have chosen your path and leave me sadly to go down to mine. Strangers are to occupy the heart that I have trained for eighteen years. But go. Console yourself as you will; midnight and tears are my portion."

Isabel clung to her mother beseechingly, the lofty look of heroism almost driven from her brow. "Mother, your parents doted on you," she said, falteringly, "as you on me, and yet you left their arms for an earthly love. How much greater is the duty that calls me from you, to give salvation to the lost and dying! O, mother," she continued, grasping her hand with kindling eye, "should I die in this enterprise, go boldly to the court of Heaven and ask for your child! How proud will be your joy to see the weak and humble girl you nurtured in your bosom surrounded by the white-robed souls she has rescued through Christ's mercy, perchance leading their hymns in Heaven as she has on earth! O, mother! will they not greet you with a new song of joy for yielding up your child? 'Welcome thou, whose child has opened unto us the Book of Life!'"

Her mother was awed and silenced. She took the dear enthusiast to her arms, stroked the falling hair from her glistening eyes, and pressing that soft cheek to her bosom, said, —

"I will resign thee; God's will be done."

The bridal was over, the few guests had gone, and silence settled on that little group, so soon to be severed by rolling seas. Isabel touched a few chords on the piano-forte. At first her hand trembled, and Rosalie, who stood by looking wistfully, wiped her sister's cheek with her little handkerchief.

Gradually her fingers became firm as her thoughts possessed themselves of her great mission, and her voice was full and deep as in her freest moments, while she sang to the tune of the " Bride's Farewell" the touching verses of Mrs. Dana.

THE MISSIONARY'S FAREWELL.

FAREWELL, mother, Jesus calls me
　　Far away from home and thee ;
Earthly love no more enthralls me,
　　When a bleeding cross I see.
Farewell, mother, do not pain me
　　By thine agonizing woe ;
Those fond arms cannot detain me,
　　Dearest mother, I must go.

Farewell, father, — Oh, how tender
　　Are the chords that bind me here !
Jesus ! help me to surrender
　　All I love, without a tear.
No, — my Saviour ! wert thou tearless,
　　Leaning o'er the buried dead ?
At this hour, so sad and cheerless,
　　Shall not burning tears be shed ?

Farewell, sister, do not press me
　　To thy young and throbbing heart
Oh, no longer now distress me,
　　Sister — sister — we must part !
Farewell, pale and silent brother,
　　How I grieve to pain thee so !
Father — mother — sister — brother —
　　Jesus calls — Oh, let me go !

Every heart was throbbing, every eye was gushing with tears, except that of the rapt singer, who sat with upward look, like a bird preparing to wing its homeward way to warmer skies. Rosalie had been cradled in her sister's arms for three years ; that night was her first banishment, and the child had sobbed herself to sleep in the little crib assigned to her by her mother's bedside.

Isabel sought the slumberer alone, for the first time almost overpowered by regrets stronger than religious duties. The little sleeper's face had resumed its tranquillity, but there was a deeper flush than usual on her rounded cheek; and as she stood by the bedside, Isabel put softly aside the tangled hair on the pillow, which was wet with her tears. Long and earnest and loving was the gaze of the missionary's bride, and as she looked, the chest of the child stirred with a trembling sob, like the heaving of a billow when the gale has died away. Isabel severed one of those moist curls from its companions, and placed it in her bosom, pressing her hand a moment on her own throbbing breast. The struggle passed away, and kneeling by the bedside, she whispered a prayer: "God and Father of innocence," she said, "as I love the soul of this little child, so may I love the souls of the young, benighted ones who are in the darkness of heathenism. Let me crush every love which would call me from Thee and my high destiny."

She rose from her knees, tearless in the might of holy resolution, and bending over the little girl, kissed her hands and forehead; then looking upward, she said again, "God bless thee, young angel, and teach me to save kindred souls."

There was one listener who drew her from that room. Could they have known the prayer that was to be wrung from *his* heart in a few short months, would they have gone forth as strong and earnesthearted as they were at that moment?

The young bride at sea! Who has not seen her gush of parting sorrow dried slowly away, as one for whom she has left all stands near to comfort her? And she is comforted. The long, long day, listless to others, is full of thought to her; for *he* watches her steps, her sighs, her smiles,—his future and hers are one. She loves to see the sunlit waves and the evening stars with him, and even the storm loses its terrors. Young bride, be it ever thus on the ocean of life! May thy trim ship tread well the waters, the sky of heaven be bright above thee, the winds waft thee kindly **on**, and he who holds the helm be true!

It was sweet to hear the hymns that rose from time **to time from the** young missionaries in the holy joy **of** their souls. Isabel's voice **kindled** in rapt delight until the roughest sailor paused and caught the religious glow. There was little to try the fortitude of **the pas**-sengers in the voyage, which was marked by the common incidents of sea-life, until they entered the Bay of Bengal. The day previous had been oppressive, and there was a stagnation in the air, as if its circulation had suddenly been suspended; and on the following morning, the experienced commander reefed his sails, though **the wind, as** yet, threatened in light gusts. A yellow haze loomed athwart **the** sun, which was strangely reflected in the gurgling **waters; this** aspect continued through the morning. **Henry** and **Isabel observed a** change in the countenances of the seamen, which **at first** they could not understand; but, as they continued **to gaze, there was** a mystery in the stillness, as **if the foot of the** Eternal might be treading on his wonderful watery creation. After a few hours, a steady gale commenced, gigantic clouds rolled like troubled spirits through the air, and Isabel shrank nearer to her husband. At twilight, the hurricane **began, and** the chafed ship, like a living thing, now sank **as in despair, now leaped** over the swelling billows. The missionaries summoned the strength of their souls, and awaited **God's** will in silence. It was a night of fearful anxiety. **No one** slept **but** Isabel, who, leaning on her husband's shoulder, dreamed sweetly of her oaken seat beside the river, and was only startled when the captain's voice was heard through the deep tones of the trumpet, and overtopped the gale. Suddenly a heavy sea struck the ship astern, and the waters rushed into the cabin. The shock was tremendous. Henry bore his dripping charge in his arm to the captain's cabin,

She was quite insensible, her lips were blue, and her frame was rigid. Henry chafed her cold hands, wrung the damp from her hair, and gave her restoratives. She opened her eyes at length, spoke his name, and laid her head on his shoulder, like a glad child.

"We will die together," whispered she; "and though we are not God's favored instruments, He will carry on the good work by other hands."

And now the uproar on deck became terrific; huge billows burst over the bows of the ship, writhing and spouting, and glittering with phosphoric light, while the lightning darted and flashed over the ocean. The captain lost his assumed calmness, and his wild oaths sounded across the storm like the shouts of a demon. Isabel shuddered at the impiety which could thus brave heaven, when seemingly so near its final judgment.

At this period the vessel was inert and powerless, drifting like a disabled swan on the waters. Isabel sat with Henry, each praying silently. At length the welcome sound of relief was heard, the vessel righted, and the waves rushed like released prisoners from the deck. The morning rose in beauty, and soon the lines of green, so dear to the landsman's heart, opened on the view.

"Is your heart still strong, beloved?" said Henry. "Are there no yearnings for friends and home?"

Isabel smiled, and pressed Henry's hand.

"The Lord has not preserved me from a watery grave that I should bear a faltering heart. I feel strong in His arm; let Him lead me where He will, so I can aid His cause."

Isabel's emotions, as she neared the shores of Hindostan, were almost dream-like, and she asked herself, as objects of strange novelty met her eye, —

"What am I who have ventured thus? An atom among the ocean. But the Lord careth even for the sparrow."

The new perfume from the flowers was among the first things that spoke to her of her distant home.

"I have to remember," she said, "that the same God scented these rich blossoms who gave the odor to my garden rose; let me not forget that he, too, is the God of the heathen as well as Christian souls."

They were touched by the picturesque beauty of the scene as they sailed up one of the mouths of the Ganges. Hindoo cottages, like haystacks, without chimneys or windows, clustered beneath luxuriant trees, contrasted in their rudeness with the more elaborate pagodas. Wide fields of rice, and grass of exquisite verdure, were spread around, while herds of cattle fed on the banks of the river. But a glance at the inhabitants concentrated the thoughts of the missionaries, and fixed them on the worth of human souls. They were willing, in the devotion of their feelings, to enter one of those hovels and begin at once the work of salvation. But new objects arrested their attention as they journeyed to the seat of the mission. A bridegroom, about ten years of age, was carried in a palanquin crowned with flowers, followed by a procession with musical instruments. Tears started to Isabel's eyes, as they followed this idle pageant, at the thought of the rational and simple rites of her own betrothal.

The next object that called prayer deep from the souls of the strangers, was the worship of Juggernaut, the wooden idol, before which multitudes assembled with overwhelming shouts. Henry and Isabel cast down their eyes at the sacrilege, and remembered the simple church at home, where spiritual prayers were the choicest gift to heaven. Their curiosity was attracted by a rude kind of basket suspended from a tree. On looking within, they discovered the partially-devoured remains of a little child. Isabel shuddered and thought of her own childhood and little Rosalie pillowed upon her mother's bosom.

But the most horrible scene to Isabel in this memorable journey was the sacrifice of a widow. In vain the missionaries tried to move away from that harrowing scene; there was a spell, even a fascination in its terrors, that chained them to the **spot, and** Isabel, sick at heart, looked **on.** A grave was dug near the river, and after a few unintelligible rites, the widow took a formal leave of her **friends and** descended into the chamber of death. It may be that she was stupefied with opium, for there was a mechanical insensibility about her that seemed scarcely human. As soon as she reached the bottom **of the pit,** by means of a rude ladder, she was left alone with the **body of her** husband, in a revolting state of decay, which she embraced and clasped to her bosom, and then gave the signal for **the** last act of this shocking scene to commence. The earth **was** deliberately thrown upon her, while two persons descended into the grave and trampled it tightly round the self-devoted **sacrifant.** During this tardy and frightful process, the doomed **woman sat an** unconcerned spectator, caressing the corpse, and she had an expression of almost sublime triumph as the earth embraced her body. The **hands** of her own children aided in this terrible rite; and when all **but her** head was covered, **the nearest relatives danced over** the inhumed body, and covered the **whole** from sight.

Before the termination of this scene, Isabel, who had lingered with infatuated interest, fainted. On recovering, she said to Henry, —

"Assist me, my husband, to hate the meaning of this act more than I do. Again and again I thought I could bear to die thus with you, rather than live without you. Will God forgive *my* idolatry?"

At length the young missionaries reached their **home, — home?** **And was this** the abode of the delicate Isabel? The late inmates had died **of the** fever, and no kind hand had arranged the few **relics** that remained. The dwelling consisted of two rooms made of bamboo and thatch, and an air of desolation pervaded everywhere. Day after day Isabel labored with those hands so unused to toil, until an air of comfort wrought its charm around her. Then her love for the beautiful broke forth. She trained the native shrubbery around the dwelling, and planted a spot on which her husband's eye might gratefully repose as he sat at his daily studies; but alas! **hunger** and heat and debility often took from her the power of more **than necessary** effort. Nothing is more wearing to an ardent person, who sacrifices everything for spiritual good, than to find himself **trammelled down** to the physical wants of life. Isabel felt this pressure a trial almost more than she could bear, and it was a day of prayerful thanksgiving for her when she was permitted by another's services to assist her husband in teaching. His labors were lightened by her active spirit, and it was a blessing to her soul to toil with him and listen to his earnest voice as he preached of salvation. How beautiful he was **to** her, as he stood with earnest eyes and gestures, breaking the bread of life to the benighted souls around them! **and** then, when evening came, they inhaled the perfume of their garden while sitting at their door and talking of their old home. Were they happy? Troubled **thoughts and** forebodings sometimes shot through their minds like **an** ice-bolt, — for death might **come and sunder** them; conversions **were slow**; brutish ignorance baffled their dearest hopes; the seed which they planted seemed thrown on stony hearts, but their faith was firm. Strong prayer went up daily, hourly, from the temple of their hearts, though all others were closed against them; faith looked with her bright, keen glance beyond the present hour, and showed them precious souls redeemed by their toils.

In the midst of these emotions, Henry was seized with the **fever** of the climate. Poor Isabel left all for him. Night **and** day **she** bent over his pillow and forgot it was wrong to idolize **an** earthly form. All memory and hope were lost in the present thought of his possible death, — but he recovered. How sweet it was to present him the first fruits of their little garden, and to bring him, one by one, his manuscripts and books; to see the faint glow of health kindle on his cheek, to aid his faltering steps, to feel the cool hand which had so lately burned and throbbed beneath her touch! Isabel sat at his feet, and looked and looked until tears started to her eyes for love and joy.

One evening Henry was summoned to his wife's apartment. She had given birth to a boy. The little one lived but to receive a father's first and last blessing, before his perfect features settled to repose. And Isabel seemed departing, too; her loving eye grew dim, the sweet voice lowered, and she called for her little lifeless baby, and took it into her arms and said, —

"Henry, if I die, *take care of the lambs* for the sake of my Rosalie and this little child. It is my last request."

And kissing her baby, she gave him back to his father's arms, and gently closed her eyes. But God had not willed that these two noble souls should yet be parted, for their double work was not finished. After a night of quiet wakefulness, Isabel fell into a deep sleep; and when she awoke, Henry felt that she was to return to duty with him; and in his turn, he had the sweet delight of ministering to her wants, and supplying her needs.

One evening, seated at the same door that was now so sacred to them, they were talking of their future, and saying how great their thankfulness was for renewed health and strength; but that if some way could only be made plain to them, practically, for carrying out their plans for the children and youth of India, it would raise them up at once to their highest dreams. Some letters were handed them, and to Isabel's delight, she read the following: —

"DEAREST SISTER: We all heard of your illness and recovery, and can only say, thank God! Oh, if I could have seen my little nephew once, — but your life is spared! Since hearing that you and brother Henry were to teach little children, and establish schools, and help the women of India, mamma and cousin Ellen, and several other ladies, have formed a society to send you out money and books regularly; and several of us school girls are going to have a fair, so as to send you a *heap* of money at once, and this is on purpose for the little sewing-girls. Hoping this good news will make you strong and well, I am your own

"ROSALIE."

After reading this letter aloud, the missionaries remained silent for a few moments, struggling with their emotions; and when they could again speak, it was to renew their vows of fidelity to the cause to which they had devoted their lives. But now they had faith as well as hope to cheer them, for they had found by experience that the true life of the missionary was to obey Christ's injunctions,—

"FEED MY LAMBS."

MR. NIBLO.

THE BASHFUL LECTURER.

FROM childhood I was a passionate lover of science. I tore my drum to pieces to examine its internal mysteries; my kites were the envy and wonder of my schoolmates, so trimly were they cut and so nicely balanced; and as they soared above all others, I felt an exaltation, a prophecy of eminence. My greatest delight was chemistry; it even rivalled the love I felt for a fair little girl, a blue-eyed neighbor, who loved me in spite of my soiled face and dyed fingers. She was a singular contrast to the young experimenter, whom she occasionally honored with a visit in his would-be laboratory; for there was a purity in her air, as if no stain of earth could dwell on her; the rose-tint on her cheek paled off to a transparent white around her chin and throat; her pencilled eyebrows lay in light arches on her serene forehead; her flaxen hair fell like a fleecy cloud over her cambric dress which emulated snow, and her hands, — how like unsunned alabaster they gleamed beside mine! Her teacher once described her thus. I was jealous of that man.

> "Behold the pupil nymph to me consigned,
> The honored guardian of her opening mind,
> In all the bloom and sweetness of eleven —
> Health, spirit, grace, intelligence and heaven!
> With beauty that so ravishingly warms,
> It seems the focus of all nature's charms.
> Yes! rival rays come rushing from the sky,
> Contending which shall glisten in her eye,
> And anxious zephyrs play her lips around,
> Soft suing to be moulded into sound.
> While still, from each exuberant motion, darts
> A winning multitude of artless arts.
> And then, such softness with such smartness joined,
> So pure a heart, with such a knowing mind;
> So very docile in her wildest mood,
> Bad by mistake, and without effort, good;
> So broken hearted when my frown dismays,
> So humbly thankful when I please to praise
> So circumspect, so fearful to offend,
> And at a glance so ready to attend;
> With memory strong and with perception bright,
> Her words and deeds so uniformly right,
> That scarce one foible disconcerts my aims,
> And care and trouble — do not name their names!
> But, yes! I have *one* anxious, sacred care,
> I have one ceaseless burden of my prayer, —
> 'Tis this; Great God! oh, teach me to be just
> To this dear charge committed to my trust!"
>
> S. GILMAN.

Well, this bright creature who could waken such a burst of enthusiasm in a pedagogue, was the chosen one of my boyhood; but I was destined to lose her early. It was her habit frequently to peep into my laboratory and ask her sweet questions about the mysteries of my craft. One day she advanced farther than usual; tucking aside her snowy dress, and stepping on tiptoe **for fear of soiling her trim white stockings, she stood amid my crucibles as unharmed as asbestos in a flame, her light** hair falling **backward, and her blue eyes upturned in pretty curiosity.** I had been preparing oxygen **gas from chlorate of potash, in a** small glass retort over an **Argand lamp, by which method it can be** obtained much purer than **by any other way. The operation was** successfully proceeding, **and the steady flame of the lamp continued to evolve the gas, as it gradually escaped through the neck of the retort, and rose in brilliant globules under the water in which the receiver stood.** Intensely occupied in watching the **decomposition of the salt, I started at the sweet tone of her silvery voice, and as I eagerly advanced towards her, with my eyes grimmed and bleared with** smoke **and heat, and extended my stained hand to welcome her, the flame unnoticed rose too** high, **the glass shivered into fragments, and the hot contents fell** hissing **around her. She shrank back** to **avoid the broken pieces, when a curl** of **her beautiful hair** caught in the **blaze of a lamp near her. My** first impulse was to throw over her **a diluted solution of nitrate** of silver (indelible ink).

The flame was instantly extinguished, but such an object **as the poor child presented!** The fast-blackening liquid fell dripping from her fair locks, and ran **down** her face and garments, **even to the** little foot that had just before trodden so daintily. **The** lovely girl's self-possession vanished, and roaring with terror, she **flew from the** apartment alarming the neighborhood with screams. **This was her** last visit to my laboratory, or even to my home; she **became** shy, and avoided me. I soon entered college, and when I returned, four years after, my blue-eyed beauty was a bride.

My absorption in technical books began to give an awkward and restrained tone to my manners and conversation, while a want of sympathy with those around me made me unsocial ; a burning love of science, however, and a hope that I might individually enlighten the world, buoyed me up with a silent kind of vanity. With these feelings, I saw my home. What wonder that I should rush to my little laboratory with intense interest. Parental fondness had kept the spot sacred ; there stood the furnace and the crucibles, and placed neatly, on one side of the apartment, the nameless articles I had used as expedients in my experiments abstracted from the kitchen and store-room, for which I had been sometimes punished and sometimes praised. There was the very spot, too, on which my first love had been inundated with that fatal nitrate.

I smiled, but it was sadly, and I began in earnest my more manly and scientific arrangements. I almost hoped such blue eyes as hers might look on me again. But I soon forgot that vision, and from that period my whole soul seemed centred in this apartment. I rushed to it with the first dawn of light, and the night lamps of heaven were forgotten for its fitful rays. Such strong and passionate love cannot long keep within a narrow channel, it will burst forth, and fertilize or destroy. Without power to utter in conversation the deep stirrings of my thoughts, I resolved to lecture, to throw myself on the public ; it seemed to me that I should be stimulated by numbers, and I was confident that in a mixed audience some hearts would beat responsive to the enlightened hopes of mine. Confirmed in this opinion, by the advice of my family, I commenced writing a course of Lectures on Chemistry. I had never tried my powers of elocution beyond the college walls, and the themes there having no immediate interest for me, were sufficient excuse to my mind for any deficiency of grace or power. The moment I began to write, an ambitious thrill ran through me, and I poured out on paper, paragraphs that I thought would go with the force of light and sound through my audience.

The morning of the day on which my introductory lecture was to be delivered, arrived. I read and re-read the advertisement inserted by my father, till I trembled and glowed like a girl. I revised my lecture for the last time, and inserted here and there slips of paper containing additional notes.

The evening came, and I stood before a crowded audience of partial townsmen. If my readers are interested in this moment, they will like to know of my appearance. I was twenty-four years of age, spare, and of middle size, pale, with somewhat sharp features; my eyes were always thought remarkable; they were of a light blue, of a singular, piercing expression, so penetrating that they often attracted attention in a crowd; and yet, strange to tell, I could never fix them on a woman's face. I felt like a startled deer when a woman's eye met mine; but this peculiarity was compensated by quickness of motion that made me see without seeming to observe. My hands were delicately formed, and my thin hair was scattered on a high forehead. I had read my lecture frequently aloud in my own apartment. I had half fancied that the walls shook under the power of my language, and that the spirits of Bacon Priestly, Lavoisier, and Black, were bending down in angelic sympathy. Thus prepared, I stood before the audience, but in how different a frame!—as I glanced around, I felt myself the merest atom. I forgot the bow that I had made twenty times before my mirror, my eyes began to swim, my teeth to chatter; the rustling of the first blank leaf that I turned, sounded like thunder. I began to speak; my voice seemed to have descended two feet in my system. I lisped, I mumbled out one page, two pages, without raising my eyes; then came a reference to one of my interlocutory notes; it had slipped out; I could not find it. In searching for it, I lost my place, began three wrong sentences, and attempted to extemporize. It was in vain, and crushing my manuscript in my hand, I retreated from the hall, hurried through the streets, and locked myself in my own chamber. There I trod the floor like a frantic man, until tears, gushing freely as a schoolboy's, came to my relief. I left my native town the next day.

But better hopes came over me. I condemned myself for attempting a lecture without experiments; they would have aided me, I thought. Attention would have been drawn away from myself to them, and I gradually came to the resolution of pronouncing the same course of lectures among strangers, with whom I flattered myself I should be more at ease. With this view I visited a neighboring city, and without delivering letters or seeking patronage, issued an advertisement. Of all seemingly simple things, an advertisement is the most difficult and perplexing. To advance one's claims sufficiently without an air of self-importance, to combine one's meaning in a few words, and those few the right ones, is no small task. Few who glance over the columns of a daily print, are aware of the waste of paper, the biting of nails, and the knitting of brows that have attended the concocting of those concise looking squares.

My advertisement appeared: —

"MR. NIBLO, *from Hawletown, respectfully* **informs** *the inhabitants of* **Cityville** *that he proposes commencing* a *Course of* **Lectures on** *Chemistry,* **and kindred** *subjects, illustrated by various interesting experiments, beginning* **with** *an* **introductory** *Essay, on Thursday evening, which will be gratuitous.*"

Here was no trick or cant, no forced comet-tail of patrons' names, following the announcement. My hearers would come from the pure love of science. I breathed hard, but commenced conveying my apparatus to the lecturing hall. On the way I broke a retort of great value and rarity. The two next days were employed in vain endeavors to supply its place. Every lecturer will sympathize with me in the horror I felt at the prospect of saying to my audience, in the midst of a brilliant experiment, "This *should* be so and so, ladies and gentlemen," instead of, "This is." In the mean time, I was stimulated and comforted by the daughter of my hostess, an intelligent girl, who possessed that class of frank, bright manners, that save a bashful man an effort, and insensibly put him at his ease.

Lucia Breck had just passed her girlhood, without laying aside her simplicity. Her feelings and thoughts gushed out like a full stream; they were scarcely wise thoughts, but I delighted in their freshness; and if ever she bordered on silliness, a just taste brought her back again. Her eyes were dark and glittering, and her brown hair lay smoothly on her forehead. Her rounded form spoke of youth and health, and her cheek was mottled with "eloquent blood." Impetuous and self-confident, she sometimes startled those who loved her, who forgot how soon the world trammels the exuberance which to me was delicious from its spontaneousness.

I scarcely knew how, but Lucia was often by my side, aiding me in my preparations, and chatting away without looking at me. Her needle was usually in her hand, and she seemed to talk as much to that as to me. Thursday evening arrived. Lucia, sweet creature, sprang about like a fawn; her eyes glittered with expression, and her jests and laughter rang out like silver bells. We went with her mother to the hall. I had visited it repeatedly by daylight, but never at night. As we entered we were struck with "the dim, disastrous twilight." A few tallow candles, like sleepy sentinels, were placed in tin hoops against the walls, and two ornamented the desk where I was to stand. Who has not felt the chill of a badly-lighted apartment, as the forms glide in and out like spectres? As it was too late to remedy the evil, my object was to attract immediate attention to my experiments. The stillness was awful, broken only by the tinkling of the glasses in my trembling hand.

"Now, ladies and gentlemen," said I, "observe this receiver. It is filled with a very peculiar gas. It has hitherto borne the name of oxymuriatic acid gas; but you will yet perceive its pale yellow-green color, which has gained it from Sir Humphrey Davy, the name of chlorine. I shall insert this small piece of phosphorus into the vessel, and you will perceive an instantaneous and brilliant combustion." Alas! for me. I had forgotten, in my hurry, that chlorine is rapidly absorbed by cold water, and I had been so long detained by the slow dropping in of the audience, that the water with which I had filled the pneumatic cisterns was entirely chilled. I might have noticed that the gas had disappeared but for the dimness of the light. Ignorant of this, and too much embarrassed to feel if the water was warm or not, I desperately inserted the slight stick of phosphorus which I had a thousand times admired. In vain; dark and quiet all remained. This was a sad failure. My assumed confidence vanished, and I stammered out a few words, endeavoring to explain. The audience, disappointed as they were, were too good-natured to manifest any strong signs of disapprobation.

I determined then to recover my fast-sinking credit, by a very beautiful and critical experiment by the union of the gases which are the constituents of water. Oxygen and hydrogen in their proper proportions, had been prepared beforehand, in a tall glass tube. The wire from the voltaic battery had been introduced, and I flattered myself there could be no failure here. Again, I called the attention of my audience.

"Ladies and gentlemen, I wish to show you an interesting and exceedingly beautiful experiment; you know what are the constituent parts of water; they are mixed in this tube" (here I held up the tube apparently empty, but filled with the invisible gases), "in their proper proportions and gaseous form; I shall explode them by a spark from the battery, and you will see a small portion of water produced by the reunion of the gases." Unfortunately, in replacing the tube, I permitted the gases to make their escape. Unconscious of this, I applied my freshly-charged Leyden vial to the eudiometer. A spark shot from one wire to the other across the tube, but no explosion followed.

The audience looked and listened with all their might; nothing was visible but empty vessels; my trembling touch had caused the gas to escape, and the experiment was a nullity. Some lecturers possess the happy faculty of filling up with fluent remarks, or jests, such awful failures; but I was overwhelmed, and as the tube, freed from its pent-up gas, shook in my trembling hand, my heart sank within me, and I dashed it away. Just at this crisis I heard an hysterical giggle from Lucia. I was angry enough to have put her into the air-pump.

Utterly defeated in this effort, I turned my attention to the electric machine. My audience gathered in a circle, hand-in-hand. I applied the battery. Not a start — not an exclamation! My wires were as innocent as lambs; my audience looked at me between curiosity and ridicule, and retired to their seats, and again Lucia's laugh met my ear. At this crisis, one of those annoyances commonly called a thief, took possession of one my tallow candles. It sank rapidly until the flame reached the paper which enveloped it at the socket. I had no extinguisher, and was obliged to stop in the midst of a sentence to puff and blow at the increasing blaze. I forbear to describe the utter *forlornity* of my feelings and appearance as I stood before the upshooting rays of that dying candle. I dismissed my audience, and almost clutching Lucia's passive arm, returned home.

It was necessary that an effort should be made to secure an audience for the next lecture, after that failure. I laid aside my noble disdain of patronage, and examining my letters of introduction, selected those which were addressed to the most influential persons, and calling on them, requested their advice. I was courteously received by all, and allowed to use names at discretion. Friendly hands greeted me, and cordial bows dismissed me with wishes and prophecies of success. I inserted costly advertisements with the formerly despised *comet-tail* of patrons, and determining that the hall should be well lit, spared no pains or expense for the perfect illumination. Lucia was sure that all would go off well.

"You wanted nothing but light," said she, "to have made the last lecture capital; besides, people knew that the matter of an introductory lecture will be repeated in the course, and they are less anxious to attend. I am sure I saw Mr. ——, and Mr. —— in one corner, on Thursday, but then it was *so* dark. But, *dear* Mr. Niblo, we will have a glorious time to-morrow!"

Sweet Lucia!

The evening came. I started, with Lucia on my arm, ten minutes before the time. We saw the brilliant lights of the hall sparkling up as we turned the square, and they burst upon us as we entered the hall, while the polished brass of my apparatus shone in their beams.

"Give me a front seat," whispered Lucia, "where I can see and hear without being crowded."

I seated her, and went behind the desk to look, for the hundredth time, if all was in order. The clock struck eight, — the appointed hour. No one appeared. Twice I was deceived by the door-keeper's reconnoitring. Quarter past eight. Not a soul. I could not look at Lucia Half past eight. An old gentleman entered and took his seat at a distance. He blew his nose. Mercy, how it reverberated! Another quarter of an hour elapsed. I dismissed the old gentleman, who claimed his money of the door-keeper, and Lucia almost led me home.

A few of my acquaintances rallied; they knew that my expenses had been great, and by dint of puffing and appealing, with a promise that I should exhibit some transparencies, a lecture was got up by subscription. A breeze was given by some leading people adding their names, and on the first of March, 18—, I stood before a large and fashionable audience. My experiments were brilliant, and Lucia's eyes were as bright as phosphorus. Applause ran through the apartment at my success. I forgot my diffidence, threw by my notes, and poured forth the tribute to science which had been burning like silent fire in my bosom.

"And now, ladies and gentlemen," I said, in a voice of unhesitating dignity, "let me call your attention to a beautiful experiment, which, though of secondary importance in science, is still attractive, like the gems which glitter over the brows of the fair."

With this flourish, I directed their attention to a union which I was about to make of nitrate of ammonia and chlorine, and which I expected would prove a very beautiful experiment, but which requires peculiar care; for, after being together for a long time, a highly-explosive substance forms, which detonates with great violence upon the contact of any oil. Unfortunately, a small portion of oil adhered to the rod which I introduced, and a most terrible explosion followed. A jar of sulphuretted hydrogen stood near, and its contents were liberally diffused, filling the room with appalling odors.

Splinters of glass with the colored mixture spirted around the apartment. In an instant the jetty broadcloth of gentlemen and rich silk of the ladies shared a common fate; groans of fright and disgust, screams and laughter, mingled discordantly; friend scarcely recognized friend, as the vile preparation adhered to their faces. I flew to Lucia; her new bonnet, her only silk frock, were ruined. As we walked home in silence, her good nature was fairly overcome; and when we reached the door, she flung herself angrily from my arm, exclaiming, that she "wished chemistry was in the Dead Sea." I said Amen, and retreated to my chamber in despair.

. . . .

I am far from wishing, by the above narration of my calamitous *debut* as a lecturer, to intimidate others. Many years have rolled away since that disastrous experience, and crowded audiences have testified to my success. The name of Dr. Niblo is not unknown in foreign academies, while he reaps at home the advantages of a successful professorship; while another Lucia, a pretty fairy, with eyes like her mother's, and the same round and merry laugh, wipes his spectacles and hangs upon his arm. **C. G.**

THE YOUNG CONSPIRATORS.

At the revolution in Naples, in 1779, two young brothers were condemned to death, and upon the entreaties of the mother for their lives, the king's attorney told her she could choose between them.

THE flames of Vesuvius were hidden in a bright morning sun that lay in glory on the noble bay at its feet, when two Neapolitan boys were seen issuing from a vine-clad way, removed from the populous city. They were followed by an attendant bearing a basket of fruit, and their laugh rang free and wild upon the morning air, its hilarity tempered by the grace of courtesy. They were brothers, alike, yet differing. When the laugh was past, a tender thoughtfulness, as when a cloud presses on dying sunbeams, shaded the face of the younger; while lines of light, like the twilight of their own clime, lingered upon that of the elder. Amid the play of youthful fancies was mingled a classic, softened grace, called out by the nature of their studies, the ancient ruins around them, and a yet softer impulse that urged them towards a widowed mother, for whose morning meal they had selected the choicest of fruits. Rosalba de Soria, who awaited her sons' return at the door of her villa, stood in the glow of perfect, matronly beauty, for the sorrow of the widow had had compensations in the mother's love. Ferdinand, the elder youth, pressed her extended hand, while Lorenzo received her kiss on his ready lips.

The education of the boys, though conducted in retirement, did not prevent familiarity with the scenes of classic interest around them. They glided on the beautiful bay, with its garden-like borders, where vineyards, groves and villages blend in delightful harmony, and they saw the skiffs darting from shore to shore, or pleasure barques with ornamental streamers and musical accompaniments, glancing like summer birds in plumage and sound.

They climbed to the heights that overlook the delicious country of Campania Felix, and their eyes wandered far over islands and seas. Sometimes Rosalba paused with them at the tomb of Virgil, awakening the love of poetry in their souls; sometimes they sojourned at Pozzuoli, where the grandeur of the sea beyond rivalled the opening glory of countless flowers at their feet; or, the wonders of Herculaneum and Pompeii attracted their curious regards. But the most delightful enjoyment was to sit with Rosalba in the balcony of their villa, and listen to the story of their brave father, while the stars twinkled above, and Vesuvius threw out its fires on the darkened sky.

Nor were they debarred access to the populous city, where their little knowledge of the world received an increase. The great street of the Toledo, itself a world, formed an exciting contrast to the romantic seclusion of their home. The following description will reveal the animated scene which was such a fascination to the young students: —

"The great street of the Toledo presents the most amusing scene. Every one has a costume as peculiar to himself as if attending a masked ball. The sun flung bright lights here and there, while the lofty houses cast their shadows in other quarters. A merry fellow, with a dozen tamborines arranged and perched upon his head, while he played on another, dressed in a cloth cap, round jacket, blue waistcoat and red-striped trousers, invited the world to buy a beguiler of tears for the baby at home. Next, a green-grocery man caught the eye; his donkey is laden with a mat sack balanced on both sides with large mouths, where cabbages, cauliflowers, salads and celery are heaped in verdant abundance. A sugar-loafed hat, flatted at the **top,** is over a worsted cap. His swarthy face and neck defy the sun. A pipe in his mouth, red **vest and short calico** breeches complete his apparel. No stockings hath he, nor shoe, nor sandal. He and his donkey seem to be brothers. A pious piper begins the labors of **the day before** some **shrine of** the Virgin, where a lamp **is burning.** His instrument of three tubes derives its melody **from a** bag of wind, which he fills from his own lungs. **His** pointed hat is clapped on the top of his bag while he plays his pro-**pitiating** prayer for success. **His** night-cap is displayed on his inno-**cent** cerebellum, his curly hair flowing beneath, and showing off his ruddy, distended cheek. His green coat, sleeveless mantle, ash-colored breeches, and linen wrapped round his legs for stockings, shows that he has not been blowing to the shrine in vain; **for** he looks a very respectable tradesman in his **way, and** need not be ashamed of his profession.

"Venders of roast chestnuts are numerous in the Toledo. They have prescriptive stations where they fix their stalls, within which a small charcoal fire burns and gives its heat **to a basket** filled with **the fruit,** placed on the top, and covered with a blanket to keep the nuts hot. These people are a thrifty set, and well-dressed. The man has a red worsted cap, silk handkerchief round his neck, yellow vest, green round jacket, pants of blue; clean white stockings, neat shoes, a stool to stand on, and one to sit upon, as business or relaxation may require. He cries out his wares at the pitch of his voice, holding his left hand **to his** cheek to render it louder.

"But have you seen **the melon** man? There is a picture of independence. A ragged suit of loose trousers, pretty good vest, yellow or sky blue, and part of a shirt, are all that he requires. A long board is balanced on his head, displaying the fruit blushing in its slices; and on the palm of his left hand, equally poised, is a shorter board, exhibiting another sample of his merchandise, while in his right hand he waves a sprig of myrtle.

"Who is he with that snug capote and hood, and pretty little baskets piled up under his arm, running along barelegged? A fisherman who sells the most delicate fresh herring in the world, just taken from the bay. The bottle vender, whom he has almost knocked down in his haste, is a still greater curiosity. Long wooden pins are stuck all round the edge of his basket, on which very thin flasks with long necks for oil or wine are attached. He looks like a high priest of Bacchus, with his merry face, always sure of a market, for the flasks are so speedily broken open that he can scarcely supply all of his customers.

"The Segretario is another picture. Seated at his table in a quiet corner of the street, with a wise-looking hat shading his gray locks, spectacles on his nose, paper, pens, ink-bottles, and and wafers in due order before him, he waits to indite a petition, or a love-letter, or a letter from a sailor to his mother, or from a creditor to a debtor, or a law paper, or a memorandum. He is prompt, methodical, confidential, and a valuable sort of person, who attracted my particular respect on account of the unwearied patience with which he waited for his customers who were too few and far between.

"The pride of Toledo, in their own opinion, at least, are the money-changers. They are generally females, who display their riches in the ornaments on their persons. The braided hair is tied under a dashing silk handkerchief, knotted in front coquettishly. The broad forehead, sharp eye and intelligent face show that if her ladyship makes any mistake in the reckoning, it will not be to her loss. She sits there before her strong box, on the top of which are little baskets filled with silver or copper coins. A pair of *real* gold rings dangle from her ears. Her open neck displays a pearl necklace. A velvet spencer, chintz gown, silk apron, and fingers covered with

•

rings, attract customers on all sides. The itinerant trader, who disposes of his stock early, and is laden with copper pence, changes his into silver at her table, on which she receives her small commission. The shop dealers that want accommodation in either way, — coppers, gold, or silver, — are sure of finding all they want at the money-changer's stall. An umbrella fixed on her counter forms a canopy over her head, to protect her highness from the sun.

"Not quite so opulent, but much more captivating, are the female venders of fried fish, — magnificent women, fresh from the seaside. You will know them by their yellow kerchiefs, gypsy faces, snow-white sleeves tucked up their beautiful arms, and their red aprons and blue gowns. Of these syrens let the fish-eater beware!

"With an earthen pan and charcoal fire she browns and cooks her soles and herring, taking the live fish from her basket of dried flags at her side. Her bony figure seated on a stool and her well-dressed feet peeping from beneath her long petticoat, St. Anthony himself would not refuse to take a fry or two from those clean taper fingers. She holds the fish on a skewer, and turns the little martyr round and round until he is done to a turn, the mouth watering while the fragrant odor breathes around.

"The egg woman is a more quiet kind of body, though she seems to be sitting for her picture, dressed in her tidy green apron, russet gown, and linen sleeves, and her ruby kerchief thrown back over her head. Next comes, shouting his 'Oil to sell!' a great farmer-looking boy, in a gay straw hat. A goat-skin sack of oil is tied round his left shoulder, through the tail of which the smooth liquid descends into a brass measure for the customers whom he serves.

"The porters, waiting for jobs, with their picturesque dress and long pipes in their mouths, form a kingdom among themselves. He holds his oblong square flag-basket always ready for the bundles of his employers. At every corner of the street macaroni is served from morning until night, hot or cold, in its own plain soup, or mingled with a savory stew boiled or baked, or in cakes, or in elongated ropes of about a mile in length. When graced by the soup it is most popular. It is handed smoking hot to the ragged customer, who, without any ceremony, takes up the macaroni between his fingers, and introducing the extremities of three or four ropes at once into his thorax lifts his hands high in air and the whole dishful vanishes in a trice. The soup is drank at discretion with a wooden spoon, or out of the dish itself, — the latter mode being generally preferred. The water-vender is met everywhere and at all hours. The ice-man is more stationary, but equally persevering. Here, the female restorer of old chairs is busy with her rushes. There, the smirking milliner's maid is tripping it with the band-box in her hand; she is wholly French, and out of keeping with her trim cap and ribbons with the rest of the scene. Every one lives in the street. The bakers' shop is so open that everything within is public. It is the same with the tinman who incessantly hammers; the blacksmith whose bellows are always blowing and urging up a fierce fire, and whose anvil never rests a moment.

"All the gay shops are in the Toledo. All the pretty women of Naples show off in the Toledo. There the idler lounges, there the merchants meet, there the military men ride or walk up and down in their splendid uniforms."

Yet amid this gay and brilliant population floated the seed of those revolutions which have so often marked the political history of Naples.

On one occasion Lorenzo was purchasing at a stall in this busy scene. Ferdinand's attention was arrested by an individual, who, unseen to others, beckoned him apart. A cloak and slouched hat concealed his face and figure; but his piercing eyes shot through the folds. Ferdinand obeyed the summons, warned to silence by the uplifted finger of the stranger. Withdrawing just far enough to keep Lorenzo in view he uttered a few words to the listening youth.

A flush of surprise lit up Ferdinand's face, followed by an air of intense interest and chained attention until Lorenzo turned inquiringly.

"Remember," said the stranger, fixing his piercing eye upon the boy, "*trust, secrecy*," and he disappeared in the crowd.

From that moment a thoughtful expression gathered on Ferdinand's brow,—something which gave it the stamp of manhood. The quiet of his home was no longer attractive; the Toledo alone engaged his thoughts, and when there, his restless eyes seemed in search of some one. At the same hour, on the spot, the next week, the stranger appeared. Ferdinand, already taught the language of deception, beguiled his brother to a distance. Then followed whispered, emphatic words, and the keen eyes of the stranger seemed to search the innermost soul of the youth as his parting words were, "*trust, secrecy*."

The next day Lorenzo went alone to the Toledo, and as he strolled carelessly along, glancing at the sights around him, he felt a slight but emphatic touch upon his shoulder. He turned, and the stranger's eyes were upon him. His first feeling was to escape; but a deep voice of authority said, "Follow me, for your country demands you."

Lorenzo shook off his fear, and with curiosity followed the figure, who, threading the crowd, led him to a retired spot. Whatever the uttered words were, they took deep hold of the sensitive boy, and as the stranger on departing uttered the watchwords, "*trust, secrecy*," Lorenzo laid his hand upon his throbbing breast and responded with a prayer.

From that day there was a struggle in his hitherto calm existence, that shook its very depths. He became reserved to Ferdinand, but a deeper tenderness characterized his manner to his mother, mingled with a fitfulness and impetuosity that almost alarmed her. He followed her footsteps like one whom he feared to lose.

It was one of those bright nights that woo to watchfulness rather than to slumber, when Ferdinand leaned from his casement, and looked upon the moonlit scene. But it was not the softness of night's smile that wooed him to where the moonlight decked the meanest leaf with a diamond glitter; nor was the glow on his beardless cheek awakened by its mellow hue, — "*trust, secrecy*," were whispered by a muffled figure retreating through the shrubbery, while Ferdinand held his breath to hear. He glanced hurriedly at Lorenzo, who lay wrapt in the innocent beauty of sleep. While Ferdinand looked, a troubled smile crossed the lips of the dreamer, and he whispered, "*trust, secrecy*." His tones were low and soft as a woman's first answer to love, but they darted through his brother's ear like a thunder-clap. His first impulse was to arouse and tax him as a listener; but the profoundness of his repose contradicted this belief, and he left him to his slumbers while with mingled emotions he sought his own rest.

At the same hour on the following night, the stranger appeared.

"Our secret is known," said Ferdinand.

"How?" cried the stranger, grasping a dagger beneath his cloak.

"Lorenzo whispered the watchword in his sleep," said his brother.

"Noble boys!" exclaimed the man, a smile crossing his dark countenance, like a ray struggling through a cloud. "No trust is betrayed. I have confided to him that I might trust you both. The time draws near for action."

"But he is so young," hesitated Ferdinand; "and our mother, — how can we risk her happiness?"

"It is a woman's fate to yield and suffer," said the stranger, moodily. "I, too, have ties to rend"; and his thrilling sigh sounded in the stillness. "Awaken Lorenzo."

Ferdinand went to the bedside and touched the slumberer's arm. His was the delicious repose of youth, which clung to him like a garment.

"Lorenzo, Lorenzo, awake!"

The boy turned languidly, half opened his eyes, and throwing his arm over his head again, fell asleep.

"*Trust, secrecy,*" whispered Ferdinand in his ear.

The word was like flame to the mine; he started wildly from the bed, planted his foot firmly upon the floor, and exclaimed, —

"Ready!"

Ferdinand drew his arm within his own, and in a few moments they were in a recess of the garden with the stranger.

There was an expression of anxiety and alarm on the countenance of the youths as he unfolded his plans.

"It is robbery," murmured Lorenzo; "robbery of a mother, too."

"Things have a different name under different circumstances, young gentlemen," said the stranger. "History will call the deed patriotism. The noble band who have resolved to rescue the state from oppression, have sworn that none of the softer affections shall stand between them and their country. If you drive away these boyish feelings, and procure me the paper from your mother's cabinet, you aid in that for which heroes have sacrificed more than paltry gold. And, remember," he continued, while a flickering moonbeam brought out the aggravated expression of a sinister countenance, "that you are *pledged, known,* to me. If our party succeed, — and success is almost as certain as that the skies are above us, — your mother will be elevated to the rank that she deserves. If, however, you stop in this movement, and I betray you, as I swear to heaven I will, she will be implicated; for who will believe, boys as you are, that you act voluntarily?"

Sad it is to unloose the first strong link of filial sympathy, when no contact with the world has dimmed the brightness and beauty of the chain. How often, through the long day that followed that night, tears started to Lorenzo's eyes, and groans, in the solitude of his chamber, burst from Ferdinand's heart!

Darkness came, — how unlike the starry nights of innocent days! Every wind seemed to murmur, every leaf seemed to swell the word "treachery, treachery."

Their mother slept; their beautiful and good mother, who had nursed them at her breast, who had watched, not betrayed, their slumbers, who had taught their lips to pray against temptation. The cabinet to which the stranger referred was in a dressing-room next to her sleeping apartment. They went together with the hurried step of young deception. As they passed her door, the moonbeams revealed her form, — they faltered, — a 'voice, low beneath the casement, was heard thrilling "*trust, secrecy*." They delayed no longer; the spring yielded to their touch, and the paper was soon eagerly grasped by the stranger.

A few weeks rolled away. Rumors were abroad of danger to the State. Many individuals were seized on suspicion of conspiracy. Rosalba knew not why, but there seemed something like a blight on her once cheerful household. A haughty defiance sat on Ferdinand's brow as he read the papers of the day, while the healthy glow on Lorenzo's cheek faded, or was brilliant with a sudden flush. Rosalba watched her boys as a mother will watch the casket where her heart's treasures are enshrined. She felt that the bitter moment had come when parental sympathy was unasked, when the moorings of youthful confidence were severed, and the barque thrust forth on life's wide sea alone. She stood like a wintry tree deserted by sunshine.

There had been a tranquil day, undisturbed by rumor or apprehension, and at twilight Rosalba and her sons sat in their favorite bower. Something of the lovely confidence of the past was restored. Lorenzo leaned with his arm around his mother's neck, and Ferdinand threw himself on the turf at her feet, his flashing eyes softened by her gentle smiles.

"How like your father you are growing," said she, as she pressed her lips on his forehead.

"I shall be jealous, mother," said Lorenzo, "for I call such kisses mine." And he turned her cheek with his hand until it came in contact with his own.

They were interrupted by strange voices, and suddenly there stood before the group several officers of police, who arrested the boys as prisoners of state. Rosalba sat for a moment like one in a dream.

"This is some strange mistake," at length she said to them. "These are mere children, and have scarcely ever wandered from my side."

The men showed their orders, — they were definite, the individuals could not be mistaken, and they were charged with conspiracy.

Rosalba turned from the men and wildly urged the boys to assert their innocence. Her heart sank within her at their statue-like silence. The movements of revolutionary periods are rapid and decided. They were conveyed to prison before her eyes, and soon sentenced to death.

Rosalba hastened to the authorities, and with tears and prayers, implored their pardon. The answer was, *that one could be saved, and she might choose between them.*

She repaired to the prison, broken-hearted. They were in different cells. As she entered the first, the light through the grating fell strongly on Ferdinand, and now flashed forth to her sight in stronger lines the likeness to his father. Those deep full eyes were his; that forehead and retreating curls were his; the compressed lip and manly bearing were his; and his, too, the smile that was to be so soon extinguished forever. She sank into his arms.

Ferdinand supported her to his wretched pallet, kissed her cold cheek, upon which his big tears fell fast, and bade her be comforted.

"Comfort! O, God! comfort!" shrieked the widow, in the first paroxysm of hopeless wretchedness; "where, where, but in the grave with my children?" and hiding her face in her son's bosom, her sobs were so strong and wild that he feared her heart was breaking.

"Listen to me, mother, listen to me," he said in tremulous tones, "and I will tell you what will comfort you,— the memory of what a good parent you have been, from the first moment I nestled in your arms until this dark hour. How you have warned and guided us, and sacrificed your wishes to ours! You have been a true mother to me, God knows; you have been an angel watching my path, my own, own mother;" and as he said this, he knelt and bowed his head to her lap, and hid his face there.

She spoke not; she even shook him off in her agony; the waves were rolling over her soul, and her life-star was gone.

He drew her gently towards him, and soothingly pressed her hands in his.

"Since I left you, mother, I have had a dream,— a strange but sweet dream. I have not thought much of Heaven before; but I am sure I was there in my dreams. We were all there, all four,— and you and father were so young and beautiful. There was a light around you, and you seemed too glorious to Lorenzo and me, until we heard you say, '*My children.*' O, mother, there were no tears in that heaven,— no death!" and his voice faltered, a shudder went over his frame, and he was silent.

"Death, death!" almost screamed Rosalba, "why did you not die in your cradle? I could have closed your eyes softly, and crossed your hands upon your breast, and strewn your grave with flowers; now, now—"

There was a pause of passionate sorrow. Ferdinand knelt still at his mother's feet, and gazed into her face with a look of pleading.

"Mother, dear mother, for mercy's sake, be composed, or I shall go wild, too;" and he pressed his hands to his head. "Mother, you forget that I must be strengthened for this great trial, and our poor Lorenzo, too."

Rosalba turned on him such a gaze of mournful admiration, as we give the meteor darting to sudden extinguishment. Lorenzo's name subdued her; it was not a moment for words, but turning from Ferdinand she knelt before a rude crucifix inserted in the wall, offered a silent prayer, and kissing him, passed to the cell of his brother. As she entered, Lorenzo rushed to her with such a scream of joy and fear that the empty vaults sent back the sound.

"You have come to save me, mother," he cried. "I knew you would not let your poor boy die!"

Rosalba turned aside in agony. He followed her beseechingly.

"Look at me, mother. I am your own, your youngest one. Here," said he, throwing back the glossy hair that shaded his features, "here is *your* likeness. My father loved me because I looked like you,—you would not have me die!" and he threw his arms around her neck and nestled as a bird beneath the parent's wing.

Rosalba sat upon the damp floor and took the boy to her heart as in days of infancy. She wiped away his gushing tears and uttered soft tones of endearment.

"You will save *me* then, my mother?" he asked, wildly.

"I can save *one* of you," she whispered, almost inaudibly. 'The sentence is, that one of you may live if I will *choose* him."

Lorenzo sprang from her arms and threw himself at her feet.

"You will save me, *me*," he cried, vehemently. "I am too young to die. Mother, my heart will break with terror if you say I must die. O, mother, I think of it, I dream of it. I am afraid; I am crazy; save me, save your poor, poor Lorenzo," and he clung to her with a piercing look of entreaty.

The agonized mother turned upon him with a kind of fierceness and almost shouted in his ear,—

"*You* say that Ferdinand is to die? *I* will it not. Thank God it rests not with me; I am guiltless!" and she stamped the narrow cell with almost maniac footsteps.

"I said it not, mother," replied the boy mournfully. Ferdinand must live, and I will go. It is fearful, but I must go," and with a frightened look he swooned away.

Three days and nights Rosalba passed in alternate visits to her children. She ate no food nor slept. The keeper's eyes moistened as she passed to and fro. Sometimes, in the horror of despair, she threw herself down in the dark passage and beat the impassive stones with her delicate hands. Sometimes she knelt, and gazed upon the crucifix, as if asking aid from Heaven. Now, low unuttered sounds escaped her, as if her reason had fled. She shed no tears. Suffering had gone deeper than their fount.

On the fourth day an eager crowd gathered to the execution of *two* youths. At the closing moment, when there was a hush in the multitude, a shriek went up from among the spectators so piercing, wild, and unearthly, that many a sleeper started that night in his dreams, as he remembered it. When the populace dispersed, a senseless female form was discovered closely enveloped in a veil. The pulse of life had ceased to beat in that fair and gentle bosom, on which was discovered the miniature likeness of two beautiful boys embracing, and a braid of dark hair encircling the name of Rosalba De Soria.

GOOD NIGHT.

Good night, mamma; good night, papa;
I'm going now to sleep;
Your little boy will say his prayers,
And God his soul will keep.

THE LOST MAIL.

A TALE OF THE FOREST.

My cousin Lewis Walpole, from the earliest childhood, was remarkable for finding things.

His companions thought he enjoyed what is commonly called good luck, but a closer philosophy might say he was particularly observing. He once found two letters in a morning walk, the reward for which filled his pocket with spending-money for a year; and as we were rambling together one day, he brought up from the mud on his ratan a gold ring. It was a plain ring, with two initials, and though no immediate reward followed, it introduced him to a friendship which was like golden apples for the rest of his days.

Once I stepped on a bit of dirty paper; Lewis followed me, picked it up and laid it in his little snug pocket-book. Six weeks after, an advertisement appeared, offering three hundred dollars' reward for that very bit of paper, which was the half of a note worth as many thousands.

It seemed to me that pins sprang from the earth for Lewis, for he was never without a row of them in his waistcoat.

If an old lady was in want of one, Lewis was always ready, and then his head was patted, and he was treated to tit-bits. If a pretty girl's shawl was to be fastened, behold Lewis' pin came forth, and then such a beautiful smile beamed upon him! If a child was in danger of losing her bonnet, Lewis' offered pin was seized, and he was caressed with lips and eyes, for her preservation from a maternal chiding.

Cousin Lewis, sometime since, removed to the far West, and I, his senior by a dozen years (though he was a stricken bachelor), went with him to darn his stockings and keep his hearth clean. We called our log-house Sparrownest, and in one way and another made it as cosey as heart could wish. What could poor cousin Lewis find now, in his wide fields and vast forests? Not pins, certainly; but one day, twenty miles from home, he did find in the wild woods a strange thing,— a pretty Irish girl about sixteen years old, all alone, wringing her hands and sobbing as if her heart would break.

Cousin Lewis dismounted (he was a noble horseman), and offered her assistance. The poor child only wept the more, crying out,—

"And isn't it alone in the wide world that I am?"

It was an awkward business; but cousin Lewis knew better than anybody how to do a kindness, so he wiped her eyes, soothed her, and bade her be of good cheer; then took her up on his saddle, and brought her home.

"What big bundle has cousin Lewis brought home?" thought I, as he rode up to the door in the twilight; and great was my astonishment to see a red-cheeked girl slip down from the saddle, with a shame-faced look. I bestirred myself and got supper, for the child was cold and hungry. When her appetite was appeased, (she ate a whole chicken, poor thing!) she began to cry.

"What can I do for you, my child?" said I.

"And isn't it of my father I'm thinkin'?" said she, sobbing and wringing her hands. "There were twenty of us, big and little, in the wagon, and him in the front one. It was with a clever old lady I was, in the after one, we to take the charge of one another, ye mind. And when the 'orses was stopped for wathering, I minded to go and gather some flowers I had never seen in my own counthry. So I sated myself down to pull some flowers, and a bit weed thereabout looked like the shamrock, and I fell a thinkin'; a kind of the dream came upon me, and I was at play with Kathleen and the girls, and thin we were for throwin' peat at Dermot, and Dermot made as if to kiss me, the impudent—, and I slapped him on the face, and thin I knew nothin' more until I started up and found

DORA.—Page 155.

myself alone. The wagons were gone, the owls were hootin', and the night comin' on. Then I shouted, and cried, and raved, and ran till my feet failed me, and my heart was jist like to break in two, when the masther (here she made a low courtesy to cousin Lewis), came along like the light on a dark night, and took compassion on the poor girl; and she will love him all her days for his goodness, she will."

With that, cousin Lewis took out his pocket-handkerchief, and I punched the fire.

So Dora became one of us, and she sang about Sparrownest like a young bird, with a natural sigh now and then for her father.

Did cousin Lewis find anything else in the forest? Listen. As he was riding on horseback, in his deliberate way, on the far outskirts of his fields, he saw something white scattered among the green herbage. He spurred his horse toward the spot. It was strewed with letters, which were dashed with mud and rain. Cousin Lewis alighted, and quietly deposited them all in his saddle-bags.

Dora and I had made a blazing fire, for the night was chilly; and while I was knitting, she trod about with a light step, laying the cloth for supper, and singing an Irish air about "Dermot, my dear." When cousin Lewis came in, she sprang towards him with such joy, and hung his hat on the peg, and put his heavy saddle-bags in one corner, and brought him water to bathe his hands, and helped to draw off his great boots. He looked very fondly on her. You would not have thought he was so much older than she, for his hair was curling, and black as the raven; mine has been gray for many years.

At supper cousin Lewis told us about the letters. I confess, old as I am, I could scarcely keep my hands from the saddle-bags, and I thought Dora would have torn them open.

"We shall have a rainy day to-morrow," said cousin Lewis, in his quiet way, "and will want amusement; beside, our Yankee clock points to bedtime."

"Masther, dear," said Dora, imploringly, "the letthers will not slape a wink for wanting to be read."

"We must keep them locked up, my love, as we do restless children," said cousin Lewis, and I think I saw him kiss the hand that struggled to take the key of the saddle-bags away from him. No wonder he felt young, for he was very straight and graceful.

The next morning, when we assembled at breakfast, the rain descended in that determined style which announces a regular outpouring for the day.

Dora and I glanced at the saddle-bags; cousin Lewis smiled.

"Have you settled it with your conscience," said he, "whether those letters should be read? There has evidently been a mail robbery."

"You would n't in rason be after sendin' the letthers away, poor things," said Dora, "when they were left in the forests. And it wasn't *that* ye did to me, anyhow!"

Cousin Lewis looked down and sighed, and smiled. I could not tell whether he was thinking of the letters, or Dora; but I noticed, when he smiled, how white and even his teeth were.

After some discussion we decided that no seal was to be broken where the superscription was legible, but that it was right and proper that we should constitute ourselves a committee to decide which of them were in a state to return to the post-office. Cousin Lewis was appointed reader. While he gave us the contents of the following, Dora amused herself by treading on Carlo's paw, who looked up in her face and whimpered.

The date was erased.

"Dear Judge: You will be surprised to learn that . . . has taken the field against us. What will European cabinets say when such addle-headed fellows form a part of our government? B—— is up and doing. You must be on the alert, and circumvent these movements, if possible. The secretaryship may yet be secured by a general canvassing. T. and J. are fit tools. Take care of S., and give a sop to old Cerberus on the island. Keep the date in mind, as — "

The rest of the writing was obliterated. The next letter made Dora stop playing with Carlo's paw.

"PHILADELPHIA, ETC.

"DEAR RUSSELL: I received the books safely, and thank you. After looking them over, I had an odd dream, and was awakened with my own excessive laughter. It is utterly preposterous that a staid lawyer, half a century old, should be dreaming such dreams.

"I dreamed that I was blowing soap-bubbles out of a clay pipe, a thing I have not done since you and I were boys at Fishkill. One after another they floated off, poetically enough; now rising gracefully in the sunbeams, and now exploding softly on the turf at my feet. At length, one, the king of the rest, grew and grew at the end of my pipe, until it became as large as a wash-basin. It fell, and lay rolling about, offering beautiful prismatic hues to the eye, when, presently, a little square-nosed pig came grunting towards it. Twice he smelled it, and tried to turn it, but retreated as it rolled towards him. Again he seemed to gather up his courage, and thrusting his square snout against it, it exploded with a noise like a pistol. Little Squarenose ran as if for life and death, and I awoke in a positive perspiration with excess of laughter.

"Interpretation of

"Your,

"JAMES COL——."

Dora shouted with glee at this droll description, and her interest was kept awake by the following, written evidently by a relation of a certain popular character : —

"Mrs Sippi
"West End of A Merry K.

"Dear Veller: Wot with my see sickness and warious causes, it's bin utterly onpossible for me to rite to you, tho' it warnt for want of thinkin' on you, as the thief said to the constable. Wos you eve see sick, cozen Veller? If you wos, you would say that you felt in the sitivation of a barrel of licker, that's rolled over and over agin its vill.

"A most mortifyin' thing happened a board the wessel. You know, my lovin' cozen, the jar of baked beans you put aboard for my private eatin'. Wot should the stewhard do, but set it atop of three basins in my state-room, and won day wen the ladies wos eatin' lunch, there came an awful lurch of the see, the wich burstin' open my door, driv the whole concern into the cabin. The beans was mouldy beyond account, and smelt werry wilely, as the pig said wen he vent to his neighbor's pen. The beans was awfully griddle about the floor under the ladies' feet, who scrambled up into the cheers. I put my head out of my birth to explain, and was taken with an awful qualm in the midst of a pology.

"Give my love to Miss ——, and tell her the Merrycans have been quite shy of my letter of introduction from her. I'm jealous she did n't move in sich respectable society as me, or else she made a mistake, as the dissector said wen he got hold of a live body. I ain't seen a drunken lady, nor a young woman married to her grandfather, nor a hypocritical parson since I left the wessel.

"I will write agin as ever I get to Miss Sore-Eye.

"Your loven cozen, Timothy."

It may well be imagined that Sparrownest rang with our mirth, for little matters move one in the country. Dora laughed until she cried; but her mood was soon changed when cousin Lewis, in his pathetic tones, read the next letter.

"Father: I take my pen in desperation, not in hope; and yet, perhaps, when you know that the body of my child lies beside me without my having the means to buy him a shroud, you may relent. Poor Edward is stretched on his hard mattress beside the boy, and his hollow cough rings fearfully through the empty room. O, father, if he had but that old sofa you banished to the garret on the night of my birth-day ball! You will think me crazy to say so, but you are a murderer, father. My boy died for want of nourishment, and you are murdering Edward too! the best, the noblest —. O, heaven! to think of the soft beds in your vacant rooms, and the gilt-edged cups from which you drink your odorous tea, with that white sugar sparkling like diamonds! I have just given poor Edward his nauseous draft in a tin vessel. I have not had time to cleanse it since my baby was ill.

"My baby, how tranquilly he rests! Would that Edward and I might lie down beside him!

"Father, will God treat his erring children as you do? 'Like as a *father* pitieth his children.'

— "O, Father in heaven, art thou like mine?"

"A change has come upon Edward, father; he is dying —— dead."

Dora laid her head upon the table in tears, but she soon wiped her eyes and listened with feminine interest to another letter.

"New York.

"Dear Isabel: You must not fail to be here on the 21st of next month as my first bridesmaid. I can take no excuse. My dress is perfect; papa imported it for me. There is and shall be no copy in the city. The pearls, too, are exquisitely *unique*. You can form some judgment of what will be necessary for your own dress by mine. Of course you must be less elegant than the bride.

" Frock, with lace trimmings, etc.	$150 00
" Veil	50 00
" Pocket handkerchief (the divine thing)	20 00
" Embroidered gloves	3 00
" Satin boots	12 50
" Stockings	5 00
" Embroidered scarf	10 00
" Set of pearls	200 00
" Bouquet of natural flowers	5 00

" Come, dearest Isabel, and witness my dress and my felicity!

"Your own ELEANOR.

" P. S. You know you must appear with me on Sunday. Mamma has bought me a heaven of a bonnet with **feathers.**"

Dora rolled up her eyes. "And isn't it feathers that's to make *that* bird?" said she. Upon which she began to speculate on her own wants, if she should be married, and decided that ten dollars would be an ample dower for her. Cousin Lewis, appropriately enough, though accidentally, hit upon a letter of good advice to a bride. I was very much disconcerted, however, at the third paragraph, to see Dora begin to nod; at the fourth, her hands fell in her lap, and her ball of thread rolled on the floor; at the fifth, her head sank on her shoulder, and cousin Lewis had to support her with his left arm.

" Don't disturb the poor child," said he, kindly, as I began to shake her.

" But cousin Lewis," said I, "it is a pity she should lose such excellent advice, particularly if she should marry a parson."

" You know nothing about these matters, Rachel," said cousin Lewis, sharply. " I will tell her all the advice to-morrow."

So his left arm continued to keep her from falling, and he read on : —

"My Dear Mary: You ask for advice on the new scenes of duty which you have entered. I thank you for the implied compliment contained in such a request. Having watched your growth from the moment that you first blessed the eyes of your fond parents to this time, when, with conscientious resolutions, and warm affections, you have become the wife of a clergyman, it is with no little interest that I answer it.

"You feel, doubtless, better than I can express, how necessary is true piety to the happiness of one whose husband is devoted to the cause of Christ. Beautiful is the spectacle, where confiding hearts move in pious sympathy, pleased with earth, yet looking towards heaven; and when the wave of sorrow comes (as come it must), and rushes over their souls together, bending but a moment with the shock, and then, with a common impulse, resuming their upward view.

"Yet I would warn you, in the enthusiasm of your aims at religious duty, not to involve yourself in your husband's sphere. Many young ladies, when wedded to clergymen, have made themselves unhappy by extending too widely the circle of their cares. Ardent in the cause of the Master they profess to follow, they imagine that they must devote their time and powers to the flock over which their husband presides. By degrees, family cares press on and crowd their time, and they lose their equanimity of temper amid conflicting duties.

"A minister's wife should show by her deportment that she is one of his *flock*, and not a leader. A constant and respectful attendance on his ministry, and a deportment which marks that her thoughts are

'For God, through him,'

will secure for her a quiet influence over the minds of his people. She should seem not to be *first*, even in good works, but skilfully and delicately promote the cause of truth through others.

"The best service you can render his people will be to make your husband's home happy; then will he go forth prepared to sympathize with them, and his free spirit will range over his wide sphere of duty in religious joy. Remember, that in common with all men,

> "'A something of submission, of respect,
> Obedience, kindness personal, he loves.
> A slighter service so adorn'd will please
> Him more, than wanting this, a greater would.
>
> *Goethe.*'

"Be not cold to his peculiar taste; if he loves books, cultivate literature, that he may find your intellectual improvement keeping pace in a measure with his own. If music attract him, forward, either in yourself, or those around you, an accomplishment which may soothe his weariness, or beguile his care; and while you faithfully study your domestic duties, either in the preservation of neatness and order in your household, or with your needle, by his side, let him see that mind is still 'lord of the ascendant.'

"I say to you, what I would say to all young wives, cultivate a gentle temper. *You* have a sweet disposition: thank God for it, as the best dower for married life.

"Riches, accomplishments, intellect, fade all away before the genuine smile of good nature. But do not trust to the gift of a sweet temper. None but a woman can know the wear and tear of feeling produced by the minute details of household care. Pray and strive for gentleness, and 'the soft answer which turneth away wrath.' Be willing *not* to have your own way. The contest for power is always a losing one for woman.

> "'Obedience
> "Is her best duty.'

"In obtaining power, she may chance to lose the sway of stronger affection.

"Farewell, dear Mary. May the God who has blessed you thus far, sanctify and accept the offering of the talents which you and yours have laid before him.

"Your affectionate aunt,
"CAROLINE."

As cousin Lewis' voice ceased, after reading this certainly excellent letter, Dora started and rubbed her eyes; it was not many minutes, however, before her sympathies were excited and her fingers beating time on the table to the musical jingle of the following girlish epistle: —

"CAMBRIDGE, MASS.

"I ought to make excuses due,
Dear Julia, for not writing you,
Since, with a kindness prompt and free,
You gave your charming thoughts to me.
But I abominate excuses,
And rank them among mere abuses,
As they come marching full and round
To tinkling instruments of sound,
Without a particle of feeling,
Mere drapery for the heart's concealing.
Your letter was delightful to me,
And made a pleasant thrill run through me,
Like that we feel in smelling flowers,
Or when we listen to soft showers
That fall upon a sultry day,
And chase our languid thoughts away.
  So you are reading Anacharsis!
How well kept up that learned farce is,
Showing us sages, states, and kings,
Familiarly as common things.
Stationed once more in this retreat,
Where leisure and excitement meet;

Where studious pleasures, happy, calm,
Show life with every softer charm.
Nothing disturbs seclusion's hour,
Which hovers with its tranquil power;
Save transient visitors, who seem
Like shooting-stars with brilliant gleam,
That dart from out a distant sphere,
Delight **my gaze and disappear.**
The Boston question, **What's the news?**
Is only answered by reviews,
Or weekly papers, letting out
The bus'ness that the world's about.
While the "last book" unfolds its page
Of interest in this bookish age.
Charles Lamb, amid some random start,
Throws out sweet whispers to my heart;
While Bulwer's strong yet poison'd **bowl**
I quaff until my senses roll.
Not to his hand the task is **given**
To lift the erring soul to Heaven;
Tartarean darkness fills the soul
That yields to his unsound control.
"Some graver things than these I find
Daily to occupy my mind.
Theology, with critic eye,
Causes my lingering doubts to fly;
And history, with reflecting pen,
Teaches of empires and of men.
"Then I have evening reveries
In gazing on the changing skies;
And walks, where, as I **look abroad,**
My soul springs **forward to its God.**
Nor even lonely am I then,
Though straying from the haunts of men;
The breeze lifts up a pleasant voice,
The streams in whispers say, Rejoice!
And Nature's tone, wherever given,
Thrills me like Nature's God **in** heaven.

> "But how I've written off my time,
> Led by the marching step of rhyme!
> Forgive this light and careless letter,
> Which leaves me still a heavy debtor
> To you for yours, with its completeness,
> Finished, epistolary neatness.
> And now, with kind remembrance true,
> Receive, dear girl, a warm adieu.
> 									EMILY."

"And isn't it nice, that?" said Dora, clapping her hands. "Och, but it dances like Dermot to old O'Connor's harp."

And now the impatient girl's fingers were again thrust into the saddle-bags; but as she drew out several letters, I observed that the superscription on one arrested her attention. She became very pale, broke the seal impetuously, and glanced at the signature. A joyous flush came over her cheeks; she danced about, waving the letter in the air, caught me round the neck and kissed me, and threw herself into cousin Lewis' arms in a passion of tears. When she could speak, she sobbed out, —

"And isn't it father's own hand writhing, darling? And isn't he at Louisville, weeping for his own Dora? And will not the masther" (here she disengaged herself from cousin Lewis, and stood before him with her accustomed courtesy) "take poor Dora to the father that's her own?"

Cousin Lewis was startled.

"I had hoped," said he, gravely, "that is, cousin Rachel and I, had hoped, that Sparrownest would have been your home for life, Dora."

Dora looked down, embarrassed, for my cousin Lewis' eyes were fixed upon her, and they were very black and sparkling, though he was a stricken bachelor.

I withdrew towards the window, but did not altogether look away.

I saw cousin Lewis take Dora's hand; I saw Dora blush all up to the eyebrows; I heard Cousin Lewis speak in a pleading tone. One would not have thought him an old bachelor by his voice. I saw little Dora tremble; her heart seemed starting from her bosom, and she began to cry.

"I will not distress you," said cousin Lewis, tenderly. "Tell me all your feelings as you are wont to do. Can you love me, and be my wedded wife?"

Dora looked up through her tears. Her eyes shone sweetly.

"I will love the masther to the day of my death, and after," said she; "but thin I will love Dermot better, and it is a sin is that."

Cousin Lewis dropped her hand abruptly, and left the room. He stayed away an hour, and then calmly prepared for Dora's journey. And now I never hear him speak her name.

MR. INKLIN:

OR, THE MAN OF LEISURE A MAN OF MISCHIEF.

Mrs. Sheridan, a happy wife and mother, having concluded the bustle of a housekeeper's morning, ascended to her bedroom with the agreeable consciousness of a neat parlor and pantry, and commenced the important business of cutting out a piece of linen. The smooth surface of a well-made bed was appropriated to this somewhat intricate process, on which, humble as it seems, the happiness of one's husband greatly depends. There is scarcely a more forlorn or pitiable object in the universe, than a man who, putting on a new shirt, perceives some radical defect, with the awful consciousness that nine, fifteen or twenty more are cut upon the same pattern. It so happened that Mr. Sheridan had detected, almost with complacency, the incipient decay of a set of shirts that had kept his neck in a vise for a year and a half, and with many injunctions to his wife to be merciful, had purchased a piece of new linen.

Mrs. Sheridan began her work with a light heart, and, humming a low tune, placed the various pieces on different parts of the bed in the most systematic manner. It is delightful to *create;* and the humble evolutions of the needle and scissors have healed many a wounded heart; but to work for those we love gives an added charm to this seemingly humble employment. Mrs. Sheridan went tripping lightly round the bed to the growing tumuli of gussets, wristbands, etc., looking back to her life of placid duty, where even the clouds that had sometimes shaded her path, were tinged with the light of love and hope.

She had not advanced far in the progress of her work, when a ring at the door-bell was heard, and a visitor announced. She smoothed down the border of her pretty morning cap, and with a sorrowful parting glance at the bed, descended to the parlor.

The visitor was Mr. Inklin, a broken merchant, who had contrived to save just enough for his support, without energy to strike into new plans, though it was his intention to enter upon some occupation at a future day. Mr. Inklin had no gift in conversation; his voice was an anodyne, and his sleepy eyes seemed wandering to the ends of the earth. Nothing is so chilling in conversation as an unanswering eye. Besides this unfixed look, he kept up perpetually a grunting kind of affirmative which destroyed the hope that a difference of opinion might stimulate his ideas. He dressed well, and made great use of his watch-key. Most men of leisure do.

The man of leisure sat down composedly, remarking that the day was fine.

Mrs. Sheridan assented, and tried to recollect if she had stuck a pin as a guide where she had drawn the last thread in the linen.

Mr. Inklin enlarged upon the weather.

"It had been warm," he asserted, "perhaps warmer than it was that time twelvemonth. Warm weather agreed with him. **He** thought it might last a few days longer, it was apt to in June."

Mrs. Sheridan looked towards him as he spoke, but it was silently to observe that his shirt collar was more pointed than **Mr.** Sheridan's.

"You have a quiet time," said the man of leisure, **"with the children all at school."**

"Yes, **sir**, very quiet," said Mrs. Sheridan, falling into a reverie, **as** she thought how well it was adapted to cutting out shirts.

Mr. Inklin went through the commonplace manner of morning visitors, **with** many a resting-place between, until he remarked that "the wind was rising."

Mrs. Sheridan had observed it too, with a feeling of dismay at the prospect of the commingling of all her shirt elements.

The man of leisure stayed an hour (he liked a morning visit one hour long), and then exclaiming, as the hand of his watch turned the expected point, "bless my soul, past twelve o'clock," **made his bow** and departed.

Mrs. Sheridan went to her chamber. The wind was whirling neck, **sleeve, and** flap gussets in unceremonious heaps; and collars, wristbands, and facings were dancing in eddies on the floor. In her agitation she lost the important boundary pin, and an error occurred in her calculations. The shirts were made, but for eighteen months her husband never took one from his drawer **but with a** nervous shudder, or **a** suppressed execration.

The Man of Leisure in a Counting-house.

The man of leisure next visited **the** counting-room of B—— & Co., and socially seating himself on a barrel, hoped he should not prevent the head clerk, who was his acquaintance, from writing.

"Not at all," said the polite clerk, putting his pen behind his ear with **a** constrained air.

"Pray don't stop on my account," said Mr. Inklin, with a patronizing smile.

The clerk returned to his accounts and letters, while the man of leisure described with somewhat more animation than usual, some herring he had eaten for breakfast. The clerk made an error in a figure, which cost Messrs. B— & Co. one week to rectify, and one of the correspondents of the firm was shortly after surprised with the announcement by letter, that an hundred bales of *pickled herring* would shortly be forwarded to order.

The Man of Leisure and his Minister.

It was Saturday night, and the Rev. Dr. Ingram sat in his study with his sheets before him, commentators and lexicons around him, and a well-mended pen in hand, when the man of leisure was announced. He entered slowly and almost diffidently, so that the compression of the Dr.'s brow produced by the interruption gave way to an open smile of encouragement. I have mentioned that Mr. Inklin was taciturn, and not only that, but that he threw an opiate over the minds of his associates. There were long pauses in that long hour, and the good words of the clergyman fell on barren ground. At length Mr. Inklin arose, saying, "I fear I have broken the thread of your argument, sir."

And broken it was. Dr. Ingram retouched the nib of his pen, listlessly turned the pages of Clark, Rosenmueller, Grotius, etc., rubbed his forehead, took two or three turns across the room, and threw himself on a seat in despair. The impetus was gone, the argument was frittered away; he stole off to bed, and dreamed that a thirty-two pounder was resting on his chest, with the man of leisure surmounting it.

The Man of Leisure and a Pretty Girl.

The man of leisure called on Monday on Miss Emma Roberts, — a pretty, blooming girl of seventeen. Emma was clear-starching.

Talk about the trials of men! What have they to annoy them in comparison to the mysteries of clear-starching? Alas, how seldom *clear!* Emma was going on in the full tide of success, indulging in the buoyant thoughts of her age; there was a soft light about her eye, as she drew out the edge of a *fichu*, or clapped it with her small hands, as if they felt the impulse of young hopes.

"I am sure Harry Bertram looked at this collar last Sunday; I wonder if he liked it," thought she, and a gentle sigh rustled the folds of the morning-robe on her bosom. Just then the door-bell sounded, and the man of leisure walked into the sitting-room, where Emma, with a nice establishment of smoothing-irons, etc., had ensconced herself for the morning.

"You won't mind a friend's looking in upon you," said Mr. Inklin, with an at-home air.

Emma blushed, loosened the strings of her apron, gave a glance at her starched fingers, and saying, —

"Take a seat, sir, suspended her work with the grace of natural politeness. In the mean while, the starch grew cold, and the irons were overheated.

Emma was not loquacious, and the dead pauses were neither few nor far between. Emma, rendered desperate, renewed her operations, but with diminished ardor; her clapping was feeble as the applause to an unpopular orator, she burnt her fingers, her face became flushed, and by the time the man of leisure had sat out his hour, a gray hue had settled over her muslins, and an indelible smutch disfigured Harry Bertram's collar.

Mr. Inklin soon called again, and met Harry Bertram. It was no influence of coquetry; but Emma rallied her powers and talked more to Mr. Inklin than to Harry, a modest youth, thrown somewhat into the shade by the veteran visitor, who outstayed him. Harry, who was not a man of leisure, could not call for several days; when he did, Mr. Inklin had "dropped in" before him, and was twisting his watch-key with his cold, wandering eyes and everlasting affirmatives.

Emma sewed industriously, and her dark lashes concealed her eyes. Her cheeks were beautifully flushed, but for whom?

Mr. Inklin toyed with her work-box, without seeming to know that he was touching what Harry thought a shrine.

Harry looked a little fierce, and bade good-night abruptly.

Emma raised her soft eyes with a look that ought to have detained a reasonable man; but he was prepossessed, and the kind glance was lost. Emma wished Mr. Inklin at the bottom of the sea; but there he sat, looking privileged, because he was a man of leisure.

The fastening of the windows reminded him that it was time to go, for he did not limit his evening calls to an hour. Emma went to her bedroom. She was just ready to cry; but a glance at her mirror showed such bright cheeks that it stopped the tears, and she fell into a passion. She tied her nightcap into a hard knot, and broke the string in a pet.

"Harry Bertram is a fool!" said she, "to let that stick of a man keep him from me. I wish I could change places with him"; and sitting down on a low seat, she trotted her foot and heaved some deep sighs.

The man of leisure "just called in" twice a week for three months. Report was busy. Harry's pride was roused. He offered himself to another pretty girl, and was accepted.

Emma's bright cheek faded, her step grew slow, and her voice was no longer heard in its gay carol from stair to stair. She was never talkative, but now she was sad. Mr. Inklin continued to "drop in"; his heart was a little love-touched, but then there was "time enough." One evening he came with a bit of news.

"I have brought you a bit of Harry Bertram's wedding-cake," said he to Emma.

Emma turned pale, then red, and burst into tears.

The man of leisure was concerned.

Emma looked very prettily **as she** struggled with her feelings, while the tears dried away; and he offered her his heart and hand.

"I would sooner lie down in my grave than marry you!" said the gentle Emma, in a voice so loud that Mr. Inklin started; and **rush**-ing to her own apartment, the china rang in the closet as she slammed the **door**. Mr. Inklin was astonished. Poor Emma covered **up** her heart, and smiled again; but she never married, nor ever destroyed a little flower that Harry Bertram gave her when it was right for **her to love** and hope.

The man of leisure bore her refusal with **philosophy, and continued** to "drop in."

The Man of Leisure and the Pale Boy.

"You'll please not to forget to ask the place for me, sir," said a pale, blue-eyed boy, as he brushed the coat of the man of leisure at his lodgings.

"Certainly **not**," **said Mr. Inklin.** "I shall be going that way **in a day or two.**"

"*Did* you ask for the place for me, yesterday?" said the pale boy, **on** the following day, with a quivering lip, as he performed the **same** office.

"No," was the **answer**. "I was busy; but I will to-day."

"God help my poor mother!" murmured the boy, and gazed listlessly on the cent Mr. Inklin laid in his hand.

The boy went home. **He ran to the** hungry children with the loaf of bread he had earned by brushing the gentlemen's coats at the hotel.

They shouted with joy, **and his** mother held-out her emaciated **hand** for a portion, while a sickly smile flitted across her face.

"Mother, dear," said the boy; "Mr. Inklin thinks he can get me the place, and **I shall have three** meals a day,—only think, mother, *three meals!*—and it won't take me three minutes to run home and share it with you."

The morning came, and the pale boy's voice trembled with eagerness as he asked Mr. Inklin if he had applied for the place.

"Not yet," said the man of leisure; "but there is time enough."

The cent that morning was wet with tears. Another morning arrived.

"It is very thoughtless in the boy to be so late," said Mr. Inklin. "Not a soul here to brush my coat."

The child came at length, his face swollen with weeping.

"I am sorry to disappoint you," said the man of leisure, "but the place in Mr. C——'s store was taken up yesterday."

The boy stopped brushing and burst afresh into tears.

"I don't care now," said he, sobbing; "we may as well starve Mother is dead."

The man of leisure was shocked, and he gave the pale boy a dollar.

The Man of Leisure on a Death-bed.

Mr. Inklin was taken ill. He had said often that he thought religion might be a good thing and he meant to look into it. An anxious friend brought a clergyman to him. He spoke tenderly but seriously to the sufferer, of eternal truths.

"Call to-morrow," said the man of leisure, "and we will talk about these matters."

That night the man of leisure died.

FAIRY-LAND

AND OTHER TALES.

BY

MRS. CAROLINE H. JERVEY.

FAIRY-LAND;

OR,

JESSIE AND HER KITTEN.

GIVE me your whole attention. Open those large, blue eyes,—not too wide, for they frighten me,—and who ever heard of violets frightening anybody? Let me see those bright lips parted in expectation, and those hands clasped, as if waiting for my words, and listen to me.

This is a regular fairy story,—none of your true and true stories, but something as fanciful as a bird in its flight, or a comet in its course, or anything zigzag and unreal in the world.

Said little Jessie Harding, one day to her mother, "Mamma, may I take my kitten and go into the woods?"

"Yes, my love; but come back before twelve to help me tie up my creepers on the arbors, and before your papa will miss his little Jessie."

"Yes, mamma," said Jessie; "I am only going to teach my mocking-bird a new song, and to wash my kitten, and to gather some wild flowers, and to—"

"Very well, dear," said the mother; "go."

And Jessie went with her kitty to the deep, still, dark, green woods. Did she ever **come back** again? *The kitty did.* **If you** shut your blue eyes a minute you can see her in imagination, **as she** runs with her kitten in her arms to the fresh, **cool stream.**

She looks almost like a fairy, for her step is so light that she scarce touches the ground. Her white dress **is** carefully tucked up at the **sides, for** a neat little girl she is, **and her** voice rings **out a childish song** of happiness and glee. **The kitty did** not like the washing much; but Jessie was very determined, and **scolded or coaxed** her until it **was all** over.

"**My dear** Arabella Victoria Marie Antoinette (that was the kitten's name), you are behaving in a very shameful manner," she **said**; "**it is some weeks since** you **have** been **washed, and I am washed every day; you must not scratch me, you** naughty thing, or I must duck you, and then you may be drowned! **No, you shall not be** drowned; there,—you are almost clean; just let me wash this disagreeable black spot from your head, and all will be over."

The kitty came out of **the** stream looking very miserable, and as if life **were** a thing **not at all** to be desired; but Jessie **rubbed her white and** black **sides quite dry, and wrapped** her in a shawl, and **the kitten** slept **as** quietly **as a tired child.**

Jessie then took off her shoes and stockings, and sitting on the bank, dipped her white and dimpled feet into the glad waters and laughed because **she** had achieved so great a thing as kitty's bath.

"**My!**" **said she,** clapping **her** hands, "**didn't she kick, and** didn't she struggle, and didn't I wash her infamous eyes and her disgraceful ears! **Come** feet, the water **is** very **pleasant,** no doubt, but home you must **go.**"

"*But home you must not go,*" said a voice near her, about as loud **as** the sound of a guitar. "You must fly over the *three perils,* for our queen has fallen in love with you, and has a seat prepared for **you on her** ivory **throne, and has sent me** to bring you **to her!**"

Jessie looked up and saw peering into her face — a fairy! Her heart beat violently when she beheld the impudent little creature seated in a bell-shaped flower, rocking away like a child in a swing, and uttering these bold words. Her heart beat quick, but she gazed steadfastly at the fairy queen's messenger, until the rocking motion made her quite sea-sick.

He was a gay-looking little fellow, with a rose-leaf twisted into a cocked hat, and a jacket of rose-leaves buttoned with dew drops. He had a reckless, determined air about him which made Jessie tremble even while she gazed. However, she returned his glance boldly, and quietly wiping her feet in her apron, she put on her shoes and stockings and took up her kitty to go.

"Put down the kitten," said the fairy.

"I would like to oblige you," said Jessie, "but I must be at home to give papa his lunch, and I have remained here too long already."

"So you won't go when our queen invites you?" replied the fairy. "You had better come, for she has ordered a bed of humming-bird's down for your ladyship, and a cup of coffee made from ground pearls. If you will not come of your own accord, I must bring you by force."

Jessie was frightened now, and clasping her kitten more closely in her arms, she prepared to run home; her home so quiet and inviting, where her parents were listening for her welcome step, and watching for her beaming smile.

As the fairy perceived her intention, he turned a summerset over the branch and stood directly in her path.

"Stir not a step at your peril," said he, sternly; and Jessie's feet refused to move at her will. He looked with his bold, bright eyes at the kitten, and Arabella Victoria Marie Antoinette dropped from her sheltering arms and sped onwards with trot, canter and gallop towards that home where Jessie's parents were listening for her welcome step, and watching for her beaming smile.

Jessie tried to follow, but the fairy's spell **was over her,** and she could not move a limb nor speak. He cruelly produced a gold chain which clanked as he wound it about her white **and** delicate arms, and binding her wrists so tightly together that **it hurt her** tender flesh, he drew her **onward** and **onward to the habitation of the** queen **of the fairies.**

Whether **it was in** earth, **or sea, or air, Jessie knew not ;** but she followed her guide blindly, with her white eyelids, **which** he had **breathed upon, closed** upon her **once** smiling eyes. There were **two words in her heart** which **she tried** in vain to utter ; they were papa and mamma ; and she thought of their intense sorrow **at seeing the kitten return alone ;** their desperate search **through the woods ;** their useless search through the world, **and their agonizing imagining** that she might be sleeping in death **beneath the deep waters of** the leaping stream.

But this mattered **not, nor stopped** her in her **onward course.** She knew the fairy's **chain** galled and **tore her** soft **arms, but she did not care for that;** she only cared **for** her home, so **quiet and inviting,** where **her parents were listening for** her **welcome step, and watching for her** beaming smile.

Sometimes she felt that the air was hot, sometimes **cold. Sometimes she** knew that it was dark, and again a light appeared to **beam** around ; but she feared no changes save the sad change in her **poor parents' hearts.**

Suddenly the bold fairy stopped, and, coming near her, breathed on her shoulders. **Two** wings instantly sprung from them, and, still guided by the chain, she and her companion soared aloft and onward, and then alighted at a brass gate, double-locked. As the fairy knocked three times, Jessie's eyes opened, and she looked around her. The immense brazen gates creaked on their ponderous **hinges,** and groaned like sick giants. They seemed a boundary to an inner and an outer world, and as she entered and they closed upon her, Jessie felt as **one would who enters** alive into a grave.

On an ivory throne sat the fairy queen, as beautiful as the day. Her sweet breath perfumed the air like a thousand violets, and her haughty and determined bearing was an embodiment of majesty. She smiled as she beheld Jessie; but the smile, so much like heat lightning over the heaven of her face, was exchanged for an expression of anger too terrible to be borne.

"Slave!" said she, glancing sternly at the fairy who had so cruelly obeyed her mandate, "is this the way to execute my commands? Did I order you to drag this mortal, whose presence I so coveted, into my court like a felon? Fie!" continued she, with increasing anger, stamping her tiny foot, "you so-called protector of injured innocence, you mirror of chivalry, begone! What, ho, guards! confine that fellow for life in the east beehive prison!"

Jessie pleaded for her late companion, but in vain; and she felt that the little queen's mandate was as unalterable as the laws of the Medes and Persians.

Oh, the dreary, dreary days in the golden jail of fairy-land! How leaden were the wings upon which they slowly sped! And yet the queen did everything to chase away the deep and settled gloom which shaded the face of the little maiden. She gathered gorgeous jewels, which grew in clusters like flowers, for the new favorite; she culled flowers more exquisite than tongue can tell, and wove them into chaplets for her hair. Balls were given in her honor, where everything bright and beautiful tempted her to return once more to her gay mood. But alas! her young head drooped, and, spite of love, devotion and pleasure, her home-sick heart sighed for the simple pleasures of her country life. Night after night the stranger devised some plan of escape from those enchanted regions, but the morning's dawn told her how useless they were. Besides the brazen gate which guarded fairy-land, the three perils arose to her imagination to shut out heaven from her view, and she knew that if she attempted to escape, death would be the penalty.

One day the fairy queen, blushing like a rich rosebud, called her into her presence and said these words:—

"Jessie, I am going to be married to the most powerful and noblest of fairies. Hitherto, I have found no one worthy of my heart; but now," added the exquisite creature, hiding her face in a sprig of Indian creeper, "I have found the idol of my dream, and I am going to link my fate with his. We are to meet in my enchanted castle, some leagues distant, and, as no mortal has ever been permitted to witness such a ceremony as the nuptials of a fairy, I must leave you here almost alone. Only two guards will remain; also, the prisoner in the beehive. He endures tortures every day, according to my commands; and remember, when I am roused, if my wrath is so terrible to my own kind, it is worse than terrible to a mortal who offends me. I love you, Jessie, and would keep you with me always. After a time your deep grief will subside into contentment, your contentment into happiness, and you will become like one of us. Beware, I say again, of attempting to escape. It is useless, utterly useless; for beside the brazen gate, which can only open to my fairy lock-keeper, yonder yawns the sea of fire which encircles this isle; next to that, the mountain of ice; beyond that, the garden of fruit, guarded by monster giants, whose frowns alone create insensibility. When I return home with my heart's delight, my chosen love, I shall study your happiness more than ever, and I shall teach him to love my Jessie, too."

"Oh, queen!" said Jessie, passionately, and falling at the fairy's feet; "I thank you for all your kindness, but I am not happy here, and I never can be happy; night after night I weep whole rivers of tears; night after night I pray that your hard heart may be softened and that you will allow me to return to my own home. Oh, if you would only let me go back, I would thank you so much, and I would tell them how good and kind you were, and how so great a queen, made herself more noble still by such a kind action."

"Silence," answered the fairy, sternly, uttering the first harsh words that she had ever done to Jessie; "a whole lifetime of prayers and tears is of no avail. Here you are, and here you must remain, for my commands are not to be disputed; and as a warning, I will tell you the fate of the only mortal beside yourself, who has ever been within these gates. I loved, as I do you, a bright, brave, frank boy, some summers older than you are, and I had him brought hither. As he entered my dominions, his sweet smiles faded, and the demon of discontent disfigured his lovely face. I warned him, but my kindness was not appreciated. My love changed to hate, and he is chained in the garden of fruit, guarded by my monster giants. Beware of the like fate!"

Jessie could only weep at this terrible tale, and when the queen motioned her to kneel upon the first step of her throne that she might kiss her brow, she did so; but she neither felt nor cared how great an honor it was to be kissed by a fairy queen.

Then the gorgeous train departed, and Jessie was left alone with the two guards and the prisoner in the bee-hive. She had heard many secrets since her sojourn in fairy-land. She had seen flowers growing; she had learned how to put seed into the ground which in one day would spring into a plant and bear glorious blossoms; she knew in what plants the fiercest poisons were centred; and the different power of poisons were known to her also, from those which would create insensibility, to those which would cause instant death.

When the bridal train went, she remembered these things and her little brain was perplexed in finding out how to turn them to advantage. She knew that a mortal could never cause the death of a fairy, nor did her tender heart desire such an evil; but she hoped to be able to create insensibility, and she hastened to gather the flowers of a certain kind, and to distil them for her purpose. This she was only enabled to do at night, when the guards were resting from their labors of the day, and when they thought that she was secure in sleep herself.

At last, in these stolen moments of trembling anxiety, she completed her work, and when it was over, prepared to put her schemes into execution. What was her work to be? Let me tell you.

Jessie took the precious vial which contained the liquid, and in the deep silence of night, proceeded to the sleeping bower of the drowsy guards. Her light tread did not awaken them. You might **have seen her eyes glisten** like diamonds, as she carefully, **but with** trembling hands, poured **a drop** of the enchanted liquid upon each eyelid of the sleepers. You might **have seen** her placid smile of content, **as she heard the** deep-drawn sigh **of each fairy, which** assured her by the knowledge she had of the **poison, that it had** taken sure effect, and that they would remain **insensible for many** nights and days.

But alas! her case was hopeless still, and she **was** almost sorry for what she had done, for there, towering up before her, were those fatal gates, and **she sat down** and wept at her own forlorn state.

Suddenly she dried her eyes, for she remembered the beehive fairy. **She** could not attempt to escape and leave him in misery; so she formed the worthy and benevolent design of rescuing him from his captivity. She ran towards the prison, and heard the poor little fellow's groans before she had quite reached the place.

"**Little** sufferer," said **she, as she** approached the formidable hive, "**can I do anything for you?**"

"Who is that," answered a forlorn voice, "who speaks so kindly? I have not heard a word of kindness for a long time."

"It is I," answered Jessie, "who have come to free you; and **if** you promise not to thwart me in my plan of attempting to escape, **I** will let you out of this miserable dungeon."

"Oh!" answered the fairy, falling upon his knees, "this **is really rendering** good for evil. I solemnly declare to you, that if **you will** have the goodness to liberate me, I will not only thank you and be eternally grateful, but I will assist you to escape; and I, who would not be safe here longer, — for my doom on the return of the queen would be death, — will go with you and help you along on your perilous path; and then when you are safe at home, I will wing my way over mountains and seas, and will find a haven of rest in some fairy tribe in distant lands."

Jessie was too overjoyed to speak, and she silently drew the bolt of the terrible beehive, not without some danger for herself from the infuriated tenants, and there the once bright and gentlemanly fairy stood before her, his gay apparel stained and disfigured, and his whole appearance altered. He again bent his knee to Jessie, and said, in accents of gallantry: —

"You alone do I acknowledge as my queen; you alone will I guide or follow, as the case may be, to the ends of the earth."

The fairy had unfortunately lost the power of flying, for the wings which had formerly glittered on his shoulders were bruised and useless; so the little mortal and he consulted together with earnest intent for a means of escape.

"If we could only get over those brazen gates," said the fairy, "half the difficulty would be over; but alas! there they stand at the very beginning of our journey, and it is impossible to pass them by, as the keeper who opened them for our entrance has gone with the queen to her marriage."

"Ah," said Jessie, "then all is in vain, and we must remain here, subject to the queen's wrath when she returns!"

As the little maiden said these words, she leaned heavily against the tall, brazen structure, grief-bowed and despondent; but her whole frame shook with pleasure as she felt the gates yield a little to the pressure of her light form. The fairy perceived this also, and upon examining them more particularly, they found that the gates were not locked at all, and that the keeper, in the hurry of his departure, must have forgotten to do his last duty. Then, with glad hearts, they opened the gate upon its groaning hinges, and gliding out, found themselves still in fairy-land, but out in the broad, uncultivated fields.

Next came the sea of fire. When Jessie saw this roaring element, this ocean of flame, raging and boiling up near her, she burst into a passion of tears. Life seemed very dark to the child, and she almost wished herself safe again in the palace; but it was too late to retrace her path, for the rage of the queen was more terrible than a whole universe of fire.

The fairy, at least, knew what to do; for he told Jessie that hidden in an immense tree, near the bank of the stream, was a boat made of asbestos. He told her, too, that this was a kind of wood upon which fire had no effect, and that it was used by inferior fairies who came to visit them, who could not fly, or for those of their own kind who had accidentally injured their plumes.

Of course his strength was not much, — for he was weakened by his long confinement, — but his will was great, and he assisted Jessie to draw the boat with its two asbestos oars to the brink; and never was vessel launched with more rejoicing.

It was a terrible thing to Jessie to find herself upon that strange sea, almost parched with the overpowering heat; but the watchwords, — father and mother! — nerved her heart and her arm, and the mute couple soon found themselves over the narrow sea, and at the opposite shore.

It was an easy thing to climb up the low banks; and setting the boat adrift, they watched it for a moment float down the fiery stream. The fairy proposed giving nine cheers, but Jessie only offered up a silent prayer of gratitude, and went onward on her journey.

It was a day's travel from the river of flames to the mountain of ice, and the new companions trudged bravely along the same road. The fairy entertained Jessie with all the adventures of his life, and

I can assure you that some were as strange as the one in which they were now engaged. He had been a wild fellow, and he was a merry and agreeable one. It was to Jessie's advantage that she had such a tireless companion with her; for, had she been alone, her spirits must have died within her, and she would have become faint in the way. She said all the prayers she knew to the fairy, into whose breast she hoped to instil some portion of gratitude for their escape; but alas! he only laughed or sung, and Jessie smiled through her tears at his antics. His voice was very sweet and flute-like, and this was his favorite song, — not very good poetry by the by: —

"Through the brass gate,
　Over the sea,
Nothing can stop
　Jessie and me.

She with her gentle step,
　I with my bold,
Onward we'll go
　Through heat and the cold.

Over the mountain
　Covered with ice,
Through the broad garden
　We'll bound in a trice.

Then through the woods,
　By the old woodland stream,
We'll find ourselves walking
　Like folks in a dream.

Then the white cottage
　We'll spy through the trees,
No more we'll be prey
　No monsters or bees.

She to her mother
　With arms wide spread out;
She to her father,
　With glad joyous shout.

I, to the ends of the
　Broad earth will go,
Feeling the sadness
　The desolate know.

Will mourn like a dove
　Bereft of its mate — "
　． ． ． ． ．

Jessie was always so affected at this point, that she never heard the end of the song; for she invariably requested the fairy to stop before the verse was ended; which request, with his usual politeness, he granted.

But at last, serious times came, and all singing was suspended; for there before them, like a huge looking-glass for giants and monsters, rose the tall mountain of ice. How were they to cross it? They themselves did not know for some time, but at last they found a way.

Jessie began as usual to cry, but the bold fairy kissed her flushed cheek, and told her to be comforted, and he would go in search of something with which to scale the **mountain**. He remained away so long that Jessie thought he would never return, and she was just **about to** give up in despair when she discovered him at a little distance, trailing along a kind of walking-stick, with a mournful coun**tenance.**

"Alas, Jessie," **said** he, "I can find nothing but this, and **your** shoes **are so** slippery that you will never be able **to** climb the mountain, and we must lie down here and **die!**"

Jessie felt in her pocket for her handkerchief (the usual refuge for the distressed), and a gleam of joy lighted up her countenance.

She had exchanged the elegant clothes the queen had given her for those made by her mother, and which she had on when the fairy found her by the stream. In the pocket, then, **of** this homely dress **she felt a hard substance, and** drawing it out discovered that it was a package of tacks which her father had given her, together with a little hammer, to make a cart which her kitten was to draw.

The desperate are always fruitful in inventions, and she called the fairy and told him her plan. It was this: to insert these little nails **firmly in** her shoes so that they might cling to the ice, and **with the staff, she hoped they might scale** the mountain.

Nor was she mistaken. But **how was** the fairy to ascend? His wings had not quite grown out and he could only fly a short distance; but Jessie volunteered to have him perch on her shoulder, which the little fellow gladly did; nor did she regret her offer at all, for when she was weary he cheered her, and when sad he encouraged her, until they arrived at the summit of the ice mountain.

They stopped **for** a while to look at the prospect. It **was** perfectly sublime. Trees of the richest dyes, birds of the gayest plumage colored the landscape. The golden sunlight played over the palace of fairy-land, which glittered with its thousand jewels. The sea of fire wound like a burnished thread through the woodlands, while the garden of fruit, although distant, sent its exquisite perfume all around.

Jessie gazed quite delighted, and seemed inclined to remain there forever; but the fairy reminded her that they still had a great peril before them. "And," said he, shaking his head and shutting his eyes, as near-sighted people do in order to see better, "I distinguish something that looks like the bridal train yonder in the distance, and we must be up and going."

It was an easy matter to descend the mountain. They slid very quietly down to the bottom, and although Jessie was almost frozen to death, and though her cheeks and her little nose were as rosy as the red clouds over the lake of fire, her heart kept her body warm, for that was burning with the love of the dear ones at home.

At the foot of the mountain the fairy brought Jessie some water, in one of her shoes, for refreshment, and a few bright-looking apples he had gathered from one of a group of rich green trees. Jessie took the proffered gifts with great willingness, for the little bag of provisions she had brought from fairy-land had nearly given out. Indeed, it was so long since her companion had tasted anything like tolerable food in his prison, that he ate too voraciously of her store to enable the supply to last very long.

After a short nap under the inviting cluster of apple-trees, which refreshed Jessie very much, she looked towards the last and worst peril, the garden of fruit-trees, and then up to heaven, and took the first step towards the dreaded spot. It was a whole day's journey to this place, and you may be sure that the travellers made a thousand plans to overcome the dangers which awaited them; but in vain. Nothing would answer; and even the fairy seemed in despair. He looked at his wings, now grown quite respectable, and he looked at Jessie and shook his head.

"No! even if I could fly," said he, "she would be left to be devoured by the giants, and I must not suffer that. Oh, no! I could not leave this gentle and generous mortal to perish here; and yet my wings have grown finely, and I dare say I might fly. I will try. Her feelings will be dreadful when she sees me about to leave her. It is too painful to think of"; and this brave, bold coxcomb, spread abroad his small wings of purple and gold, and soaring up into the air, gave one thought to liberty and a happy home in distant lands, and another to the child who stood looking up with wonder in her innocent eyes, and in a minute more he was by her side.

Poised, for an instant, between heaven and earth, the noble fairy formed the resolution, for the sake of Jessie, not to go. He placed his white and dainty finger upon his brow for an instant, as if in deep thought, and then said to his companion, as if struck with a new idea, —

"Have you the vial, and is there any more poison in it?"

"Yes," said Jessie, gladly, holding up the vial which she had in her bosom, "enough to make twenty giants insensible, if it could have such an effect."

"Certainly it would," returned the fairy; "and you know that they always sleep standing at the entrance of the garden, in order to be better prepared against intruders. This is my plan: I will take the vial, and, while they slumber, fly near enough, with noiseless wing, to drop some of the liquid upon the eyes of each; and, if all prospers, we shall be free. But remember, my little lady, that this is an undertaking of great danger, and it will require the boldness of a Bonaparte, the skill of a Wellington, the caution of a Washington, and the everything of a fairy; and it must be done in the night, when the giants are dreaming of breakfasts of little children, dinners of boys and girls, and suppers of men and women. We can hear their snores, and we shall know by that when to approach. If the plan succeeds, they will remain for some time insensible, as if they were dead; and when they awake, hurrah! we shall be far, far away from their dominions. Do you fully appreciate, madam," continued the fairy, bowing, "the dangers that I undertake for you, and the way in which I risk my most precious life for your sake?"

Jessie turned away to hide a smile, and then, with a lovely grace, thanked her companion for all his trouble. It was really a most peculiar undertaking; but as they heard the snore of the giants beat the air like thunder, the fairy bade Jessie an affectionate farewell, and mounting high in the air, with the precious vial in his hands, was soon out of sight.

Thump, thump, thump, went Jessie's heart as she stood behind a tree, as if that could shield her from the rage of a giant, and she trembled so that she wished the ground might open and take her in. She clasped the tree with her shaking hands, and, closing her eyes, awaited her doom.

Hush! hush! what is that sound, like an earthquake, that stuns her where she stands? And, hark! yet another, and a groan that seems like the voice of a multitude! Jessie could bear it no longer, and giving one long and hopeless scream, fell upon the earth fainting.

When she recovered from her death-like swoon, she opened her eyes upon the fairy, who was bending over her, with anxious looks, and sprinkling water upon her white face. He clasped his little fingers, with an air of gratitude and, bending on one knee before her, said:

"Queen of the woodlands, we are free! But your majesty cannot praise me too much for my valor and discretion. Yes, *I* dropped the liquid upon their eyes; *I* saw them fall, and *I* flew here to tell you the tale, and

> To take you home to your parents' arms,
> Where you shall be safe and free from alarms."

Oh! how exquisite the dawning of that day was to our little flower, Jessie! Hope raised her bowed head; hope directed her willing steps; hope nerved her tired frame; and her voice burst forth into song, as she entered that delicious garden, the garden of fruits. She turned away her head from the prostrate giants, not caring to look upon anything so repulsive and disagreeable, and her light feet kept time to the music which her voice uttered:

> "Mother, mother, I come to thee,
> Open thine arms to welcome me;
> Press me to thy yearning breast,
> And let me there delighted rest.
> Mother, I come to thee!
>
> "Father, father, with voice so mild,
> Welcome, welcome thy truant child;
> Let me ne'er leave the home I love,
> Till called to the brighter one above.
> Father, I come to thee!
>
> "My flowers, my birds, my kitten dear,
> For you has been shed the bitter tear:
> No more shall I pine, or murmur, or sigh,
> As my steps to the portal of home draw nigh.
> Sweet home, I come to thee."

As Jessie sung the last line of that song, which gushed out of her heart like the trill of a bird, a voice took up the measure, but in a tone so sad, so broken, that the tears streamed down her face as she stopped to listen. It said:—

> "Sweet home, sweet home!— no more, no more
> Shall I see the home that I adore!
> My mother's prayer, my mother's smile,
> In dreams alone my heart beguile.
> Mother and home, good-by.

> "I have been years imprisoned here —
> My youthful heart is old and sere:
> I ask not joy, and the whole world's charms,
> But only death in my mother's arms.
> Mother and home, good-by."

Could Jessie hear that song, and not search for the broken heart which uttered it? I think not. The warm tears stole down her cheeks, and her hand stayed from gathering a golden apple which hung temptingly near her. She looked above, below, and around, and at last, chained to a luxuriant nectarine tree, whose fruit was too high to be reached by his emaciated hands, she saw the being from whose despairing soul that song had issued, — the veritable boy who had so incurred the fairy queen's anger, with his dark eyes cast down in despondency, and the fresh morning air playing with his damp curls.

Was there ever such a bound as that which Jessie gave to his side? Was there ever such a pitying look as that which she cast upon the chained child? Never! But, then, — was there ever such joy on any human face when he told her that the key which unlocked the chain was hidden under a large stone near? I must say again, *never!* Jessie lifted it; how, I do not know, for it was a very heavy stone; but we can do great things sometimes when urged on by love; and, while the fairy ate, with inexpressible satisfaction, the choicest of golden pippins, she set the prisoner at liberty.

And how did the boy act when he felt the great load taken from his heart, and his body unshackled? First, he thanked God, and then, opening wide his freed arms, welcomed Jessie to them, as a brother would a sister; but the fairy would not let them ask or answer any questions within the precincts of fairy-land.

And then they began to travel in good earnest, never stopping to gather one of the golden apples which tempted them on their way, but only looking with admiring eyes upon the rich green foliage which clothed the glistening fruit with greater beauty.

Of the trio, the fairy showed the most happiness, for he was here, and there, and everywhere, talking, laughing, and singing; but I am sorry to say that the burden of his song was always his own bravery or his own beauty. The joy of the others was more subdued and heartfelt the nearer they advanced towards the magic spot of home.

Jessie learned that the boy's name was Ernest, and that he lived a few miles from her father's cottage. She vaguely remembered a poor, desolate widow, who, a long time ago, had come to the homestead to inquire after her lost child, and her hopeless and despairing glance still remained on her memory.

And has Jessie, indeed, so nearly reached the end of her homeward journey; and is that indeed the stream where she was torn away from all that was dear in life? Truly she has; but the fairy is no more there beside her like a tyrant urging her on her way towards fairy-land; but as a suppliant on one knee before her, he implores her in the most affecting manner to forgive him, actually forcing a tear into each eye. And Jessie freely forgives him all.

My little reader, have you ever been tired and sleepy, and have you found rest and sleep, *at home?* Has unkindness made you miserable, and have you found sympathy and happiness, *at home?* Then you may know how, in a small degree, to sympathize with those children who stood one night — their long journey over — looking through the window of the cottage at the scene within.

I shall look with them, and tell you what they saw and heard. The soiled, white muslin, which draped the casement, shaded them from view, and they listened as for their lives.

They saw a poor fire burning upon the hearth, and a group of three around it, — Jessie's father and mother, and the childless widow, who had been so long robbed of her son. They saw a look of care on the brow of each, as they conversed together. Jessie's flower-pot graced the low mantle ; but alas, the flowers were withered and uncared for. Cages were there, too, but the birds had long since pined and died, while a solemn-looking cat moved about uneasily and unnoticed. The father heaved a long,. deep sigh, the widow sobbed aloud, while the wife silently wiped her tears away.

"It is of no use," said the father, at last, "to give up to this deep, deep grief any more. The loss of my child should not make an idler of me. I must not waste my years unprofitably, but must go about my daily concerns and try to make the cottage more comfortable, and the farm more productive, for those who are dependent upon me. Wife and neighbor, I am ashamed of these tears, and will begin to-morrow to work in truth."

"Yes," replied the widow, "as you say, its no use to sorrow ; for God's will must be done. A brother and a sister have you been to me since you met me in our mutual search for our children, and God will reward you for offering a home to the stricken and broken-hearted."

And Jessie's mother said nothing but, " My child ! my child ! my child ! "

"It is all dark and mysterious," said the father, "and some day, here or hereafter, we shall know more about it ;" and then a tender recollection overcame his manliness, and he sobbed, "yes, here, night after night, in these arms did her gentle form rest, her willing feet were never tired of doing for others, and her sweet voice gladdened the hardest heart."

And then the widow passionately exclaimed, "O, my lost, lost Ernest ! how often in illness have you been my help and stay ; how often did your hand smooth my pillow or my throbbing head ; how often would the music of your voice lull me to sleep, or cheer me with accents of joy and hope. Ernest, come back once more to say ' good-by,' and I will be willing to part with you forever. But why do I dwell on that which never again can be? Hush, heart; hush, rebellious heart."

And Jessie's mother said naught but " My child! my child! my child!"

There was a knock at that cottage door, and the boy and girl stood before them in all their youth and beauty. Poor parents! poor, deluded parents! they thought that it was a dream come to mock them, and they smiled at each other and at the blessed vision, afraid to move, lest they should disturb the exquisite loveliness of that phantom picture. But ah! it was no dream, husband, wife, and widow; those children were human, and yours, — and to your hearts you took them, and perfect joy and perfect love spread their white wings over that humble cottage.

When all the rapture of the meeting was over, then came the story of the adventures of each; and the fairy received the thanks and admiration of all to his heart's content. His relation of all that had happened was listened to with great reverence, and nobody blamed him for making himself the hero, and everybody loved him for his daring and constancy. Even Arabella Victoria Marie Antoinette, when he had ended all that he had to say, gave a mew of approbation, and rubbed her silken sides against this most potent hero.

The end of my story is, that that night the fairy disappeared from the happy group, and was seen no more.

LOST AND FOUND.

ON a bright, soft autumn day,
 Two glad children took their way
  To the woods through pleasant fields,
Just to see the bird's-nests there,
And to taste the berries rare
 That the shaded valley yields;

Just to see the pretty flowers
In their quiet woodland bowers,
    Or the trees' deep, changing green;
Or to look at azure skies
With their own blue, tender eyes,
    And the glittering sunlight's sheen.

But, alas! when the first star
In the twilight beamed afar,
    Sad, feet-wearied, worn and tost,
Down they sank forlorn and cold,
And the truth all trembling told,
    That they knew that they were lost.

Lost,—and weeping bitter tears,
Lost,—and growing wild with fears,
    Sinking hopeless on the ground!
Hark! a voice comes on the air:
Has a mother traced them there?
    Yes! give them joy, *they're found!*

THOUGHTS ABOUT THE MOON.

OH, saw you the moon as she gleamed in the west
When the stillness of eve gave a feeling of rest,
Like a slight silver thread on the soft glowing skies,
Down floating serene where the setting sun dies?
As you gazed on her waving so clear and so bright,
Oh, throbbed not your heart, as mine throbbed, with delight?

And did you not see near her brightness a star,—
A beautiful jewel in twilight afar?
Oh, I wished for the crescent, so rich and so rare,
To crown the soft waves of a sweet maiden's hair;
Oh, I longed for the star's burning ray in the west
To place as a brooch on her pure and white breast.

A thousand such fancies came into my mind
Each night as **I saw** her more clearly defined ;
Till over the **world** she uprose like a car,
And I yearned to be sailing within **her** afar
With one that I love in the clear azure even,
With one that I love, in the moonlighted heaven.

Then rounder and brighter and **rounder she seemed,**
More golden and larger and orb-like she beamed,
Into life sprang each tree as she looked upon earth,
And to numberless dew-drops her brightness **gave birth ;**
And she walked o'er the sky in her train pearly white
Like the queen, as she was, of the beautiful night.

Then fainter and paler her drapery showed ;
A circlet no more in the wide heavens **glowed ;**
I watched with eyes tearful each night as she waned,
And her fast-fleeting roundness my loving heart **pained,**
Till again the curved car cut the darkening blue,
And closer **their curtain** the solemn skies drew.

Oh, she came like night music, first faint to the ear,
Then nearer **and nearer,** distinctly and clear,
And her full **orb to** me was the melody sweet
Brought near **to** my window by on-coming feet,
And her fading, the notes and their echo, that fell
Far departing, **a** mournful funereal knell.

I know not, I know not, I never can say
If the clouds or the brightness **her** beauties display ;
For sometimes she modestly **shades her sweet eyes,**
And **I** jealously **long for the mist to arise ;**
And then when each cloud steals reluctant away
I wish that their veil, so becoming, would stay.

Oh, when shall **I** see her again in the clouds
Peering out, and white fringing their mystical shrouds ?
When she comes, her frail beauty with pleasure I'll greet,
Her form as a loved one long absent I'll meet ;
And I'll watch for that thread in the soft-glowing skies
Down floating serene where the setting sun dies.

WHAT BECOMES OF PINS?

BY THE AUTHOR OF THE "LOST CHILDREN."

"My gracious!" said Sally Starlington, "where do the pins travel to? It is only a little while since I bought a whole paper, and now I can't find one; the paper, to be sure, is here, but that is not exactly the thing. I shall never get to the party to-night; and if I don't, what consternation there will be! Mrs. Goodhue will say, 'Why, what can keep Miss Starlington?' and there will be such amazement on every face at my non-appearance, that it will be by no means a successful party. The ice-cream will certainly not freeze, the custards will curdle, and everybody will blame Miss Starlington, Miss Starlington! Betty, you *must* find me one pin to secure this sash."

Poor Betty took the last pin from her own handkerchief, which no longer kept the towering height on her head, for which Southern waiting-women are distinguished, and gazed in admiration upon the lovely girl before her, — and lovely she really was; the glass said so, and I say so. She was a fat little body, quite rotund, which, you know, is anything but fashionable; and the dimples in her cheeks were large enough to hold a drop of water. And her looking-glass said, —

"Sally, my dear, you have funny little flat brown curls all over your head, that look just as if they had been ironed; and your brow is very smooth and white; and your eyebrows are fairy bridges; and your eyes two stars shining and twinkling; and your nose the sweetest little pug that ever ornamented human face; and your mouth and teeth, darling! Why, rosebuds are nothing to the first, and the last shame all the pearls in existence!"

So, as this was the talk of the glass, Sally believed it more than ever on the night of the party; and courtesying to her other self in a dignified manner, and stumbling over Betty in an undignified manner, she gave her mother a parting kiss, and, after the fashion of great ladies, threw herself into the carriage, and in a languid tone desired to be taken to Mrs. Goodhue's.

Mrs. Goodhue walked with rather ungraceful haste up to the little girl and expressed a hearty welcome.

"My dear Miss Starlington," she said, "how overjoyed I am to see you! Nothing in the whole range of existence could have given me more pleasure than your arrival on this evening, my Mimi's birthnight, — and how very pretty your dress is! — but pray stop a minute; your sash is not fastened; the pin has probably dropped out; I wonder what has become of it? Pray do not look for it," continued Mrs. Goodhue; "I will send up-stairs for a fresh paper bought this morning, and you are welcome to any quantity of them."

"It is the strangest thing," commenced Sally; but Mrs. Goodhue interrupted her.

"What could have kept you so late? Is not my supper-table charming?" and any one would really have thought that Sally was of some importance; for Mrs. Goodhue took her to look at the arrangements of the supper-table, and ten very young gentlemen asked for the honor of her hand for ten dances. And she was so self-important, and yet so sweetly agreeable, that everybody blessed her little round face. She spoke to all the old ladies who had come to look on, and was so polite to them that she won their hearts at once. She allowed her mop-looking head to be patted by the old gentlemen, and looked up so confidingly in their faces that they wished that they had just such a little daughter; and then her laugh, — why, it was as necessary to the room as gas-light was to make it bright and cheerful; and here I must pause a moment to tell you what some poet unknown to fame has said about

SALLY'S LAUGH.

Did you ever hear our Sally laugh? No?
How strange, when the melody gladdens us so!
Well, as I was sitting near yonder tree,
The grace of her pretty ways to see,
Watching the shadows chasing each other,
And playing together like sister and brother, —
I dare say you've seen them so, just at twilight,
Ere day shut his sleepy eyes dreaming of night, —

Our Sally was sitting quite close to the brink
Of the rivulet where her pet lamb goes to drink,
With his bright blue ribbon buried low
In his fleece, as pure as new-dropped snow;
Her feet low down in the water dipping,
And her pet of the same clear streamlet sipping,
While bursts of merriment, clear and free,
Came borne on the air to gladden me.

First a rainbow-like smile flitted over her face,
Which gave to her dark eyes a beautiful grace,
And then came a shout of such joy-giving glee
That my footsteps drew nearer our Sally to see;
Like a murmur of water, like music's full swell,
She laughed, — but at what, that *I* never could tell,
And neither could she any more than her pet,
But that sweet laugh at *nothing*, I'll never forget.

But see her! Who but Sally ever before looked pretty while eating? Her appetite was good, and she certainly did justice to Mrs. Goodhue's excellent supper; for first, through her rosy lips disappeared chicken salad, then sandwiches and lemonade and ice-cream, with innumerable sugar-plums. Nor was she so selfish as to forget her companion, Willie Parker, with whom she kept up at intervals the following conversation: —

"What warm weather we are having," said Sally.

"I was thinking it was rather cool," said **Willie**.

"Yes; I meant it was cool," said Sally; "**but the weather is** *so* changeable."

"Very," answered **her** companion; "but don't **you** admire the moon above all things?"

"Oh, yes!" returned Sally; "and the sun, — isn't that sublime? I declare one evening it was as handsome as one of mamma's best China plates."

"Oh, that must have **been elegant!**" said Willie.

Then came a long pause; after which the old subject came up again, "Don't you think we **are** having very warm weather?"

"Very," was the answer; "but do, Willie, help me to **a sandwich**; they are so delicious! O, Mrs. Goodhue, how very nice your supper is! you always have everything about you *so* **French.** I do admire anything that is French so much!" And **yet little Sally** herself was Dutch in the extreme.

Mrs. Goodhue was pleased **of course, and said so;** while Ned Young, who prided himself upon his wit, said, —

"Sandwiches! Are you talking of **sandwiches?** Did **you** ever hear this conundrum: 'Why could people who travel in the **desert** live without taking any provisions there?'"

"**Nobody** could answer this deep question, and Ned **replied,** triumphantly, —

"Because they could eat the sand which is (sandwiches) under their feet."

"How **unrefined Ned** Young is with his anecdotes and loud laugh!" whispered Sally; and yet who could laugh more loudly than she?

"Miss Starlington," said Ned, still bent upon being witty, "was the moon shining when you came?"

"I didn't look," replied Sally.

"**Well,**" was the answer, "**you don't** know, then, if it was **as light as** the old woman **said** it was?"

"And pray, how light may that be?" asked Sally, with a curl of her lip.

"Only as light as a cork," replied Ned, amid the shout of the bystanders.

After this, the company moved to the dancing-room and a joyous time did they have. Sally, however, slipped on a piece of orange-peel; but she arose gracefully, hid her blushing face in her handkerchief, which was filled with sugar-plums, and then danced away again as briskly as ever.

The party did not last very long, for Miss Starlington, from a time-honored custom, did not approve of dancing after supper, and Sally was soon ready to go; but a pin she must have to fasten her hood.

"Wait a bit," said Mrs. Goodhue; "here, you shall have one from my cape"; but no! there were the loose ends dangling, and the pin not there. Mrs. Goodhue wished to send up-stairs for the paper again, but Sally would not on any account think of that; so she held the hood until she found herself again at home, standing before her looking-glass, ready to undress, and answering Betty's and its numberless questions.

"Well," said the glass.

"Perfectly delightful," said Sally.

"You have a rich crimson glow upon your cheeks and your eyes are brighter than ever."

"I danced a quadrille with Dick Cross, a charming polka with Charlie Graves, and intended to waltz with John Bell and Dick; but they quarrelled about it, and so I took Mary Davis instead."

"That look of scorn becomes you as heat-lightning does the skies," said the glass.

"And I told them that I should *never* dance with them again for behaving so, if I lived two hundred years; but I could not exactly keep my word, you know, when they promised never to do so again, as long as they breathed the breath of life. Oh, I forgot to tell you,

Betty, that Willie took me in to supper. What a very agreeable person he is, so intellectual and refined; but what a delightful old lady Mrs. Brown is. I stood near her for a long time, hearing her tell of some poor children who are in great want; I am going to-morrow to give them some old dresses; but Betty, make haste, I am so sleepy and tired; there, you have bent that pin quite crooked, and you might as well throw it away; no, on the whole you had better *not*, they go away fast enough themselves."

So it came to pass that after Sally had said her nightly prayer and folded her dimpled hands, her white lids closed in sleep. Her breath at first came slowly and then more quickly and troubled, so that one might well imagine that she was dreaming some almost unutterable thing. But I shall try to tell you about it. She dreamed that a little fairy perched herself upon the top of one of her bedposts and said to her, abruptly, —

"*I will tell you what becomes of pins.*"

The little woman looked very important as she said this, and being dressed in the most approved fairy fashion, Sally, who had always wished to see such a personage, was instantly interested. Her gypsy hat was a rose-leaf, most coquettishly bent over her ears, from which two brilliant diamonds hung. The hat was tied under her chin with the softest shades of the silkworm's work. Her dress was of woven gold, and upon her breast shone a single forget-me-not. What struck Sally as very peculiar and quite out of taste was a *cushion* attached to her side, which contained several pins, small and large, dull, shining, or rusty.

"We are great people," said the fairy, "and we live in a great country. From the nature of our soil and the character of our atmosphere we require pins for use or embellishment. For instance, all our fencing is done with pins; our pavements are pins firmly fastened in the ground, their heads being a secure and elegant walk, and we make use of them for the roofs of our houses, enclosing our trees, and in a thousand other ways. Everybody acknowledges that all mankind and fairy-kind are dependent, more or less, on each other for something; the doctor on his patients, the merchant on his purchasers, the minister on his people, so we are dependent on you for *pins*. Consider for a moment; since their introduction, we, an immense race of people, not knowing how to manufacture them, have been gathering them for our beloved country, which sparkle with their borrowed light. How busy the scene! Miles and miles in the distance one sees sparkling fences stretched out over well-cultivated lands; beneath the feet our pavements invite the evening promenade. Myriads of fairies arrive each moment laden with their precious spoils and deposit them in a storehouse, built with an almost inconceivable magnificence, while authorized officers report the increase to the king, who rewards or punishes according to the industry and activity of the pin-gatherers. That our king is sometimes severe, I must confess, and so much is he wrapt up in the idea of progress and improvement, that I will relate to you an occurrence which happened in his domains. Upon each mortal of the softer sex, yourself for instance, there attends an invisible fairy endeavoring by every art to abstract pins from her apparel. Should you arrange your sash in fancied security and soon perceive it be unfastened, you may know what influence has been at work; you constantly miss pins from your toilet; you will know after this to whom to trace the loss. You purchase a paper to-day; in a short time they all disappear, — now you will well know in what way. I must not leave you unenlightened on one point, however, that attendant fairies never take pins either from boxes or papers; they consider this below their genius, and it would not be at all sanctioned by the king. But to my sad recital. Not long ago, our monarch sent out his subjects with particular injunctions to bring home a large harvest, as he wished to enclose a piece of land for the sport of the royal children. We all came in well laden at the appointed day, except one fairy, who was the attendant upon a young maiden who determined that for three months she would use only those pins that she could pick up, as she found that she was too extravagant in these useful articles of the toilet and wished to economize. Very wroth indeed was the king when he saw Violetta almost empty-handed return from her expedition. His usually smooth brow was clouded, and he ordered her to be brought to the hall of justice. Heavens! how we trembled at his rage and the strange mood in which he was. The darkness of a coming storm covered the land and vivid lightnings made the scene more terrific. Violetta drooped like the flower whose name she bears, and besought, on bended knees, for mercy; but in vain. They dragged her by her beautiful hair, soft as the finest silkworm's thread; her exquisite form swayed to and fro with the agony of helpless grief, like the willow in the wind, and her blue eyes filled with tears.

"Violetta," said the king, sternly, "what hast thou to answer for thyself?"

She told her story with a voice broken by heart-rending sobs, but nothing availed; some demon seemed to be ruling our monarch, and he commanded that she should be empaled for twenty-four hours upon one of the very pins which she had brought. Right glad were we when the delicate creature was released from her torments, and we watched her recovery with tender love. Since then I think that the king has repented of his harshness, for he often looks kindly upon her and does not require such heavy tasks from her, and the queen loves her like a sister.

Poor Sally groaned at this recitation, thinking, perhaps, that she was the maiden in question as she had often made such resolutions.

"Sweet Violetta," murmured she, "if it is upon me that you attend, take as many pins as you please, if it will free you from punishment."

The fairy softly glided from the post and proceeded to the toilet upon her plundering expedition. Successful she must have been, for

Sally saw her smile upon the fairy in the glass with quiet approbation.

"Farewell, little lady," said she to Sally; "come whenever you choose in dream-life to our fairy land and you will be welcome."

Betty, coming in to say that breakfast was nearly ready, awoke the sleeper, and the fairy had disappeared, although Sally had formed many plans for keeping her for a pet in an old bird-cage which she had. She dressed herself quickly to tell her mamma cheerfully all that had happened at the party, and as she descended the stairs in her white morning robe, she was a picture of purity and grace.

"O, mamma," she said, "I had such a delightful time last night; the music was enchanting, and my dress so neat and pretty — but the supper! O, mamma, you should have seen that! It was so nice that I am afraid I eat a little too much, for I had such a queer dream, and Betty said that she heard me groan just before she woke me this morning."

"I am glad that you enjoyed yourself, my dear," said her mother, "but sorry that you should have eaten so much. I thought that I had warned you upon that point quite often enough; but, Sally, if you looked neatly last night, that is not exactly the character that I would give you now, for your dress wants a pin sadly, and I fear that I have none to offer you. It is not a month since I bought a paper of the best English; but now there is not one left. I know that I have taken them out myself; but then, they disappear so strangely. I do wonder what becomes of pins?"

"I will tell you, mamma," said Sally, clapping her hands. And she told her mother about the Pin Fairies.

THE RICH CHILD AND THE POOR CHILD.

Why do you look so white and wild?
Your eyes so blue and your face so mild
Are full of the traces of tears and wo, —
What is it that troubles and wearies you so,
      Little child?

I thought that your eyes were a brilliant blue,
But they seem to fade from their first bright hue;
What is it that gives you that haggard air,
Your cheeks are as pale as my roses fair,
      Poor child!

Don't tremble **so**; your white, thin hand
Is cold and weak as you shivering stand;
Your long brown hair is silvered with rain,
And you fill my breast with wonder and pain,
      Dear child!

Can it be that you're hungry, with want are you cold?
Ah, yes. Poor thing, with my question bold
I have brought a blush to your pale, pale cheek,
And your lips with pleading earnestness speak,
      Tired child!

'Tis a sad, sad tale of woe that you tell,
But my mother with comforts will make you well;
She will feed your sister who sickly lies,
And your brother who almost of hunger dies,
      Famished child!

Why glows your face with that radiance bright?
Your small hands, why are they clasped so tight?
Who has wiped the tears from your tender eyes,
And scared from your breast those long-drawn sighs,
      Gentle child?

You say 'tis **our kindness to** yours and to you,
That our gifts will clothe you and feed you too;
Say rather, 'tis GOD who THROUGH US has given,
And let your sweet thanks rise from earth to heaven,
      Happy child!

THE MOUSE WHO WENT TO SEE THE WORLD.

A MOUSE and her mother, Mrs. Silverskin Mouse, lived in a closet remote from cities, where they had plenty of cheese to eat and the nicest white bread. Then for dessert they had apples and nuts, and very often they gave large country parties, inviting the mice for miles around, and they treated them, especially at Christmas, with mince pies and other dainties which people usually have at that time, and on thanksgiving days they eat so much at their family dinner parties that really it was rather uncomfortable to themselves than otherwise. Viewing the whole matter at this distance, one feels inclined to ask " what more *could* mice want? " but strange to say, Miss Jeteye (that was the name of Mrs. Silverskin's daughter) languished to see more of life and the wide, wide world; languished for a broader experience than a country closet, and pined for more extensive views of society at large; so she took to fits of melancholy, and the better to attract her mother's attention, eat little, slept less, and was generally to be found moping in corners, with her fair head resting upon her paw in an attitude of deep dejection. Her mother at first did not regard these words, and thought that they would pass away like cheese before a hungry mouse, or mist before the morning sun; but one day, when Miss Jeteye positively refused a slice of toasted bread made palatable by the nicest butter in the universe, her mother went up to her and said, carelessly, —

"My dear, what is the matter with you? Is the butter not to your liking? are the raisins in this pie not properly stoned? is the cheese too strong? Tell me, my darling, pride of my life, what ails you?"

"Mother," said Miss Jeteye, suddenly and passionately; "none of these things affects me. I want to travel; I want to see King and

Queen Mouse and Lord Long Whiskers and Lady Soft Skin, who make such a noise in fashionable life ; and then I hear that there is *such* cheese in the royal palace ! O, mother, I *must* see the world ! Won't you let me go? Don't say no, best of mothers ; nobody ever wanted *so* much to see the world. Isn't it a *very* large place, mother ?"

"O, my child," said the old lady mouse, seriously, "don't, don't go there ! It is a place full of trouble, and traps lie all about for the careless and unwary ; and then you will break my heart if you leave me here alone, with no company. An individual at my time of life is sadly dependent upon cheerful society, such as yours, my dear. No, you must never leave the domestic hearth !"

So when Jeteye saw that Mrs. Silverskin was weeping bitterly, she promised her solemnly that she would not leave her ; but the deceitful little thing was not telling the truth ; for she meant some day, not very far off, to go and look for the world ; and that night she dreamed that she went on her travels, and was everywhere praised for her grace and beauty, and that King and Queen Mouse invited her to a select dinner party. "Surely," said she to herself, when she awoke, "this dream will come to pass ; it *shall* come to pass ; *I leave this closet to-day.*" So she arranged every hair of her soft gray fur to her satisfaction, and went to say a few words to her mother, who unfortunately was not well, having eaten a thought too much of rich plum cake.

"Mother," she said, softly, "I'm sorry to see you indisposed, but I hope that you will be better when I return ; I'm going to take a short walk, as I need exercise, and will be back directly."

"Don't go far, Jeteye," said her mother ; "don't go beyond the store-room, my child."

"*Not for the world!*" was the deceitful answer ; and shaking her parent's paw, she departed. She couldn't help looking back once or twice, for, said she to herself, "my mother grows aged, and

I may never see her again." Then a few salt tears dropped from her eyes, but she wiped them away suddenly with the tip end of her polished tail, for she saw Squire Long Ears, another mouse, coming along.

"Where are you going, Miss Jeteye?" he said.

"Only to see the world," said she.

"I will go with you to the ends of the earth," said he, and away they went together.

They had a rough, hard journey, and perils not a few; and often they lost their way, and had to eat most miserable and unwholesome food. One day, when they were eating some lunch in a fine pantry, which they took for a tavern, Miss Mouse had the misfortune to fall into a jar of sweetmeats. She thought that she was dying, and moaned so piteously that Squire Long Ears was almost mad with grief and consternation; but eventually he encouraged her with many a cheering word, though he could give her no help in her critical situation; and at last he had the satisfaction of seeing her climb upon a very large preserved peach and then out of the jar, trailing along after her a line of best clarified syrup, until they gained a safe hiding-place. There they had to wait several days, for Miss Mouse would on no account consent to travel until her skin had become soft and clean again; and during this time they felt the greatest terror, for a big black cat, with green eyes, often looked lovingly into the hole where they had taken refuge. At length, one day when he was absent, they fled and went on still farther in their travels to see the world. But fate seemed determined not to let them go along peaceably, and they met, before many days had passed, with another sad adventure. Quite tired and hungry, they went one night into another tavern to get something to eat; and after they had helped themselves largely, they spied a tempting barrel of flour, in which they thought they might obtain a long rest, and be ready for their journey again the next night. But alas! no sooner had they ensconced themselves comfortably in their new quarters, than they were awakened by the voice of a giant rat, who asked them what they were doing in his flour-barrel. He called them very hard names, and used very coarse language; and in his fury bit off a long piece of Squire Long Ears' elegant tail; and then, to add insult to injury, ordered them out of his domains, thus forever putting a blot upon the white page of rat hospitality.

Mortified and hurt, Squire Long Ears said that he could not think of travelling in that plight, for a tailless mouse would never be respected at court, and he begged Jeteye to go back again to her home with him, especially as she had met with such formidable dangers; but she said no,— that she would not be faint-hearted now; that she thought the royal residence must be so near; and as she had come so far, and being of a romantic turn of mind, she suggested that she might fare even better without than with the Squire, as no one would think of molesting unprotected innocence, and a protector might be raised up to her at every turn. Then she remembered that the young ladies in whose house she lived in the country spoke in such raptures of the world, and went out to it and returned in so short a time, and painted such glowing pictures of its fascinations, that bidding Mr. Long Ears farewell, she turned her pretty head away and went on alone. "Alone!" she had not to repeat that cheerless word long before she thought she knew that she had arrived at the end of her venturesome journey. It was in a grocer's store that she arrived at this proper conclusion. "At last," she exclaimed, raising her fine eyes in an ecstasy, "my dream is realized!" As she uttered these words, she was conscious of being gazed at by a splendid mouse with most regal whiskers, whom she recognized at once as King Mouse, and close behind his kingship appeared another of the softer sex, whose sumptuous aspect declared her at once to be the queen. She told them what she thought, expressing at the same time great admiration of their majesties and their palace ; and after telling her that she was quite right, and whispering to each other that from her appearance she must be "somebody," perhaps some country heiress, they invited her to take up her abode with them for a season and visit their court.

Imagination is too poor to paint how her little heart beat at these words. "Now," she said to herself, " I am thought of as I deserve ; my beauty is admired, and I shall be a countess, may be ; and then I shall send for my mother (who must be polished up, by the way, before she comes to court, her ways and looks are so old-fashioned) ; and won't she be astonished to see how high I have risen in the world !

The king gave a ball that might do honor to the distinguished stranger, and much company there was. The most delicate fare was offered to the charming young guest, who swept through the hall with such enchanting grace ; in fact, so much attention was never before paid to a foreigner ; for at that court they were naturally suspicious of foreigners, as they had rumors of attention being paid in neighboring palaces to strangers, which were ridiculed by the guests upon their return to their own country, and this made them very cautious of being treated in the same way. But suspicions vanished in the presence of Miss Jeteye. The courtiers wished to claim the honor of her hand, and even the king danced with her in a new court polka, and made poetry to her fine eyes ; while the queen could not but look with admiration upon her feet, which she said were the smallest she ever saw, and a sure sign of her being high born. Then she had such a confident, self-satisfied air, that they came to the conclusion that she was no country Miss, and therefore they neglected to tell her, in fact they thought it would be in rather bad taste to tell one so experienced, of the dangers she would be apt to meet with, and she was too silly and proud to let them know that she had lived in the country all her life. Alas ! poor Jeteye !

After a most delightful supper upon all the dainties in creation, and at an unusually late hour, the guests departed and the royal party retired to rest. The queen pointed out to her ladyship, as she called Jeteye, her apartment, and desired two maids of honor to attend to any of her wants; and after having dismissed them with many gracious words, she felt curious to investigate her apartment of state, as the queen had named it. It was in a snug little corner behind a box of prunes, westward of a jar of sweetmeats, and eastward of a box of fresh Italian biscuits, a delicacy just introduced into the royal residence. "You will find this apartment most convenient," remarked her majesty to Jeteye, when she had designated her place of rest, "and it even has an advantage over the royal apartment, inasmuch as you will observe that it has *two* entrances. Should you hear any noise indicative of robbery or intrusion, remember this fact; there will always be safety in one of these outlets; so good night, your ladyship; sleep well; and remember, don't be too fascinating on the morrow, for," added she, playfully, "you have turned the heads of half my court, and I must begin to look to my honors."

So, as I said before, the young lady began to look about to see the curiosities of a palace chamber. She did not see anything extraordinary therein; *she* did not see any elegance in that close place behind that rough box of prunes. If she became hungry in the night, there was nothing there for her to eat, for she could not, from old associations, abide sweetmeats, particularly peaches; and biscuits were too common for *her* refined lips; and then, not far off were a low set of common mice, who *might* be there for the purpose of keeping guard; but they made such a noise with their eternally nibbling the remains of the feast, that it was impossible for her ladyship to get a wink of sleep. She preferred the country for one thing, — its quiet; and so she put her graceful head out of one of the entrances to see if possibly the queen might not have made a mistake, and have put her in the wrong apartment. She had no sooner done this, than her bright eyes spied the prettiest little contrivance in the shape of a sleeping room imaginable. She thought that it was a love of a place, the most curious work of art that she had yet seen on her travels; and now she felt certain that the queen really had made a mistake; so she determined, instead of having them mortified to death the next morning by hearing that she had slept behind that plebeian box of prunes, to take possession of this treasure of a dormitory at once.

"How pretty it is," she said, softly; "I have never seen anything exactly like it before; those arched wires are so graceful, and that cupola on its top suits the style so well; then what a charming entrance it has; and, as I live, the royal family have honored me by placing within a slice of the best English cheese." And in my lady went, quite delighted with her new quarters.

However, she did not quite like the "click" which met her ears as she entered, and a far off vision of her childhood came across her, almost as indistinct as a dream, of a story told her by an old uncle on her mother's side, of a thing called a *trap*, into which he had been imprisoned by accident, and from which he had escaped with difficulty. This little adventure, she remembered, had been accompanied with the loss of his tail; and in telling his story, he had always dwelt forcibly, and with a kind of spiteful malice, upon the "click" which did the mischief; but after all, *that* was not in a royal palace, and her uncle had seen nothing of the world; and in the cheese, which was most delicious, she forgot her terror, and having partaken largely of it, she went quietly to sleep, thinking what a fascinating thing an apartment of state was.

How long she slept I know not, but she was awakened by a sound which she thought seemed familiar, and, I am sorry to say, not entirely agreeable to her under her present circumstances. That familiar sound was her mother's voice, and it said, "My daughter,

O, my daughter! how cruel you were to leave me! I have come to take you back to our secure and quiet home."

"Indeed, mamma," said the spoiled maiden, "you might have spared yourself that trouble. I dare say that that vulgar fellow, Long Ears, sent you after me. But it is of no use; I find the world **so pleasant, that** I am never going to return. But, my dear mother, your dress inspires me with feelings of horror, and your tone is excessively drawling and countrified; then you want polish sadly. **Oh,** what is to be done! Was there ever a being so tried, **so** straitened as I! The king is most particular as regards **pedigree, and** none but aristocrats in decent appearance have entrance into *this* court. My unfortunate mother, pray step into my chamber, and at least *try* to make yourself presentable; or, perhaps, I might offer one other suggestion to which you would not **object.** Could you not, could you not return *at once*, my dearest parent, to your much prized 'quiet home?'"

Jeteye's dearest parent drew nearer, **to see if** it **was indeed her** gentle and obedient daughter who thus addressed her; and who **can** describe **that** mother's feelings when she saw her child's situa‐ **tion. She** was speechless for a moment with fright and horror, **and then, in her** anguish, she exclaimed, "Mistaken child, how **came** you here? Do you know? Ah! you cannot be aware of your fate! That luxurious chamber, that fretted dome, that classic entrance, is **a trap!**"

Ah! there was no misunderstanding that frantic mother's words, and in an instant flashed upon Jeteye the truth. She remembered her mother's long years of experience; she thought of the sad story of that tailless uncle on that mother's side. She suddenly awoke to the full reality of her situation. She was wild with terror! **She** bit her wire prison-bounds; she hurt her head against **the hard steel**; she tore the skin from her delicate form in trying **to get out** where she got in. She made the circuit of her wiry cage one hundred times, and she called upon her mother, in piteous tones, to release her. But what could her parent do? Nothing but bewail and lament over her future solitary life in her quiet country habitation ; nothing but wring her fore-feet and cry aloud about that place called *home*, to which pleasures and palaces are as a drop to the ocean ; and wheresoe'r an individual may roam there is no place like it. Occasionally she would break out into a wail, the burden of whose song was an aggravating, "I told you so!" which cut Jeteye to the very heart. But even mother mice have a law of self-preservation ; and when the first streak of daylight appeared, Mrs. Silverskin Mouse disappeared, after casting one passionate look of anguish and regret upon her forlorn and exhausted offspring.

"Oh, ho!" said Mr. Storekeeper, as he opened his doors at sunrise, and took up his trap to see if it contained any of those disagreeable customers called mice ; "here is a fine, fat, sleek intruder. This is the last time, my friend, that you will come stealing *my* stores. Here, Dick, take the vile creature to the pump and drown it speedily, and be sure you set the trap again for other poachers. 'Tis a nice, gentle-eyed thing, though, and the prettiest little animal I ever saw ; it is almost a pity to have it drowned. However, whoever thought of pitying a mouse? Yes, a mouse ; the little thief. Here, Dick, don't let it suffer a minute more than you can help,— *but go it must!* Everybody must take care of himself, or there would be no getting along in the world."

"Alas! the world!" sighed Jeteye.

Those were her last words.

NICE HABITS.

1.
Bathe your body
  Every day,
Put your clothes with
  Care away.

2.
With a penknife
  Your nails pare,
Clean them nicely
  With due care.

3.
In the morn and
  Evening too,
I will tell you
  What to do.

4.
You must brush your
  Teeth so white,
And you'll keep them
  Clean and bright.

5.
Wear an apron
  When you eat,
And sit upright
  On your seat.

6.
Speak no harsh nor
  Wicked word,
No cross answer
  Should be heard.

7.
Love your brothers,
  Sisters too,
And they always
  Will love you.

8.
Be to servants
  Ever kind,
And your every
  Word they'll mind.

9.
Ne'er forget, each
  Night and day,
With gentle voice
  Your prayer to say.

10.
If you always
  These things do,
Every body
  Will love you.

Ne'er forget each night and day
With gentle voice your prayers to say.

BAD TEMPER AND ITS CURE.

HALF FACT, HALF FICTION.

CHAPTER I.

THE GOOD AND EVIL SPIRIT.

"There, I told you so! You have at last let my beautiful glass peacock fall upon the floor, and it is broken into ten thousand pieces! you little, worrying, bad, mean, disagreeable girl, you!"

Would you believe that Florence Somers said these words to her little sister Ellen? Scarcely, and yet it was so. How could such a refined-looking girl utter such words? I will tell you all about it. Florence had put her peacock on the table, and had told Ellen not to touch it; but then, little children are very curious, and Ellen took it up, when, alas! it fell to the ground.

Florence was lying on the sofa at the time, reading a book of fairy tales, and no one could have desired to see a more charming picture than she was. Her face was bright with pleasure and her hands as white and soft as an infant's; her cheeks were colored with red and her lips redder than her cheeks; and there was no denying that she was in reality perfect in face and form. But, alas! all this beauty did her no good, gained her no admiration from those who knew her, for it was marred by the worst temper that ever was known. It made every one in the house miserable; it made her dear mother often weep bitter tears in the silence of the night, and her father wished to send her away to a boarding-school in order to have her out of his sight; and it made the servants dislike her and shrink from the fiery flash of her eyes; and her poor little sister and brother, whom she should have loved and cherished, were never comfortable in her presence, but always dreaded some outburst of passion from Florence, which would send them away from her terribly frightened.

Thus, when the peacock fell, out came the thunder of her wrathful voice upon Ellen; and going to the poor, trembling child, she first shook her violently and then struck her twice, bidding her pick up the pieces, which the little creature did as well as she could, and then she thrust her violently from the room.

After she left, Florence paced the room with an angry flush upon her lovely face.

"What is the use of little children?" she said, aloud; "they are always in the way and should never be allowed to leave the nursery; everything I have is ruined by them; and now, to crown all, that busy-body Ellen has broken my beautiful glass peacock. I don't think she cares about it much, either; but I'll *make* her care, that I will; and I'll break her Bohemian tumbler to-morrow, just to let her know how it feels to have what one most cares for destroyed." And with this cruel determination, Florence lay again upon the sofa and opened once more her book of fairy tales. She had just reached that place in Bluebeard where he gave his wife the key of the closet and told her not to enter it upon pain of death, when the book slid from her dimpled hand, and she fell asleep. She had not slept long, when she was awakened by a strange sensation in each hand; that on her right hand was soft and cooling, like the fall of dew upon a rose-leaf; that in her left was as if melted lead were being poured upon it in hot and heavy drops. She opened wide her drowsy eyes, and holding up her hands to see what possibly could be the matter, she beheld a strange little being standing in each palm and looking into her face. She tried to shake them off in vain; and after her first fright was over, she became quite angry and said some very rude things to her new visitors. Just in proportion as her temper increased, so did the sharp pain in the left hand increase; and when she found that anger produced no effect, she softened her voice and said, courteously: "Well, little people, what on earth brings you here and who and what are you?" As she said these words, softly and gently, she was conscious that the pain in her left hand subsided, and that the gentle pressure in the right was stronger than before.

At length the individual (if such he might be called) in her left hand spoke his mission. Never was there so hideous a being created. He was only about as long as Florence's little finger, and yet she could not, for his very ugliness, look at him. His hair was flaming fire; his forehead like that of an old man, all wrinkled and marked with sin and woe; his nose shapeless, and his mouth, as he opened it, was full of small snakes. Out of his eyes came a disagreeable green fire, and he had four hands of different colors, in each of which he held a looking-glass, which magnified his own terrible image, and his feet were turned backward and shaped like the claws of a bird. But when he spoke, horrors! how Florence shuddered; it was as if her ear had been pierced with the scraping of a knife upon rough glass, and the sound of it amounted to a pain.

"I come, maiden," he said, "to wait upon you; and I am happy to be in your service, for you are the most beautiful mortal in the world. But while you are outwardly so very fair, I claim you to be my sister; for in your heart you are just what you see me, — a demon. I am the prince of my tribe and Bad Temper is my name; I attend you ever; and in future you will *feel* my presence whenever your unfortunate fault, which makes me your brother, overmasters you; for I shall always be with you in the same manner in which you knew of my presence a while since, more or less according to your mood."

Then Florence experienced the sensation again, as if a hot iron were searing her hand; and she would have screamed with pain, had not the flute-like voice of the little creature who occupied her right hand arrested him in the midst of his torture.

"Demon, desist," she said, softly; "you have given evidence enough of your power."

"Oh, what a relief it was to Florence to see the mild eyes of that gentle being turned reproachfully upon the hideous dwarf monster; she felt as if she had one friend in the world, and was not utterly forsaken.

"Hear me, Florence," she said; "I am the queen of Good Nature and Self-Conquest; this crescent on my brow betokens mildness; these white robes, purity; these tears, which flow for those I love, repentance. I have a powerful enemy in the demon Bad Temper; we are fighting a hard fight; one of us must conquer even unto death. The seat of that fight, Florence, is in your heart. What is the use of your beauty unless you have good inward gifts? It cannot make you happy when you know that over it all that frightful wretch has such power. Then listen: whenever you allow the fiend of bad temper to overcome you as you did to-day, upon your left hand you will feel his burning presence; whenever you subdue an evil thought, check a bad impulse, repent of violence, or restrain yourself from doing wrong, you will feel my gentle presence in your right hand. Farewell. When you desire my aid, call upon me and I shall be near to protect you."

Then the strange shapes seemed to melt away into the air, and Florence fell again into a deep sleep and did not wake until she heard the voice of her little brother calling her to take her afternoon walk.

"Have I been dreaming or not?" she said to herself; how real seemed those two little shapes upon my hands. Oh, of course, it was a dream! and yet it was so vivid, that if I had not been asleep, I could almost fancy it to have been true. What strange sleeping visions people have sometimes! and mine just now was passing strange!"

Then she went up into her own pretty little room and smoothed her glossy ringlets, smiling at herself the while in her mirror; and she looked so lovely and pure, that her brother kissed her sweet lips and told her always to look thus; and her mother wondered that such beauty was ever disfigured by passion and frowns.

CHAPTER II.

THE GLASS TUMBLER.

FLORENCE did not forget that Ellen had broken her glass peacock; she never forgot anything which she thought was an injury; her revenge was not hasty, but deliberate, and she waited for a fitting opportunity to indulge it. One evening Ellen told her with great glee, that a little friend was coming to take tea with her, and that her mother had promised her a pitcher of lemonade, which was to be served out in her little glass tumbler.

"Now is my time," she muttered between her white teeth; "your tumbler will not hold *much* lemonade to-night." But suddenly she remembered her dream; and as she thought of it, she felt a little frightened at the memory. "After all, suppose I let her off this time? Yes, I think I shall. Perhaps she did not mean to break my peacock; but when you trouble me again, my little lady, woe be unto you and your glass tumbler."

So Ellen and her friend had their lemonade in peace, and Florence became interested in their happiness and even helped to make it, and to show them how to strain the lemon seeds from the liquid; and all the time that she was so busied, there was a cool, soothing sensation in her right hand, which she could liken to nothing but a fairy's kisses; and it seemed to her as if she had felt the same before.

Her cheerfulness made her surpassingly beautiful on that evening; and little Ellen's friend went home very happy and told her mother what a good sister Florence was, and how she wished for one just like her. Alas! she wished too soon. At another time she would have fled far, far from her presence.

CHAPTER III.

THE PARTY.

For many days Florence was all that her parents could wish, and they were so delighted with her amiable conduct, that they determined to reward her with a birth-night party. Invitations were sent to the children; and as the evening was bright, they all came, and no pains were spared to please the little guests.

The supper was delightful, and upon the table, in elegant order, were all good things; and at each end of the well provided board stood Florence and Ellen.

Now they had a good uncle who loved Florence very much; and while they were busy enjoying the nice things, in came the old gentleman, accompanied by a servant, who bore upon a silver tray something covered with a white napkin.

Everybody of course was delighted to see Uncle Phil; and he went round and shook hands with the forty children, twenty girls and twenty boys, and he looked as delighted as they did. Then the old gentleman turned round towards the silver tray, and there was a deep pause when he spoke.

"I wanted to make you happier even than you appear to be, little people," he said, in a low voice; "and so I have brought you a splendid cake with a diamond ring in it for the little girls. It is to be cut in twenty pieces, and the one who gets the piece with the ring in it, to her it shall belong. Then I have in my hand here for

UNCLE PHIL. — Page 224.

the boys a four-bladed, pearl-handle knife; and he who can make the handsomest bow shall have the knife."

Then uncle Phil stopped talking, and you never heard such a buzz of little voices in your life; the girls said, "Oh, I wonder who will get the ring!" and the boys said, "I wonder who will get the knife!" then they all wondered together.

After a few minutes had passed, Uncle Phil said he would give the knife first; and the boys all stood in a row, and Uncle Phil called them out one by one, to see which could make the most graceful bow.

First came bashful Bill Somers; but he didn't get the knife, for he turned in his toes, and that was contrary to all rules; then Jim Sanders tried, but he held his shoulders up to his ears, and Uncle Phil said that that would never do; then William Blake was called out, but he made such a sudden and ungraceful jerk with his body, that the spectators could not help laughing; and then Tom Banard made a bow so much like a lady's courtesy, that they would not admit that it was a bow at all, and they all went through the order, until Richard Rose alone was left standing upon the floor.

"Dick will get it," they all shouted; and he blushed scarlet, for he wanted the knife very much indeed; but as several good bows had been made, one in particular by Arthur Gray, he feared that he could never surpass them; but he would try his best at any rate, he thought. So he tossed back his waving curls, let his arms fall gracefully and naturally, and made such a bow, that the best dancing-master in the world would have found no fault with it.

"Bravo!" said Uncle Phil; and everybody echoed his praise and said that Richard deserved the knife; and Uncle Phil himself, making the funniest old-fashioned bow you ever saw, gave it to him amid the congratulations of the bystanders.

"Now, girls," said the old gentleman, "it is your turn"; and turning round towards the cake, he ordered the servants to put it upon the table. Then he called them all up by their ages, the youngest coming first, and gave them each a slice, one by one. Mary Dill was the youngest, but the ring was not in hers; nor in Jane Price's, nor in Mary Thompson's; and all the girls thought, when eighteen slices had been cut and no ring had appeared, that the old gentleman had forgotten to put it in at all,—but it was there, for all that, as you shall soon see.

Only two slices remained, and the last competitors for the ring were Mary Bell and Florence.

"The piece nearest me," said Uncle Phil, before he cut them apart, "is for Florence, the other for Mary. We must understand this before it is divided, for we must have no dissatisfaction or contention. Does every one know exactly how the matter stands before the cake is cut,—that the piece nearest me is for Florence?"

"Yes, yes," said every body, and Florence and Mary said, " yes, that is right; but *do* uncle Phil make haste."

Then Uncle Phil cut the cake down exactly in the middle and something hard seemed to grate against the knife and stop its way, and sure enough it was the ring.

"Oh, ho!" he said, "this is curious enough, but wait awhile, young ladies, stand a bit farther off and we will settle this difficult matter. It is not to be supposed that the ring lies just half way between the slices. I will cut it very accurately, and that little girl shall have it in whose slice it is most buried. Answer me again, does that seem fair and right to all present?"

"Yes, yes!" was the answer.

"Does it seem right to Florence and Mary?" asked Uncle Phil, "for they are most concerned and must answer for themselves."

"Quite right," was the reply from both.

Then Uncle Phil cut regularly, slowly, and softly, through the rich cake, and everybody saw that the ring just grazed Florence's slice, while its glittering circle was almost all imbedded in Mary's.

"The ring is Mary's plainly, it was all fairly done and Mary is the fortunate gainer," he said.

Then the little voices shouted, "yes, Mary is the gainer!" but amid the din, one voice shouted above them all, in tones of angry passion, "*no sir, it was not fairly done!*"

It was the voice of Florence who stood a little apart from the circle, her hands clenched, her eyes flashing with rage; "no sir, it is as much mine as hers, — more, for this is *my* house and *my* party. If Mary Bell dared to touch that ring I shall hate her forever and ever. *It is mine.*"

"Florence," said her mother chidingly, "you forget yourself, my child;" and her father laid his hand upon her shoulder and told her to be silent or leave the room.

"With the ring only," she said haughtily,. "the ring that should have been mine and has been stolen from me."

"Leave the room instantly," said her father leading her towards the door. "I confess, my young friends, with a saddened heart, that I am ashamed of my own daughter. Perhaps punishment and reflection will bring her to her senses."

As Florence reached the door, she gave a look of scorn to the company, and closing it after her with a bang that set all the glasses tinkling on the well-filled table, she went to her room and burst into a flood of passionate tears.

"That frightful Mary Bell," she muttered, "has won the diamond ring which should have been mine. It will look finely, indeed, on her coarse finger, when it was meant for my delicate hand," — *my delicate hand*, — scarcely had she said the words, when a quick, burning sensation like the scorching of a red-hot iron, seemed to blister and scar it, and there, adhering to the rosy skin, and not to be shaken off, stood the frightful prince of bad temper,

"You called me and I have come."

In vain she tried to shake the little monster off; in vain she plead, scolded, wept. "What shall I do?" she exclaimed, bitterly weeping; and the little fiend laughed in a mocking manner at her despair. "Oh! I would do anything in the world to have him away."

"Anything in the world?" questioned a sweet voice; "then go down where your guests are assembled, humbly confess that you have done a great wrong, been disrespectful to your parents, forgotten the rules of hospitality, and tell Mary Bell that she is welcome to the diamond ring."

"Oh, I cannot," said Florence.

"You are too proud to do so," said the good fairy; "then farewell, perhaps forever," and she left her with the horrible demon, but Florence's cries soon brought her back. The torture was too great to bear.

"I will go down," said the haughty beauty, now humbled to the ground; "only send that dreadful creature away, and come yourself with me."

Great was the astonishment of all when Florence entered. Her attitude was one of sadness, her eyelids swollen with weeping, her voice trembling, but not with passion.

"I have come," she said, "to ask forgiveness of each and all for my conduct this evening; to tell my parents that I am sorry for being disrespectful to them; and to say to my dear friend, Mary, that I have no claim upon the diamond ring, and that it is hers, henceforth and forever."

Then she left the room again, but all the time she could feel the soft kisses of the fairy upon her hand. Her father and mother were too delighted with the change to blame or punish her, and thinking that reflection was the best thing for her, they allowed her to remain in her own apartment during the rest of the evening, but the charm of the party was over; there was no longer any life or spirit among the children, and when they went away, both the entertainers and the entertained felt that it was quite a relief.

CHAPTER IV.

THE DRESS.

Not very long after the eventful party, Florence was invited to perform in some charade. She had set her heart upon going, as she acted well, and her beautiful face never showed to more advantage than when some fantastic fancy dress heightened her picturesque appearance.

The part which she was to have taken was the Angel in the Game of Life. The picture represents two men playing a game of chess. One is Satan disguised, playing for his opponent's soul. Elevated above the players stands the angel protecting the young man. The brightest light is thrown upon the angel, while the other figures are rather in the shade. Clothed in purest white, with her beautiful hair falling around her and a serene smile upon her lips, the angel looks down upon the players. Her hands are crossed upon her breast and her long, loose sleeves have the appearance of wings, as they fall back and leave her white arms bare.

Florence knew that this was just the character for her and she had taken infinite pains in arranging her flowing white robe, and it was laid neatly upon the bed, with every fold in order, long before the hour had arrived when she was to dress herself in it, and Jessie had been warned not to disturb or touch it. Now Jessie was Florence's little maid, a poor girl who had been rescued from starving by Florence's mother.

The child was very happy generally, and so fortunate as not often to incur the anger of her young mistress; but seldom, if ever, did she give her cause for anger; for gentle, obedient, and faithful was the child, looking upon Florence as a superior being and watching her every look and motion.

As the dress lay with its exquisite folds upon the bed, so snowy white, so graceful, Jessie could not help stopping as she was passing by to admire it. She held a candle in her hand which was insecurely fastened in the candlestick; and in leaning over a little, the candle lost its balance, fell upon the dress and set it on fire.

Nor was this all. Half frantic with fear, she rushed for a pitcher of water (her first thought) and deluged the beautiful dress, ruining it past all recovery. Poor girl, she only did what seemed to her to be right; but at that moment Florence entered.

One look told her all; she did not waste words, but pushing her from her with frantic violence, Jessie fell, striking her head against the sharp corner of the open door.

Florence followed her and was about to inflict a blow upon her with her clenched hand, when she felt it forcibly opened, and that old sensation, not to be misunderstood, — that red-hot searing of an iron, — caused her to pause.

Was the demon there again? Yes; more hateful than ever, and pointing with his four different-colored hands to the spot where Jessie lay.

"Ha, ha, ha! you have killed her, my beauty!" he screamed; "you're a sweet creature, just after my own heart; for you never stop until you kill, kill, kill!"

"Merciful heaven!" exclaimed Florence, sinking down to the prostrated child, from whose temple the blood was slowly welling. "I did not mean to hurt her much; oh, what would I not do to have her back to life again; on my knees I ask forgiveness for my sin and promise to try to curb this dreadful temper of mine which leads to such horrible results."

"Sprinkle her with water and raise her gently in your arms," said a sweet voice and Florence, only too glad to obey it, did as she was desired.

"Dear Jessie," she said, as the poor girl unclosed her eyes; "forgive me, forgive me for my wicked act, and teach me to be as uncomplaining and gentle as you are."

FLORENCE AND JESSIE.—Page 231.

Jessie could not speak just yet, but she kissed her young mistress's hand most tenderly, and pointing to the ruined dress, hid her eyes from which tears trickled slowly.

"Never mind, Jessie," said Florence, "never mind the dress, so that you are not hurt."

"I am not much hurt, Miss Flory," said Jessie, feebly. "I did not mean to let the candle fall and spoil your beautiful dress, so that you cannot go to the party to-night. Please forgive me, dear Miss Florence, and I will try never to be so careless again."

It was a sad and pretty sight to see them mutually exchanging forgiveness. Florence leaning over Jessie who was pale in contrast to the beautiful being who was now so watchful and careful of her, and whose expression was more angelic in its compassion than it could have been that night in the far-famed "Game of Life." The demon of bad temper fled far away and the good fairy nestled in a bouquet on the table, smiling upon the scene.

Florence did not go to the festival, nor did she regret it, for she spent the evening with Jessie, who became every minute more free from pain, and was able the next day to resume her accustomed duties.

CHAPTER V.

DANCING SCHOOL.

"COME, Florence," said kind Mrs. Fraser one night at dancing school, "it is ten o'clock, and I promised your father to bring you home at that time."

"Just one more dance, Mrs. Fraser, please."

"That is just what you said a half hour ago, my child, when I told you to think about going."

Florence's partner approached, and away she went to the dance. Mrs. Fraser sighed and sat down once more. The old lady was very weary; and her granddaughter, Annie, was sitting shawled by her side waiting patiently for Florence, with a great deal of sleep in her young eyes. The dance appeared to them terribly long, but at last it came to an end. Florence did not approach the place where Mrs. Fraser was sitting, but took her seat at the other side of the room and was gaily talking with her young partner, while another of the dancing-school youths was pleading for her hand for the next dance.

Florence had just given her consent, forgetting all about Mrs. Fraser, when she approached with her shawl.

"Now, Florence, come," she said, "I cannot stay any longer; not one dance more will I wait."

"But I am engaged for the next."

"That I cannot help; you must break your engagement, for your father's command should be regarded before a promise to dance. Come, Florence."

But Florence did not stir.

"Are you *not* going with me?" said Mrs. Fraser.

"No, ma'am, I am not," she answered; "I am engaged for the next dance, and I do not see what difference a few minutes will make"; and then the deluded girl turned aside and said in a whisper to her partner, "I hate overbearing duennas."

The whisper was just loud enough for Mrs. Fraser to hear, and, bending upon Florence a stern look, she said: "I shall leave you then, Miss Somers, to your fate for I can do no more, and remember that this is the last evening that you shall come here under *my* care. I shall take Annie home in the carriage, and then send it back for you, and to-morrow I shall call upon your father and tell him of your disrespectful conduct, and decline any more to be your chaperone."

Florence colored crimson at being thus publicly rebuked, and the fiend bad temper took possession of her.

"You may do what you please," she replied, with a toss of her beautiful head. "I scorn you and your protection; pray do not trouble yourself about my welfare. Come, we are losing that beautiful quadrille."

Mrs. Fraser went away more grieved than hurt. She had heard something of Florence's character, but had never seen it in its full development until now, and she pitied the parents of the wayward girl, who were her warm and fast friends.

Florence's partner looked at her for one moment in amazement, but said nothing; he thought everything. He thought,—"how very beautiful she is, how perfect her form, how pretty her foot; but, oh, what a black, black heart she must have, to treat her friend and protector so. I am glad you are not my sister, Miss Florence, and pretty as you are, this is the last time that I will ask the honor of your hand in a dance. I wish I did not have to go through with it now, it was bought at such a fearful price, and that I was dancing with sweet Emma Johnstone, over there, who, though not beautiful as an angel, is a gentle and amiable girl."

Florence tried her best to be agreeable, but two things prevented; first, the silence and inattention of her partner, who was watching sweet Emma Johnstone; secondly, a sharp burning pain in her left hand which she too well understood.

As the bad fairy never made himself visible except when she was alone, she wished for once that she had gone home with Mrs. Fraser, for she dreaded the ride by herself. And had she known what was to happen she might well have dreaded it.

"Miss Somers' carriage has come," said the servant, after the dance was over.

"Just one more, just one more," said two or three aspirants for her hand.

"Not another," whispered the demon in her ear.

"Not another," said Florence trying in vain to smile sweetly upon the supplicants.

"If she had only said that awhile ago when Mrs. Fraser urged her to go home," thought her last partner, "how lovely she would would still be; but now she is nothing to me but **a** disobedient girl, one who must make her home unhappy; one, I know, who is not kind to her sister, for she is too selfish to be so, and who must make her brother's time pass disagreeably enough. Yes! thank my stars she does not belong to my home. I would not have her there for the world. Then he added as he handed her to the carriage, — "Good night, a pleasant ride to you"; and Florence answered, "thank you, good night"; and the carriage rolled off with its beautiful occupant, who saw by the light of the lamp which they passed her left hand demon more terrible than ever, **and of whom she in vain asked** mercy; for the pain which he seemed maliciously to take **pleasure in** inflicting was more intense than she had **ever experienced before.**

CHAPTER VI.

AN ACCIDENT.

The coachman was not in a very good humor at the idea of **hav**ing to return again to the dancing school and drove carelessly and furiously through the streets, until, on turning rapidly round a corner, he came in contact with another carriage which was going at **a rapid rate also.**

Florence heard a crash and many words, then a swifter whirling through the silent street; then a knowledge seemed to come over her that there was no coachman upon the box; and she heard the mocking laugh of the demon and his voice, which said, "You will pay dearly for that last dance, my lady;" **then** another crash met her ear, and she became unconscious.

When she awoke to consciousness again, she was in her **own room. It** was darkened; but she could see Jessie sitting down by her bedside sewing, and her father and mother in earnest consultation with the doctor. A bandage was on her forehead, and her left arm was bound up with long splints, and when she tried to raise it, the agony was terrible. She tried to remember what had happened, and at last the truth flashed upon her and she closed her eyes once more.

Then Jessie came and applied some healing ointment to her face, and in a whisper to herself bewailed the loss of her dear Miss Floy's beauty, and abused that "horrid coachman" for allowing her lovely face to become so bruised and her arm to be so badly broken; and then, to Jessie's delight, Florence opened her eyes and spoke.

"Is it so very dreadful, Jessie?" she said, and burst into a fit of weeping.

"The worst is over, now," said the doctor approaching, and Florence felt her mother's kiss upon her face and heard her father's "God be thanked," and she knew that she had escaped from a great peril.

Her beauty gone, what had Florence now to do? Everything. That long period in her quiet chamber taught her many things. What had she to do with pride now? nothing; how could she best learn to be like dear, patient Jessie? By considering the wants of others. How could she heal Mrs. Fraser's wounded feelings? By sending for her, which she did, and asking for forgiveness which was freely granted; and so it came to pass, that Florence was more beloved with her bruised and disfigured face and mutilated arm, and bandaged forehead, then she had been in all her pride of exquisite beauty; and when Jessie spoke in troubled accents of her departed loveliness, Florence would check her by saying that it was all for the best, and her smile was so sweet when she thus spoke that Jessie would clap her hands and cry out, "There, I know that my dear mistress will be beautiful again!"

CHAPTER VII.

THE FAIRY'S LAST VISIT.

WERE you ever ill, little reader, and do you remember how patient you had to be, how forbearing, how, when any one but stepped across the room it sent a pang to your aching head, and you had to calm yourself and suppress the quick angry word of impatience that rose to your lips? Well, Florence passed through just such a trying experience. It was hard, oh, how hard at first! but day after day it became more easy.

"There," she would say after a day's trial; "I think I have done pretty well, Jessie, only two cross words have passed my lips to-day; once when brother whistled very loud, and then again when he shut the door so violently that it seemed to make every nerve in my frame quiver. Am I not improving, Jessie? Do give me a little hope."

And Jessie would answer, "Dear Miss Floy, *that* you are, and everybody says they never saw such a change."

"Such a change indeed," sighed Florence, thinking of her lost beauty; "but then," she whispered softly to herself, "have I not in reality been a gainer? What a sweet thing it is to be loved so much!"

And so it came to pass, that Florence improved in health and appearance every day, and Time, the great healer, restored her beautiful forehead to its original whiteness and smoothness, and the bones of her broken arm were firmly knit to their old symmetry again.

She had not yet left her chamber and was alone at twilight one evening, musing over her past and present life. The shades of night gradually deepened and the fire-light flickered upon the walls, casting grotesque shadows around.

Suddenly soft music seemed to fill the room, and Florence perceived exquisite perfumes in the air; the light grew brighter and brighter, and she saw that the apartment was filled with gay and airy shapes; while two, more beautiful than the rest, unrolled a scroll upon which was written in plain characters, *Florence, you have conquered the Demon of Bad Temper; he will be your companion no longer.*

Florence felt a thrill of pleasure as she read these words and looked at the fairies who flitted about; but greater was her joy when she was conscious that in her right hand she held her old friend and counsellor, the Queen of Good Nature and Self-Conquest.

"Yes, Florence," her sweet voice murmured; "you have indeed conquered; hard has been your trial, but greater your victory. Continue to be ever as you are, the pride of your parents, the delight of your friends. You have no need of me more, and I go to assist others who are as you have been. Do not weep, sweet girl, for though you will not see me visibly as you do now, in your heart will be my home. Farewell."

Florence stretched out her arms to embrace the beautiful shape; but it faded in the air, and ever after, when she was praised for her sweetness and gentleness she would answer, "Ah, but how can I help it, when you know that I have a good fairy in my heart."

This is only fiction, my young friend, and yet, if you choose, you can apply it to yourself when you feel that bad temper has overcome you; and you can, like Florence, cherish a good fairy in *your* heart.

LILLIAN.

AGED FOUR MONTHS.

LITTLE floweret,
Over the sea,
List to a murmur
Of song from me.

Gentle Lillian,
Wonderful child,
Who shall declare
Your virtues mild?

Tell me, Lillian,
  Whence came those eyes,
With their fringèd lids?
  From the summer skies?

Your father affirms
  Intelligence gleams
From their earnest depths,
  Like sunset beams.

You have learned the way
  To win our hearts,
And don't depend
  On tragedy starts,

And aches and pains,
  To have your will;
But deep in thought,
  You lie quite still,

A picture child —
  While you hear us tell
Astonishing things,
  You **know** full well

Are not *quite* true;
  For, *entre nous*,
You have your faults
  And wrong things do.

You close your lids
  With a sleepy grace,
To hear us speak
  Of your "perfect face";

To make us stare
  At your splendid eyes,
You raise them up
  With a *sweet surprise;*

With a dreamy gaze,
  A poetic air,
You smooth the waves
  Of your silken hair;

**Your mother too, sees
  In the** perfect curve
Of your pencilled brows,
  Resolve and nerve.

And friends exclaim,
  "Expression rare!"
And, "Behold the light
  In her waving hair!"

"And her taper hands,
  See, their rosy tips
Have **the crimson tinge**
  Of **her pouting lips."**

Like a common child,
  You scorn to show
The common ills
  That babies know.

With an absent look,
  Your ivory feet,
You enraptured hear
  Called dimpled and sweet.

All this is fun:
  Hear some earnest thing
Before you sleep
  Or my thoughts take wing.

You will hear us speak
  Of the lilies rare,
Called Jesus' flowers;
  Of the fields **so fair.**

Be like to these,
  Beloved child!
As white and pure,
  · And as undefiled.

And in life's morn,
  In the time of youth,
Keep close in your heart
  The light of truth.

And as time steals on,
  · And your leaves unfold
To the heat of day,
  Or the night's drear cold,

Be a lily still.
  Christ's Lillian be,
Arrayed in the robes
  Of His purity.

A STORY FOR CHILDREN.
"I WISH I HAD."
A REGULAR FAIRY TALE.

George. — I wish I had a room full of money, and piles of gold and silver up to the very ceiling. Oh, I do wish I had it!

William. — And I wish I had twenty race horses, all fine animals, with long tails and small heads; papa likes horses with small heads.

Mary. — Well, I wish I had fifty singing birds, yellow, purple, and gold, with diamond crests and ruby eyes, in beautiful golden cages with balconies all round.

Susan. — You would be quite welcome to the birds, sister Mary, if I only had a whole bookcase full of elegant books bound in calf, with gilt leaves. My! wouldn't I read! I would never care to play; George might count his money all day; William ride to the north pole with his fiery steeds: and you might listen for hours to your diamond crested birds; only give *me* books. Oh! I wish I had them now, — to-day.

And so when the children had all wished for what they most wanted, they sat down and began to think and think and think what they would do with their money and horses and birds and books, and their little voices were hushed, and there was a dead silence.

Presently they heard somebody knocking — bam, bam, bam, at the door.

"Come in," they all said, and an old gentleman, whom they had never seen before, entered. He was very small and shrivelled and had long white hair like blown glass, and a white beard reaching to his knees. And then his teeth shook so fearfully, that when he opened his mouth the children were afraid that they would tumble out upon the ground; his eyes were green and his eyebrows and eye lashes were green, too; and altogether, he had such a queer appearance that the children moved closer together, although they were not exactly afraid of the old gentleman, but only astonished at him, as they afterwards said.

So when he reached the middle of the room he shook hands all round, and then sat down quite at home, and crossed his legs and laughed heartily. But the funniest thing about the old gentleman, was, that instead of talking, he sang all he had to say in a sort of chant which was like the growl of a cheerful lion, and which seemed to come from the very bottom of his chest; and the worst of it was, that there was no tune nor time in the song.

"Well — little — children," he sang, "I — heard — you — a — wishing, — and — I — have — come — to — give — you — what — you — want. But — first — we — must — make — a — bargain — (then he turned his eyes slowly from one to the other); should — you — have — what — you — desire, — would — you — be — willing — to — do — without — other — things?"

"Oh, yes, yes!" they all exclaimed, "what a nice old gentleman; if we only had the money, the horses, the birds and the books, we shouldn't want anything more in the whole world."

"Very — well," said the old gentleman.

Then the children joined hands and danced round him for joy;

but he shook his head very solemnly all the time, and his eyes and eyebrows and eyelashes turned from green to blue.

Then he told George to come with him into the next room and lo! George had his wish, for it was all filled with money, and gold and silver.

"How delightful!" said George; "what a first-rate old fellow you are M, — what's your name!"

"That's — not — my — title," sang the old gentleman; "but — as — you've — heard — my — name — before — may — be — you'll — not — find — it — difficult — to — pronounce. Folks — call — me — Mr. — Wishihad."

"Well," said George, scarcely listening to him. "This is what I call happiness; nothing shall stop me now from buying the gold watch at Mortimer's, or a doubled barrel gun, or the yacht James Willis valued at so high a rate. Why, I could buy the world.

George didn't quite like the tone in which the old gentleman sang out. "Now — could — you?" nor the queer look he gave him; so fearing that the money might disappear as it had come, to make sure of at least some of it, he stooped to fill his pockets. But lo and behold! his arms, his hands, the very end of his nails were stiff and paralyzed, and though the glittering coin came in contact with his fingers, not a piece of it could he pick up.

"Look here, sir," he said, turning toward the old gentleman; "there's no power in my hand, sir, my fingers won't bend to gather it up; somebody will come and steal it all, sir."

"As — to — that," said the old gentleman slowly, "it's — of no — consequence — at — all, — for — you — said — that — you — would — not — want — any — thing — but — money — and — piles — of — gold — and — silver," and he went out and shut the door, leaving George in the midst of his useless riches crying with vexation, and trying to pick up the slippery gold in his stiff fingers, in vain.

Then Mr. Wishihad went back into the room where the children were, and sat down quite at home again.

"George — has — his — money," he sang, twisting his long white beard round and round. " I — think — that — fine, — brave — looking — little — fellow — over — there — said — that — he — wanted — horses."

"Nothing but horses, sir, nothing," said William; "maybe you've never been on a horse sir, and don't know much about horse-flesh; but nothing can come up in my opinion to a canter on a full-blooded animal, gentle as a lady, sir, and yet fiery as the lightning. Oh, horses! shouldn't I like to have some horses!"

The old gentleman seemed to have caught some of William's enthusiasm, for while he was talking his eyes changed from blue to fiery pink, and his eyebrows and eyelashes turned pink too, and every time they changed color he looked as if he had a new face.

"You — shall — have — your — horses — my — boy," he sang, slapping William upon the back in quite a familiar manner. "Come — with — me."

So he took William to another room, and told him to look out of the windows; and lo and behold, there were his twenty race horses, all full-blooded animals, and every one worth a fortune, almost.

"Are — they — not — beautiful?" chanted the queer old man.

"Beautiful?" exclaimed William, feeling all the pride of ownership; "that's too tame a word for them, sir, they are splendiferous, first rate; how proud they look, how graceful, how daintily they lift their feet from the ground; what fine nostrils they have, and then their heads, how small! There, — do you see that one yonder with a black star above the eyes — that's the fellow for me; if you are not afraid, sir, please step down a bit into the yard and see me mount him. I'll borrow father's saddle and just try his gait you know; you might take that roan, sir, he seems quite gentle enough.

"To — oblige — you — I — will," — Master — William; — come — along, — let — it — never — be — said — that — I, — Wish i had —

was afraid — of — horses," sang the stranger; and off he walked towards the door.

"Stop a bit, Mr. Wishihad," said William; "it seems to me that I can't walk. I have a dreadful pain in my legs. Oh, dreadful!" and down George sat on the ground, unable to move.

"Come — along," sang the old gentleman with variations.

"Oh, I can't, sir. You don't know what pain I suffer."

"As — to — that," returned the old man very slowly and quite out of tune, "it's — of — no — consequence, — for — you — said, — didn't — you, — that — you — wouldn't — want — any — thing — but — horses?" and he shut the door, and left him alone with the pain in his leg and the sound of the full-blooded horses trotting about the yard.

Then he went back in the room where the girls were, and they both noticed that his eyes had changed from fiery pink to pale yellow and that he was very, very ugly.

Then he looked right at Mary and chanted in the same way as before what was in his mind.

"You — are — the — little — Miss, — I — believe, — who — wanted — birds; — you — shall — have — them, — come"; so he offered his arm to Mary very politely and he carried her away to a third room, and sure enough there were the birds; but words couldn't describe their beauty; they were moving jewels, all ruby and topaz, and emerald and gold. And their cages! why, you never saw such cages, with a golden cupola on the top of each, with a diamond arrow to tell which way the wind blew, and balconies with silver railings for the birds to walk on, in the cool time of the evening when the sun was not very hot; and then their cups for water, — even Mary's mother's best company's glasses were not equal to these. So when Mary saw all these delightful things and felt that they were all her own, she couldn't help saying to the old gentleman with beaming eyes and grateful voice, "Oh, sir, you have made me very happy, I am so much obliged to you, I don't know what to do."

"*Singing*-birds — I — thought — you — said — you — **wanted**," began the old gentleman; "listen, — there — they — go"; and sure enough the **birds** quite drowned his voice in their exquisite strains, in which the music seemed to trill **and** quiver and gush **and** float, and **rise and** fall **and** swell **and fade** and die and come to life again.

That was not **a song,** but only a kind of introduction, at least the old gentleman thought so; for when they stopped, his gruff voice was heard in these words.

"None — of — your — rigmaroles, — and — quivering, — and — quavering, — give — us — **a — regular —** tune. Now — that's — what — I — call — music; — just — listen — Miss — **Mary**"; and the old gentleman began to keep time with his feet, and the little birds sang with all their might and main, and twisted about their brilliant throats, and looked so proud with their jewelled crowns, that any one **would have** imagined **that they thought** the world had never heard such music before, and **in truth the world** never had. But alas! though Mary saw that they were singing, not one note did she hear; she was stone deaf.

"Oh, sir," she said. "I'm so frightened, indeed, sir; **I am afraid you** will not believe me, but I think — I must be deaf. **Is** n't it dreadful, sir? Something has stopped my ears; you **are so great** and powerful, sir, don't you think that you could unstop **them?**"

"As — to — that," bawled out the old gentleman very slowly close in her ears, in the loudest bass voice that ever was heard, "it's — of — no — consequence — whatever, — for — you — said — you — would — not — want — any — thing — in — the — world — but — singing — birds, — and — those — certainly — are — **singing —** — birds — are n't they?" and he shut the door and **went** back to Susan.

Susan was so busy reading when he went in, that she did not see him until he came quite close to her, and then she noticed that his eyes, eyebrows, and eyelashes were bright purple. She had never seen purple eyes before, and as she thought them very strange, she looked quite down into their mysterious depths.

"I — never — saw — such — a — reader," — sang the old gentleman; "why — she — is — even — reading — my — old — old — eyes — I — think —*you* — said — you — wanted — books."

"Oh, yes, sir; I have quite a passion for books. When my sisters and brothers are playing with their toys, or walking or riding, I care for nothing but reading. But I am so tired of the books I have; I have read mine over and over again. Oh, dear me! I do wish I had some new books!"

"You — shall — have — them," was the compassionate answer; and sure enough the floor groaned and cracked beneath their feet, and he told Susan to stand a little farther off, and up rose the most beautiful bookcase in the world. Then the floor mended itself again, and the case stood firm and elegant on its four handsome legs. It was made of the clearest crystal and inlaid with gems.

These gems were grouped together in such a manner that they were likenesses of all the great men and women in the world who had ever written books for children, and then when the old gentleman touched a spring, the crystal doors opened, and he showed Susan the books that she had been longing to read, "for ages," she said, all in splendid large type, with pictures on nearly every page; and then on each side of the bookcase were two golden candlesticks with perfumed candles, which lit themselves when the sun went down, and a drawer of book-marks with every motto on them that was ever wrought on book-marks in the universe.

"Oh, — ho," sang the old gentleman; "this — is — even — finer — than — I — ordered; — they — are — bringing the — art — of — book — making — to — great — perfection; — now, — only —

look — here — Miss — Susan — at — this — fairy — tale ; — how — handsome — the — pictures — are, — why — the — young — ladies — are — dropping — real — pearls — and — **diamonds** — from — their — mouths."

Susan looked, but alas! she thought, she *knew*, that she **was blind.** What a horrible thing!

"There ; — this — is — most — extraordinary," continued **the old** gentleman. "I never — did — see — the — like ; — how — bright — sweet — Blanche's — eyes — are ; — and — how — perfect — is — the — foliage — which — seems — to — wave — on — those — **trees** ; look — Miss — Susan!"

"Oh sir," said Susan, in piteous accents, "**I cannot see, I am blind** all of a sudden ; if you could only open my eyes."

Then the old gentleman sang as before very slowly ; "Oh — as — to — that, — its — of — no — consequence, — for — you — said — you — would'nt — want — any — thing — else — in — the — world — but — books" ; and he shut the door and left her feeling the pretty bindings and dropping bright tears on the rich leaves.

And George remained in his room with his shrivelled hands and his money ; and William in his with his crippled limbs, listening **to** the trotting of his full-blooded horses ; and Mary in hers, deaf with her birds singing famously around her ; and Susan leaning her head **with** her blind eyes against her crystal bookcase weeping for a whole day.

After a time the old gentleman knocked at **George's door,** and George, glad to see anybody, said "Come in."

"**Do** — you — *wish* — *you* — *had* — anything — else, — George?" he sang.

"Oh, yes, sir, one thing only ; make my hands well and strong again, and I shall be satisfied without the money and the **piles** of gold and silver" ; so the old gentleman blew upon the treasure and it disappeared ; and then upon George's hands and they were quite well again, and they both went into William's room.

"Is — there — anybody — in — here — *wishing* — *they* — *had* — *anything?*"

"Oh, no, sir," exclaimed William. "I only wish to be **as I once was**; I should like to walk freely again, and I should be willing to give up all the horses"; so he flourished his stick over William three times and then out of the windows three times, and the horses and the lameness disappeared, and William gave a loud hurrah and then all three went to Mary's room.

"Can — I — do — anything — for — anybody — here?" he bawled with a loud speaking trumpet at Mary's ear; "*does — anybody — wish* — for — more — cages — and — singing — birds — in — here?"

"Oh, no, sir," said poor Mary; "I only wish to hear once more all that is going on about me and to lose this dead life of deafness, and I'd be willing never to see the singing birds again."

So the old gentleman coughed three times and Mary's deafness left her, and the birds broke up the cages into bits and flew away, and then Mary began to sing herself for joy; then they went to see about poor blind Susan leaning against the crystal bookcase and crying.

"Poor — little — soul," sang the old gentleman in a sad minor key, while shaking his white beard solemnly; "she — is — very — sorrowful, — truly. Little — Miss — Susan"; and he lifted up her bowed head and looked straight into her sightless eyes. "Can — I — help — you — to-day? Have — you — enjoyed — your — books, — or — do — *you* — *wish* — *you* — *had* — anything — else, — my — dear?"

"Oh, sir," she answered, clasping her hands; "don't talk to me about books, please, just yet; only let me see my dear brothers and sisters, and I will never wish for a grand bookcase again."

It was very pitiful to see her, and so the old gentleman took some blue powder out of a paper in his pocket and sprinkled it over the books and Susan's eyes, and the books and the bookcase all turned to ashes, and Susan could see as well as ever.

Oh! how delighted they all were at feeling, walking, hearing and seeing, once more. Again they joined hands and made a ring round the old gentleman and were very joyful indeed. Then he asked for a pair of scissors and cut off a long piece of his white hair and gave it to each, and while they were wondering if it was hair or blown glass, *bam, bam, bam,* went his stick, and the floor opened and down he went, the children thought forever.

"How strange," said George; "what a funny old man."

"How much power he has," said William; "how rich he must be. I wish I had as much —"

But scarcely were the words out of his mouth than the floor opened again, and out popped the stranger's head.

"Did — anybody — call — one — Mr. — Wishihad?" they heard him sing; "because — if — they — did, — he — can — come — at — any — time."

"Oh, no, no, no," they said, and down he went again.

"We must be careful," said Susan gravely, "what we wish for and must be content with the blessings that have already fallen to our lot. At any rate, I suppose there's no harm done when I merely say I wish I had contentment."

"Not — much — harm," and out popped the head again; "I — certainly — heard — some — one — repeat — my — name; — oh, — I — was — mistaken. Well, — good-by, — nobody — wants — me, — then?"

"No, I guess we don't," said George, looking rather frightened at the old gentleman's perseverance. "Come, let us leave the room and have a run on the lawn, it is much better than staying in here and wishing we had what we have not."

Then they all went out; but when they reached the stairs they heard somebody calling loudly "children!" and they went back once

OUR FATHER WHO ART IN HEAVEN. — Page 249.

more, just in time to see a wave of the old gentleman's hand as it disappeared through the floor, and to catch the tones of a departing, rumbling voice, the burden of whose song was

Don't — Wish — You — Had.

OUR FATHER WHO ART IN HEAVEN.

Oh, Thou our Father in the skies,
  Thy blessed name we praise,
That earth may be as pure as heaven,
  Upright should be our ways.

Oh, may we always do Thy will,
  As it is done above,
Still send to us our daily food
  And bless us with Thy love.

And may it ever be our care
  To treat a foe like friend,
And so thou wilt our sins forgive
  And no temptations send.

Keep every evil from our path,
  The whole wide earth is Thine,
And might and glory come Thee from,
  Thou art alone divine.

Forever and forever be
  Thy praise far sounded then,
Till all the earth with one accord,
  Together say, Amen.

MORNING AND EVENING PRAYER.

MORNING PRAYER.

I thank thee, God,
  For rest so sweet,
And that this morn
  My friends I meet.

EVENING PRAYER.

A kind "good night"
  To all I love,
Watch them and me,
  Great God above.

THE WISH GRANTED.

It was a very rainy day. Little **Isabel** had read until she was weary, and sewed until her tired fingers refused to pull the needle through her work, and at last she went to the window and flattened her little nose against the glass pane. She did not know that any one was in the room, but some one was; her uncle, a rich old gentleman, who heard her say softly; "oh, I do wish that I had twenty dollars; I know that I should be *perfectly* happy!"

"Would twenty dollars make any body perfectly happy? well here they are, Belle, at your service."

Isabel could scarcely believe that he was in earnest, but he was, indeed.

"Oh, Uncle, please take them back. I am afraid that you are robbing yourself."

"No, my darling," said her uncle. "I have hundreds and can well spare twenty dollars; come, my little lady, sit on my knee and tell me what you are going to do with your fortune."

Belle's eyes glistened and grew larger and larger with surprise and delight.

"Oh," said she as she sprung upon his knees, "I am going to buy a baby-house and a rocking-horse for Willie, and some books and — but Uncle, just come with me to-morrow and see what I will buy."

"Very well, Belle, — be ready at twelve, and we will shop to your heart's content."

So when the morrow came, Belle put on her gypsy hat and laced her pretty gaiter boots, took her purse which contained her twenty dollars, and tripped along the street with her kind uncle.

Just before a cake shop, peering into the well stocked window, she saw two ragged little boys whose hungry eyes looked longingly at the nice cream cakes and rich rolls within.

"Oh, uncle, may I?" she asked, looking towards the boys.

"Do what you please, Belle," said her uncle; "the money is yours, not mine."

Then Belle, with a glad smile, took a gold dollar from her purse and handing it to the boys, said: "Here, little fellows, take this and buy some cake."

The boys stared at her and thought that she was only in fun; but, when her uncle said, "take it," they scraped and bowed at a great rate, turned the money over and over again and at last disappeared in the cake shop, quite wild with delight! Belle and her uncle watched for them until they came out, and at last saw them each with a bundle; one was eating a cream cake, the inside of which was streaming down his chin, and the other had his mouth so full that he could not utter a word; but they both looked so happy that Belle whispered to her uncle: "Oh, uncle, isn't it nice to have money?"

"Yes, my darling," said the old man; "and it is very nice to give it away."

Belle looked back once more at the little ragged boys, and could not help laughing at them; for one was standing on his head with his feet against a fence, and the other was turning a somerset for very joy.

"Well, where now?"

"To the toy shop, *of course.*"

I do believe that Belle did not know or care about any other shops in the world.

"Anything in my store that pleases your fancy, little Miss?" asked the shopwoman.

"Everything," thought Belle, but she asked first to see some dinner and tea-sets put up in little white boxes. Real china they were and cost a great deal. Her uncle wanted to teach her not to be extravagant, so he asked her if a blue and white set, less valuable, would not suit her as well. They did suit her and she bought them for one dollar and a quarter. Then she wanted some dolls. "Oh, that one with blue eyes and flaxen hair was a love of a doll; no matter what it cost she must have it," she said.

Belle was growing very grand with her riches; so when the shopwoman told her that it could open and shut its blue eyes by pulling a wire and that it cost three dollars, she laid down the money and took it.

"What are you going to name your doll?" asked her uncle.

"Waxiana, certainly, uncle; that is a beautiful name."

"Well, anything more?" asked uncle.

"Yes, next on the list is a rocking horse; that will be about three dollars, for mamma told me so." And the rocking horse was bought, not one with real horse-hair and a fine flowing tail, costing twenty dollars all by itself, but a wooden one about a yard from the ground, upon which her little brother could jump without help.

Then she bought a set of drawers for fifty cents, and a washstand with a pitcher and basin for seventy-five, and a dolls' looking-glass for twenty-five.

"Now, uncle," she said when she had made these purchases, "I want to make you a present and I must give you something; what will you have?"

"Plenty of your smiles, Belle, nothing more."

"Oh, yes; *do* let me give you something."

"Well, Belle, you may."

"I should like to give you a paper-cutter which you can use for a book-mark too." So the shopwoman brought out some, and Belle selected a very pretty one costing fifty cents, which she gave to her uncle. Oh, it was so sweet to give!

By this time Belle felt very hungry and proposed to lay out some of her money in ice cream and cake, to which her uncle readily assented.

Then they went into a garden where they sat in a cool arbor with fountains playing about, and called for ice and cake.

"How nice it is to treat you, uncle," she said, as the white pyramid of ice-cream disappeared through her rosy lips. "I feel so very grand."

Her uncle smiled sweetly on his little pet and felt happier than he had been for a long time, for it made him so to see her joy.

They took two ice-creams apiece, and the cake cost twelve and a half cents; this brought her bill at the confectioner's to thirty-seven and a half cents.

As it was getting late, her uncle thought that she had better go home and count over her money, returning again to make her purchases; but the little lady pleaded so hard to go to a bookstore that he granted her request.

In a bookstore money goes plentifully, for a good book is a costly article; and Bell first purchased a Bible for herself for which she paid two dollars. It had clear large type and gilt leaves, and was well worth the money; for who does not like to own a Bible with large print?

Next came a little book for Bessie who was learning her letters, a nice strong primer which cost twenty-five cents. Then for her dear father she bought a beautiful penknife, one dollar; and portemonnaie for her mother, one dollar also.

Belle's bill was mounting up so fast that her uncle told her that she might overspend her money; but she shook the purse and told him that there was some there yet, and that she must have a book of Fairy Tales for the story about The White Cat was torn out of her cousin Tom's book; so the Fairy Tales were bought for one dollar.

Now just guess how much Belle found that she had spent when she reached home. I will put down all the things for you and then maybe you can add them up for yourself.

Ragged boys . . .	$1 00	Confectionery . . . 37½
Tea set	1 25	Bible 2 00
Horse	3 00	Primer 25
Drawers	50	Penknife 1 00
Washstand, pitcher, and basin	75	Porte-monnaie . . . 1 00
		Fairy book . . . 1 00
Looking-glass . .	25	
Paper-cutter . . .	50	$12 87½

There, you see, she spent twelve dollars eighty-seven and a half cents, and had just seven dollars twelve and a half cents left.

How impatiently she waited **until** the evening for her packages to come, you little readers know about as well as I do. She took up a **book** to read, but Waxiana's blue eyes seemed to gaze at her from **every** page. She took out her sewing, but the unfinished story of The White **Cat sent her thoughts far** away from the frill which she was hemming.

"How long they do take!" she kept saying.

"Make your baby-house look nicely for the **new lady who is** coming," said her mamma, "and for the pitcher and basin and drawers."

So Belle went **up stairs and set the** house in order, dusting it nicely, and making up the little bed with clean sheets, and putting on a fresh pillow-case with a tiny ruffle around it. Then she played **that there was a fire in the** little chimney-corner, and put on fresh sticks to welcome Waxiana, and brightened the brass andirons **until** her face shone broad and smiling on the polished surface.

But that was not all! **She went to her mamma for** some sugar, cake and biscuit, and put them in her little store-closet in the dolls' house, ready for the new comer.

Now I must tell **you about the dolls' house.** It was **made by** James Harris, the carpenter, who **lived** near her father's, **and to** whom her father and mother had been very kind. Little Sukey Harris **had** the scarlet fever, and Belle's mother sent a **good** physician to her, paid the bill when she got well, and every day tempted the little girl, who was recovering slowly, with jellies and good things.

Out of gratitude, James made a complete dolls' house for Belle. It was three stories high. The upper one was the chamber, the second, the dining-room and parlor divided in two, and the lower one, the kitchen. Then it had mantel-pieces and closets and fire-places; and the parlor was carpeted and everything was just like a real house.

No doubt, then, Miss Waxiana would be glad to see what a nice place she was going to live in and be mistress of.

After Belle had arranged everything to her liking, she took the cook from the kitchen, where she had been standing straight and stiff against the wall, put a nice apron on her, and made her look very tidy for her new mistress.

"Now, Binah," she said, "you must behave well when Miss Waxiana comes; you must do your duty as a cook; never send anything into the house burnt or smoked; always have your coffee of a bright brown, and never allow your green tea to boil. Then your breakfast cakes must never be heavy, for heavy cakes are very unhealthy; and, above all things, always keep a nice kitchen; so nice, that when the lady of the house comes to show you how to prepare any delicate little tit-bit from the receipt-book, she will not soil her dress nor her hands."

No doubt Binah promised everything; for when Belle put her back again, standing against the kitchen wall, she looked like a very proper cook, and as if there was nothing in her department that she could not do except to sit down.

There was one little trial, however, that Belle had to go through; she did almost with tears: it was to tell her old doll, Clementine, that a new lady was coming, very grand and elegant, who would take her place as mistress of the house; and that she, Clementine, must in future be the house-maid.

Indeed, it was quite a trial to Belle; but what could be done? Clementine had once been quite a handsome doll; but now her nose was broken short off; the mice had bitten off four of her fingers, and one of her eyes had sunk **so** far into her head, that **it** was impossible to bring it back to its place again; and, indeed, **at** every attempt of Belle's to bring it forward with **a pair of scissors, it** went farther and farther back.

"**Yes,**" **said** Belle, **softly and** tearfully, "it would not do for you to remain seated in **the parlor** when Waxiana comes, Clementine." **(while** she made a **final attempt** at the lost eye, more unsuccessful **than any yet,** for it disappeared altogether in some deep recess of head or neck), "you really are handsome no more; but you are very dear to me still, and I am sure that you will do *your* duty as housemaid. After you have done your work you must go into the **kitchen** with the cook. I am sure that she is a very agreeable cook; and though it will be very hard at first, you poor one-eyed creature, to be a servant where you have been queen, yet, as mamma says, there must be ups and downs in this world, you know."

So Clementine took her seat in the kitchen, for she could sit, though the cook could not, and Belle fancied that she saw a tear dropping from her remaining eye. Belle cried a little to see her there so forlorn; but, then, what could she do? It passed **through** her mind that she would put her to bed, and play that she was sick all the time; but then that would hide the sweet, ruffled pillow-case; so after all, when she had dusted the last speck of dust from the mahogany centre-table, and given one final glance to see if all was in order, she heard a ring at the street-bell. It was a gentle, timid ring,—not a thundering one, such as would denote that her package had come; but Belle leaped down stairs, and met the servant coming in, not with her bundle but empty handed.

"Well, Sarah," she said, "who is it? what is it?"

"**Oh,** Miss Belle, **it is** only a poor woman with a **baby** in her arms, come to beg; and I told her that I would let mistress know and maybe she would give her some money."

Some money! "Ah!" thought little Belle; "why could not I give her some money too, to buy a dress for the baby and some bread for herself?" So she went to the door and told the woman to come in and take a seat in the hall.

Belle saw at a glance that she was very poor and sick too; and the baby, though sleeping calmly, had a look of death about its white face.

"Poor little thing!" said Belle; "is it sick?"

"Not so much sick, little Miss," said the woman, "as hungry. I am too sick myself to work; my husband died last week with the fever, and it is the only comfort I have in the world to think that baby and I will soon follow him."

"Oh, no, no, poor woman!" Belle answered, with tearful eyes; "mamma will give you victuals and clothes; I will go and ask her now." So off she ran and met Sarah coming from the pantry with a plate of bread and meat, and a bowl of milk for the baby, while her mother followed and told the poor woman to go into the kitchen by the fire and eat some food.

The poor woman's eyes glistened when she saw the nice white bread and milk for the baby, and went into the kitchen as Belle's mother had told her. Then she woke the baby, who uttered a sharp cry of pain; and before she eat a morsel herself she fed the little sufferer, who soon smiled on Belle and played with the ribbon on her silk apron.

Then the poor woman ate heartily and Belle's mother came in to hear her story. It was a very sad one and she was so interested in the woman and thought the little baby so pretty, that she told her, as she said she was a good seamstress, to come and live in a nice room in her yard and she would give her work to do.

How happy the woman looked at this kindness; and Belle's mother gave her some money to pay a man to bring her trunk to the house.

The woman departed with many thanks, but just as she got outside the door she heard a little voice saying, "Stop a minute, here is something to buy you and the baby some nice dresses." The woman turned and there was Belle with two gold dollars which she dropped into her hand. She had then four dollars and twelve cents left.

"God will reward you," she said, softly, "in giving to the widow and fatherless"; and Belle felt when she turned to go back into the house that not one of her purchases had made her so happy as those heartfelt words. Besides, though she did not know it, her uncle was peeping at her through the parlor blinds and blessed her over and over again for the kind and thoughtful act.

Before Belle had quite seated herself in her little chair by the window, there was another ring, and the books arrived. How pleasant it was to open the package to give to her little sister her primer, and to her father and mother their presents, to cover her new book with a sheet of white paper, and lastly, to sit down to finish the story of the White Cat.

But before she had bent many minutes over the book, the bell rang again, and in came a basket from the toy shop filled with her purchases. Everybody came to look at them and there was quite a little crowd collected around as Belle opened her treasures; her father, mother, uncle, brother, little sister and the housemaid, while the cook, with her hands full of flour and a white apron on, peeped in at the door, and even a little kitten's bright eyes looked admiringly upon the scene.

Everybody admired everything, and Waxiana was handed about and her curling hair and blue eyes praised very much. Charlie was so delighted with the rocking horse that he could not be tempted to get off of it, and when the servant came for him to get his supper and put him to bed she found that he had gone to sleep sitting upright, and if she had not taken him in her arms he would have fallen off.

Then Belle took Waxiana and the drawers, the looking-glass and the watch-stand to the dolls' house, and put them in their proper places. Waxiana looked delighted at everything and never ceased smiling with her crimson lips and staring with her blue eyes until Belle took off her fine gauze dress and putting one of Clementine's best night-gowns on her, shut her eyes and placed her beautiful curly head on the ruffled pillow till the next morning. Then she told Clementine to be sure to be up bright and early and the cook to prepare one of her best breakfasts, shut the door of the dolls' house and went down to her fairy tale of the White Cat.

"Well, Belle," said her uncle, "shall we go out again to-morrow to finish our purchases?"

"No, uncle," she answered, "I have been thinking about it. I find that I have about four dollars left. That I will not spend just yet but will keep it and see what I really want, and maybe, too, some poor people may come to beg, and if I spend it all I will have no more to give."

"You are right, my darling," he answered; "if you make such a good use of your money always as you have of your twenty dollars, it will be a pleasure to give you more."

Belle finished the story and went to bed, dreaming that night of wax dolls and poor women and kind uncles and one-eyed servant-maids, all mixed up in grand confusion.

I cannot close this little story without wishing that all my readers had such rich and kind uncles, and were such good children as our Belle.

THE LITTLE GARDEN.

"Come see my little garden,"
 I heard sweet Mary say,
"A white fence circles round it
 To guard the flowerets gay."

And by the hand she led me
 Around each verdant bed,
"Now, *this* is bright verbena,
 And this a Pink," she said.

"And those that seem so common
 Are Four-o'clocks, you know,
They're closely shut at morning,
 And bright at evening blow.

"There, hides a blue-eyed Violet
 Beneath a rare Tea Rose;
And yonder stately flowers
 Are Dahlias set in **rows**.

"And there, around the railing,
 With tendrils green and fine,
I've trained with care and patience,
 An upward-climbing Vine.

"This little **plant so** crimson,
 With that so pearly white,
Is called a Lady's Slipper —
 But 'twould not fit one quite.

"And here's a bending Willow,
 Its drooping branches wave
Just like the tree, that watches
 O'er Charlie's little grave."

That name brought tears like dew
  drops
 Upon her rosy cheek,
And then she tried to wipe them,
 And cheerfully to speak.

She told me many **a story**
 About this plant or that,
While near her little garden
 Upon the grass we sat, —

That humming birds **so tiny**
 Came sipping honey there,
And joyous bees went buzzing
 Among **the blossoms fair;**

And that in summer evenings
 Before **the sun sank low,**
When home the cattle wandered
 In herds **with** footsteps slow —

That when each little birdling
 Sought, twittering, his nest,
And all the sky was crimsoned,
 With sunset in the west —

She'd wander to her garden
 To tell the flowers 'good **night,'**
And bid them be up early
 To greet the morrow's light.

And as her bright smile lightened
 Her pure and lovely face,
And while her every gesture
 Was full of youthful grace;

I thought, sweet is your garden,
 Its pretty blossoms too;
But, ah, no flower within it
 Is half so sweet as you.

TEN STOPS.

When you are going to say an unkind word to your brother or sister — stop!

When you are going to say what is not true — stop!

When you are going to be cross to your nurse — stop!

When you are going to do what your father and mother have told you not to do — stop!

When you are going to take anything which does not belong to you — stop!

When you are hurrying away from a poor child who asks you for something to eat — stop!

When you are going to say something against another person — stop!

When you are going to break the holiness of the Sabbath day — stop!

When you are going to deceive any one in any way — stop!

When you are going to do that which you know God would not approve of — stop!

THE SCHOOL-GIRLS' QUARREL.

One day a teacher picked up in the school-room a note which contained these words from one school-girl to another: —

"Miss Smith, —

"I rejoice to say that I have quarrelled with you; I do not like you at all, and I hope that you will never come to my house again. You have said words that I cannot forget; and as long as there is a sun in the heavens or water in the ocean, I will *never* speak to you again.

"Yours (not at all in kindness),

"FRANCES PRATT."

"These are fierce words," thought the teacher: "too strong, indeed, for one school-girl to use to another, or, indeed, for any one to use. I must try and make up this quarrel, and I will watch these two girls well." So when they came back again the next day, she inquired all about it.

Cordelia Smith, it appears, had told one of the other girls that Frances Pratt was a disagreeable girl, and Frances had heard it. Now, as Cordelia and Frances, before these words had been said, had been the best friends in the world, always sitting together, always helping each other with difficult tasks, always sharing their good things at lunch-time, it was a wonder that they, of all people, should have fallen out. They were both wrong, I think; Cordelia, to say what she did, and Frances to resent it by such a harsh note to her friend; she should rather have showed by her pretty and gentle ways, that there was no truth in the offending words, and thus have led Cordelia to think differently; but this was not to be.

The girls passed each other by in lofty disdain; and even though they sat at the same desk in school, they scarcely looked at each other, though in the heart of each there was a desire to be friends again. Frances was the best arithmetician, though Cordelia was the best parser in school; and now, instead of assisting each other, they either applied to some other girl, or recited their lessons in each branch imperfectly. The kind teacher reasoned with both, but with no effect. She could not make Cordelia take back her words, nor could she make Frances say that she was sorry that the note had been written; so she concluded that she would let things take their course for a while, as continually bringing the quarrel into notice would make it more lasting, and then trust to chance and time to bring about a reconciliation; and, true enough, it all happened as she wished.

It was quite a rainy morning, one day, and very few of the scholars had come to school; but Frances and Cordelia were among those who were present. The rain and mud which had been brought in upon the scholars' feet had rendered the steps which led down stairs into the entry quite slippery; and as Cordelia was going down stairs, she slipped and fell, uttering a sharp cry of pain, for she had hurt her ankle very badly. Frances, who was sitting near the door, alone heard the cry, not knowing, however, that it was Cordelia who had fallen, and hastened to the assistance of the sufferer. When she saw who it was, she half turned back; but she could not long keep her resolution, for Cordelia gave her a beseeching look, as if to say, "I am in pain; do come!" and half forgetting their quarrel, she hastened towards her. "At any rate," thought she, "I can help her without saying one word, and I'll try very hard not to speak." She then raised Cordelia up and supported her to a seat; then she bathed her ankle in silence and rubbed it gently; and when she had done all that she knew how, still as mute as a statue, she rose to go, but Cordelia caught her hand and held it fast.

"Frances," she said, "speak to me! *Say something*, even if you say an unkind word; only do break this chilling silence!"

"I wonder you want *disagreeable* people to speak to you!" answered Frances, trying to draw herself away.

"Oh, you are *not* disagreeable!" sobbed Cordelia; "I was very, very wrong to say so! How gentle you have been — how patient with my sprained ankle! Oh, I will take back that word now, at once!"

Then Frances' eyes brightened, and she said, "And I will take back the words of my note most willingly."

And so, in the new-found pleasure of making up, in the recitation of a hundred little things which had happened to each since their estrangement, they almost **forgot school** and rose to go back again, Frances supporting Cordelia as she walked ; and as they entered the room, with their arms twined around each other, the scholars smiled with pleasure, **and** their teacher did not **blame them** for whispering a few kind words to each other, for she knew the sweet pleasure that she had had once in her own youth, of a *reconciliation* after a *school-girls' quarrel.*

THE WIND.

"Say, where are you going, where are you going,
      Fickle Wind?
What do you see when you're roaming about,
      And what find?"

"I go on the waves and I play with the sea
      And the foam ;
And I fill the white sheets of the glittering sails
      When I roam.

"Then I fly to the woods and I toy with the leaves
      On the trees ;
And I sing as I go — you have heard of the song,
      Of the breeze?

"Then I whistle a tune on the old house top
      When it rains,
And I shake like a rattle, with terrible din,
      The loose panes.

"And I sigh 'mid the flowers and bend their slight stems
      To the ground ;
Then quietly sinking to rest, in some cave
      I am found.

"Then I wake and touch softly your neat, shining hair
    Boy or girl,
And I lurk like a fairy among the bright rings
    Of each curl.

"I am fickle, I know, but remember, I now
    Promise this —
When the summer comes round I will cool *your* hot brow
    With a kiss."

THE BIRD THAT FLEW IN THROUGH THE WINDOW.
A MEMORY.

It left the woods, the quiet woods,
 Poor frightened little bird,
And the beating of its restless wings,
 Against the walls I heard,

I opened wide the windows all
 To aid its homeward flight,
And said, "poor bird, go to your home
 Before the coming night."

But the beating of its restless wings
 And the wild glance of its eye,
And the continual, troubled chirp,
 Was all the sad reply.

I was a child, my heart was full,
 I thought, "Why comes it here,
It flies as if pursued by foes,
 Oh, wherefore does it fear?"

We tried through casements opened
  wide,
 To drive it to its nest,
But still against the ceiling high,
 It flew in its unrest.

"And could you speak," I said with tears,
 "And tell the tale to me,
That brought you to these prison walls,
 Far from the woods to flee, —

"Would you but sing *one* joyous note,
 And change that suffering tone,
To say 'twas not unhappiness
 That brought you here alone?

"And let me smooth your ruffled wings
 And gently bid you go,
Then I might smile and welcome you,
 But ah, not now — not so!

"Suppose that I, dear little bird,
 By grief and anguish toss'd,
Were wandering through the dismal
  woods
 A child forlorn and lost;

"And that my father, mother dear,
 With sorrow deep and wild,
Were weeping for their truant one, —
 Their lonely, lonely child;

"Suppose that with the briers sharp,
   I tore my tender feet,
And that my aching head like yours,
   I 'gainst the hard trees beat,—

" Would **I not thank** the gentle hand
   That **set the captive** free ?
Oh, yes ; sweet little **bird, now go**
   And even thus thank *me***."**

But 'twas in vain ; **we could not reach**
   The tender suffering thing,
And through the long, long summer day,
   Its **piercing** cry did **ring.**

" O bird, O bird ! " I weeping said,
   " Was there no rest for you
Beside the deep stream's quiet flow,
   Or by the violet blue ?

" Was there no peace **upon the tree**
   Where stood your **downy nest,**
And did it not a **refuge give**
   To calm your throbbing breast ?

" Was not the whisper of the wind
   A melody **for you,**
As through **the tall pine's** rustling boughs
   With mournful sound it blew ? "

In thoughts like these, in childish thoughts,
   I questioned oft **the bird ;**
But still that melancholy **pipe**
   My saddest feeling stirred.

I held my little apron wide,
   To catch it should it fall,
And often tried to imitate
   The mother-bird's shrill call.

I brought a branch of fragrant green
   To tempt it to alight,
But ah ! vain my endeavors were,—
   It quickened still its flight,

Until at twilight's misty hour,
   When hopelessly I cried,
It fell unanswering at my feet
   And there in **silence died.**

THE BROKEN NECKLACE;

OR, THE FALSEHOOD.

I SHALL never forget Lilly **Manvers !** She was like a dream of beautiful girlhood. Her very name was **a spell** that awoke a thousand pleasant recollections in the hearts of her school-fellows. Her parents were poor, and when they looked on their child and saw the rich treasures of her mind daily opening under the influence **of** her instructors, **they** denied themselves even the comforts of life to perfect her education in the excellent school to which they had sent her, in order to make her a companion for them in their old age. They had commenced life with wealth, but the old story of a contested inheritance involved them in a lawsuit which promised a favorable issue; but when their hopes were about to be realized, the persons interested on the other side procured false witnesses, and they saw their whole property swept away. The law determined the affair against them; but the world in general, who had seen the transaction, was convinced of the justness of Dr. Manvers' claim, and his freedom from the cruel charge which was brought against him, — that of fraudulent attempts to retain the property which belonged not to him. Thus they were bereft of all but each other's society and that of their child, which solaced them for their broken dream of the past.

And Lilly? Her golden ringlets played about her head like a halo, and many a time have I smoothed their glossy brightness around my finger with a feeling of love which I thought could never fade away. There was a look of trust in her deep blue eyes, and an innocent expression in her child-like smile, which few could withstand. Oh, what great friends we were! People called us Night and Morning; for they said that my pale face and black hair, near her brilliant and aurora-like countenance, were a strange contrast; and as the years of childhood passed away, we, who were linked together by the sweet ties of friendship, wished that life might ever continue thus. I sigh when I think of the past, and I shudder when I reflect how one fault can make us unhappy forever; and I tell this tale of early sin, overcome though it may have been by years of penitence, more for its moral instruction than aught else. Yes, those blue eyes *deceived*, those bright lips *deceived*, that pure-seeming heart *deceived*.

I remember the day, as if it were but yesterday, when there first arose in my mind a doubt of her! I was sitting on the grass, weaving a garland of gay flowers for her hair, when I perceived her running towards me. Down she fell upon the smooth sward by me, and, half laughing and half crying, told me her joyous story.

"Carry," said she, throwing her **arms around me with an embrace** even more vehement than usual, "put down that wreath and hear me talk. **Do you hear?** We are so happy at home, **for** uncle has come, — far, far from distant lands! from the deserts of Ethiopia, maybe!" said she, laughing; "and he has brought, — Oh, so many beautiful things for his 'Lilly of the Valley,' as he calls **me**, that I am almost wild with joy! But he is very sad, for he has lost aunt Mary, and four dear children of his have died abroad. **He has so much need of love and comfort, that he wants me to be his own** Lilly till he dies."

The few tears which coursed **down Lilly's cheeks were soon** dried, and we hastened on to the house to see **the** beautiful presents. I think now, but I did not think then, that she seemed to be more **overjoyed** at the sight of the rich articles than at **the meek, subdued-looking** old man, who showed by his face and form that a storm of **grief had** passed over him. He gazed at her for a while in silence and tears, and then, with a sudden impulse, clasped **her to his** breast, murmuring some words about how they would **have** enjoyed the bright array of costly gifts. Lilly was scarcely happy in his heart-felt embrace, for she seemed too glad in her newly-acquired treasures to be interested in anything **else. She twisted a silver-**fringed scarf around her head, and tied a costly **shawl about her** waist with the air of an empress, and walked proudly to the mirror to behold her curious and gorgeous appearance. I thought that she had never appeared half so lovely before; but as I turned to the mirror, I perceived that the vanity was in earnest; and from the first vain act, unchecked, there arose a root of bitterness which made her girlhood, for a time, a blight, and her heart old. Her father and mother were looking the happiness they could not **find** words to express. It seemed as if their cup was suddenly running over with joy, for their broken-hearted brother was to find refuge and a home with them, and had brought with him luxuries and wealth for their beloved child.

The time arrived for my return home, and Lilly volunteered to walk half way back with me. As soon as we left the door-steps our talk commenced, and our hearts, *mine*, at least, opened.

"How delicious it must be to be rich!" said I, with a burst of girlish enthusiasm; "one could feed the hungry, clothe the poor, and do all kinds of pleasant things; and then how glad you have been made, Lilly, by your uncle's presents; but, seriously, do you think that if he had come poor and happy instead of wealthy and miserable, that your feelings would have been the same?"

"Pooh!" replied Lilly, with contempt; "certainly, certainly; but you are always asking strange questions, and giving old-fashioned lectures about right and about wrong, which would sound better in the pulpit than they do to me, your one hearer. I wish you would let such things alone."

"Then, my dear Lilly," continued I, unmindful of the interruption, and proceeding with my sermon, as she thought it, "you must take this singular good fortune as a gift from God, and reflect that you have the means in your power of making your poor uncle once more smile happily, and by your kind attentions to him enable him to forget his own sorrows. It would be a noble work," said I, warming up, and feeling all the romance of such an undertaking.

"I will do all I can," interrupted Lilly; "and now let us talk about the party."

At that word *party*, my own thoughts wandered far away from the solemn old man. Yes! I was going to give a party on my fourteenth birthday; and we were to have dancing and tableaux, and fun and frolic, and good things. The prospect seemed to us like enchantment; and we talked of what we were to wear, and whom we were to invite, until we parted, and then we each thought silently of it until we reached home.

As time progressed, a pleasant intercourse arose between Lilly and her uncle. He was so gentle and affectionate, and she so grateful to him for his kindness, that not a doubt had as yet arisen between them to mar its brightness. I had been perfect in my lessons at school for one month before my birthday, and the time was really set for the promised party. Fifty of my friends had been invited, and my heart fairly danced with pleasure at the prospect. We were talking of it, Lilly and I, and the world did not contain two happier beings. "In the eastern scene, in one tableau," said I to Lilly, "what shall we do for jewels? Mamma has two breastpins that you shall have, but they would not look very queenly all alone; however, flowers will do as well, and the idea will be very pretty."

"Flowers!" answered Lilly, scornfully; "do you think that I, reclining on my damask couch, with an embroidered dress and a gold lace veil, would be content with flowers? No, indeed! jewels I *must* have." Now, the picture that was before us was from an old annual, and it represented a Persian scene of singular beauty and interest. A lovely young girl was half reclining, and playing with an open box of jewels, and a glittering chain was carelessly thrown about her neck, while her attendant, whom I was to represent, was looking with wonder at their richness and costliness; and a guitar, upon which she had been playing to amuse the fair young creature, lay unnoticed upon her knee. This picture pleased our fancy, and we selected it from a hundred others, as most worthy of our genius. The golden curls of the young Sultana attracted Lilly, as being like hers; and perhaps, in *my* vanity, I traced some resemblance in the dark eyes and glossy hair of the attendant maiden to my own. "Yes, flowers *will* do," said I to Lilly's scornful reply; "I can get a beautiful bunch of exotics for you, and maybe our audience will prefer them to jewels." Lilly mused for an instant, and shook her head. I knew her determined spirit, but I feared no evil from that passing cloud. She talked awhile to herself, and I heard her say these words, "Mrs. Meredith and Smith the jeweller." But I did not think that they had any connection with the subject, and I thought of them no more. The next day I was with her in her little room. Her uncle's care had fitted it up for her in a neat and appropriate manner. Pretty pictures hung against the walls, and the white quilt and curtains were as pure as her own soul should have been. A portrait of her uncle, too, looked at her with its loving eyes, just above her writing-table, where, like all girls of her age, she had fancied herself a poetess, and scribbled sonnets to the moon, and letters to dozens of imaginary friends. There was a quiet tap at the door, and her uncle, with his slow and solemn step, walked in and took a seat near me, while Lilly sprang upon his knees. Something very like a smile played over his face, and there was a peculiar beauty in it, for I had never seen him smile before; and then Lilly said, coaxingly, "Uncle, I have a favor to ask of you; and you cannot, must not say no to your little 'Lily of the Valley,' even if your other pet, Carry, says flowers will do."

"What is it, my child?" replied he, as he parted her fair ringlets and looked into her pleading face.

"Well, you know," she began, — and she made an urgent case about the jewels, and convinced herself, at least, that she could not do without them.

"I have jewels," murmured Mr. Milward, "but they belonged to her whom the cold grave covers; perhaps it is a weakness in me not to let the dear child have them, but the sight of them would quite unman me; and ah, no, it cannot be quite yet! No, Lilly," said he, aloud, "it must be just as Carry thinks; the flowers will do as well."

A shade of disappointment passed over Lilly's face, and she commenced to plead afresh; but the anguish which her uncle appeared to feel, and his abrupt departure from the room, assured her that she had no hope of having her wishes gratified by him.

The night of my party was a lovely one. The full moon watched the more active portion of the young people romping upon the lawn, and the bright glare of lamplight within revealed us at more quiet games. In spite of the sad memories of that evening, I look back to it with some kind of pleasure, for so many hearts were happy and amused. And Lilly, in our youthful circle, was the most loved, the most admired. There was a strange excitement in her eyes, and the flush upon her face increased her natural beauty. At one time she was among the dancers, excelling them all; and at another, she left the young to say a word to the old people, as she called them, who had been invited to witness our pleasure. We had in vain urged her uncle and Mr. and Mrs. Manvers to join us on that evening. The grief of the former was too deeply seated to enjoy such gayety, and the latter preferred remaining at home with him. All watched Lilly's graceful movements, and blessed her angel-like countenance. I remember one interesting scene, which I cannot pass by without recording.

Twelve of our party had gathered round a table to look at some prints, when an old gentleman who was present offered a reward of a beautiful box of *bon-bons* for the best poetical address to the moon, not to exceed eight lines, and to be produced in ten minutes. Some of our attempts were very queer. One ran thus:—

> " The moon in heaven, which shines so bright,
> Does nothing at all but blind my sight.".

That certainly would not answer; another made moon and town rhyme, but it was against all rules of rhythm; and one gallant youth, with upturned eyes and expanded arms, eloquently exclaimed:—

> " Oh, Moon, you are the only she
> That does inconstant and fickle be!"

Even I, with my sober, unromantic ideas, attempted something, so great was my desire for the promised prize, and I also signally failed; but Lilly, as usual, triumphed; and after ten minutes she arose, calm as the moon itself, and led us all to the balcony, where, with her blue eyes raised, and with a touching sweetness which is past description, she recited the following original lines: —

> " Look down, O gentle Moon, with tender love !
> Stoop from the azure skies so clear above,
> And watch our joy this night ;
> Upon each grateful heart, Oh, do thou shine ;
> Shed in our hearts thine influence divine,
> And we will bless thy light."

"Two more lines!" we all shouted ; and she, with a smile in her eyes, said, mischievously, still looking upward to the "Queen of Night," —

> " To tell the *truth*, I want the offered sweets,
> And so I lay my verses at thy feet."

The laugh which followed this address was long and loud, and Lilly shared the *bon-bons* among all the aspirants. I must say that I watched Lilly with a kind of uneasiness. She seemed almost demented in her manner, — at one time so composed, and at another so flighty and incomprehensible. I tried to talk with her alone, but she slid from me, and joined some group of which she became the life and light. The evening really seemed too short for us ; and after supper, when mamma beckoned to me to call the tableaux actors, I felt as if the last of the pageant was about to be performed, and after that there would be silence and darkness. The lights were all adjusted, and the show began. First, there was a village scene, and the boys, with large straw hats, rakes, and scythes, looked very picturesque. Then Flora, the goddess of flowers, appeared, personated by a young girl, whom Flora herself would not have disdained to acknowledge. The boys were bashful, and only a few would perform; but we had sailors and soldiers enough. Then came a sweet scene of Little Red Riding-Hood, which made all the people laugh, for a mischievous boy crept in behind the frame, on "all fours," and said that he came to inform "his friends and the public that *he* was the wolf," and he growled like a veritable inhabitant of the woods. But the grand closing scene was the "young Sultana." Lilly and I had dressed in separate apartments; and, as I had completed my toilet first, mamma, with approbation in her looks, told me to place myself within the frame before the curtain was raised, in the attitude which I was expected to assume. I was habited in a dress of pure white muslin, with flowing sleeves; on each arm I had a plain band of gold paper as bracelets; while on my head, in contrast to my dark hair, was placed a white turban, with a single gold star in front. My trousers, too, were confined with anklets of gold, and my satin slippers just peeped from beneath their ample fold. As I looked up, after I had taken my kneeling posture, with the guitar clasped tightly in one hand, I knew, by mamma's quiet "bravo!" that so far all was right. Lilly had delayed her toilet longer, I thought, than was necessary; but at last I distinguished her approaching footstep, and I heard her distinctly say to the attendant, "One instant after I take my seat, and without any signal from me, lift the curtain." She entered, and the whole scene seemed to me to be enchanted. I looked at her, and the very sentiment which I was required to express by my looks, was stamped upon my features. She raised her jewelled finger to her lips, with a stern glance at me, which I could not resist, and I felt that she demanded silence. Gliding past me, she threw herself into the most graceful attitude imaginable, half lifted an exquisite string of pearls from a small jewel box, and the curtain rose slowly. I know not which of us excited most the admiration of the spectators, — I, with my true expression of wonder, or Lilly, who reclined there, queen-like in her royal beauty. Her dress, which her mother had prepared for her with all a mother's pride, was precisely what it should have been. The embroidered slippers in which her small bare feet were encased, the full satin trousers, and the unique head-dress, with the gold-spangled veil which floated over one shoulder, were in keeping with the original picture. Her long golden curls shaded her rosy cheeks, and her drooping eyelashes curtained her half shut eyes. I saw them all, and I saw the jewels which she had obtained. A large diamond gleamed from her tiara like the eye of a serpent; her slight fingers were covered with rings which she had borrowed from her young companions; and a golden chain glittered around her neck, and that exquisite necklace of pearls which she held so loosely in her grasp, where could they have come from? thought I. There had been no applause heretofore, for mamma had rather checked than encouraged any demonstrations of the kind; but now, after a short silence, I was stunned and frightened by the noise and exclamations of delight, and I could endure the strange dream no longer. I made the signal agreed upon, although Lilly looked as though she could have remained motionless forever, and the curtain dropped. We were loudly called upon to reappear, *but I could not;* and in endeavoring to draw aside the green baize at the back of the apparatus, I believe I felt faint, for I caught too suddenly; and a lamp which was placed insecurely on a side stand came down with a crash, and in a minute, cries of fire and tones of terror sounded on my ears. The light drapery was in flames, but by great exertions it was soon extinguished; and Lilly and I, half crushed by the crowd, found ourselves in the piazza, with the cold, unconscious moon looking down calmly upon us. I grasped Lilly's hand, and heard myself say, but with a voice that sounded nothing like my own, "Where did you get those — " I could not finish the sentence; for, with a cry of anguish, she bounded from me, exclaiming, "I am ruined and undone!"

The company departed with regret at the sad ending of so pleasant an evening; and Lilly went home, under the care of a faithful servant, in her uncle's little carriage. As she came to bid us good night, the diamond, which appeared to be set in a ring, gleamed fiercely in her crushed tiara, and her hand still held the jewel-box; but the pearls had been trampled on, and she could only gather up a few from among the confusion which the fire had caused.

"It is a great pity, dear," said mamma, in her sympathizing tone, "that your beautiful pearls are lost; but I suppose that they were your uncle's; and his love for you will forgive you anything. Are they *not* your uncle's?" she continued, as Lilly did not appear to hear her.

I saw her face turn scarlet; and when at last she replied, with an effort, "Yes, they are uncle's," I felt that she had uttered a lie; but I could not then speak what was passing in my breast; and kissing her coldly, I told her that I would endeavor to find the rest of the pearls and bring them to her.

I was detained longer than I had expected, the next day, at home, and did not arrive at Mr. Manver's house until an hour before their dinner time. Her mother pressed me to stay; and, independent of the love I bore them all, I wished to see the end, if end there was, to the mystery of the pearl necklace. I waited until I was alone with Lilly before I dared venture to present her with the loose pearls I had collected, and she received them with a trembling hand, but offered no explanation. We talked over and over again the incidents of the past evening to amuse her parents and uncle; but, by a kind of mutual, tacit consent, we avoided mentioning one word about the jewels. The day was very long and miserable to me, for I read Lilly's face, and could see the effort she made to appear gay and happy in the home circle. She was cold and reserved to me; but I forgave her for that, as I did not yet see clearly the nature of her struggles. It was towards sunset, and we were sitting by an open window facing the street. The sun cast a yellow glare over the buildings, and faded in the distance to a pale straw color, inspiring that indescribable sensation of peace which the coming on of autumn occasionally brings, and which the youngest child sometimes feels. We were conversing cheerfully when we were interrupted by the sound of a heavy carriage, and a gorgeous equipage wheeled up to the door, while a lady, superbly dressed, alighted from it. She scarcely awaited the announcement of her name, but walked in. She was very beautiful, but there was a look of pride and insincerity about her which I did not like. I had never seen her there before, and I watched her intently. She bowed gracefully to the two gentlemen, looked at me with a well-bred inclination of the head; and when I turned to see how Lilly regarded her, I perceived that the place she had occupied by my side was vacant. She must have departed from the room as the lady had entered it. This lady, then, on whom my eyes were turned by a kind of fascination, approached Mrs. Manvers, and, with charming courtesy, said, "At last, Mary, you have descended from your stern reserve, and you are sorry that you ever separated yourself from my friendship. You cannot forget the love of our early years, and the pleasures we have shared together. I am glad to see that you seek me once more. We have each of us a great deal to forget and forgive."

"Madam," returned Mr. Manvers, before his wife could utter one word, "if a thousand years should pass over our heads and you still stood there asking me in those winning tones if I had forgotten the past, I should say, never! I have forgiven you as I hope to be forgiven for my own sins; but I cannot forget that you procured false witnesses against me in that fearful hour which accused me of fraud, an accusation, which has blackened my innocent and spotless name and robbed my very life of its sweetness. The *world* I know acknowledges me to be *not guilty*, for your accursed plot extended not beyond the so-called "administrators of justice.' For the loss of property I care comparatively little, and I had rather be here as I am now, conscious of my own integrity, than raised like you upon the pinnacle of earthly riches which are not your own, and which have been obtained by the ruin of another."

A strange and subtle smile covered the lady's face as she answered: —

"You care not for my countenance, — my riches, — why then did you send your daughter with soft words, and with her face of perfect beauty, to charm me while she asked the loan of a few paltry jewels for a child's pageant. On her forehead glistened my diamond, and round her white, and pure, and youthful neck, coiled a golden chain which has been often wound round mine."

"Just heaven!" said the father, "can this be so? If you are honest, madame, you came but to insult us; if what you say of my daughter be untrue, there should be a greater distance between us than ever."

The lady deigned no reply, but scornfully sweeping by us re-entered her carriage. I, at least, felt that her tale was correct, and that Lilly was on the brink of an abyss, into which she must certainly fall, and my breath seemed to leave me as she entered the room at the summons of her father.

"My dear child," said he mildly," you have been accused of an action which your trembling mother, there, and I, consider in the light of a sin against us. Did you borrow Mrs. Meredith's jewelry, so that you might glitter with splendor in the show of last night?"

She could not say "no," for she knew not how much might have been revealed; but her head fell heavily upon her breast, and her father knew that it had been so. He did not chide her for her fault, but he inquired sternly into all the particulars, asked if the jewels had been returned, and receiving an answer in the affirmative, bowed his head upon the table and wept. Mrs. Manvers stood motionless with surprise and mortification, while the uncle opened his arms to his adopted child, trusting her even against hope, and finding some excuse for her, even when her guilt was beyond a doubt. Soon there was a knock at the door and a note was handed to Mr. Milward. Oh, what varied tidings do these " white winged messengers " bring! At one time joy and happiness, at another prostration of hopes and eternal misery. The wretched father and mother had left the room to commune with each other upon the conduct of their child. After all, they could only accuse her of the sin of disobedience which might be atoned for by after acts. It was a hard struggle, though, to think kindly of her, for she knew that a ban had been laid upon any intercourse with Mrs. Meredith, and she knew, also, what had estranged her parents from so designing an individual.

Mr. Milward glanced at the signature of the note with an indifferent air as if he cared not to disturb the beloved child; and he called me to him, and bade me go to the light which had just been brought in, and read that troublesome business letter for him.

" Dear sir," I began : " Excuse the liberty I am taking this evening, but I would esteem it a great favor if you would return the set of pearls —." I stopped short, for I would not read anything which I thought would condemn Lilly. Poor thing, as I looked, she slid from her uncle's arms to the floor and seemed the personification of despair. " Go on, go on," said Mr. Milward, " there is some strange mystery in this ; the man is mad. I know nothing of his pearls," and he attempted to raise Lilly once more to his arms. " If you would return the set of pearls," continued I, " as I have the prospect of a sale for them. Again I request you to excuse this liberty.

"I remain, dear sir, your obedient servant,

"J. SMITH."

Now then, thought I, and before the affair had become public, it was the time for Lilly to come forward and explain. If the beads had been perfect as she had at first received them, no doubt they would have been returned in the morning ; but mutilated as they were she felt as if she must have a day for thought, and therefore, she put off until the latest moment any plan which might have occurred to her. What she most dreaded was the enormous sum for which she knew she was responsible. I came to all these conclusions in less time than I have taken to write them; indeed, on that evening, I appeared to be endowed with the judgment and foresight of a woman. Mr. Milward called for his desk and sat down to answer the fatal letter. I was so excited that I leaned over his chair unconsciously and watched his hand which guided the pen. He wrote the word "Sir," then stopped as if uncertain what to say. His brow became wrinkled and his hand clenched with passion. I turned for a moment to look at Lilly. Let me take her picture for you. She was on the floor as he had left her, thinking, in his innocence, that she was mourning for the grief that she had occasioned her father and mother by her conduct towards Mrs. Meredith, and he was not unwilling to see her penitent for that. She was sitting in a drooping posture with her face buried in her hands, and her long curls hanging over her. I touched her gently and said to her, in a whisper, "Lilly, if you have anything to say, now is the time." Look there, continued I, pointing to her uncle. Her eyes were instantly turned towards him. She arose and leaned over him as he wrote. As he signed his name to the indignant reply, she laid her hand on his shoulder and said in a tone I shall never forget, for every syllable trembled ere she could utter it: "Stop! uncle, it was *I* who borrowed them."

"Just heaven!" ejaculated the old man, "Has the whole world forsaken me? Explain quickly, Lilly, or I believe that I shall lose my senses."

I knew by her agonized look that she was true *then*, that each word she uttered was sincere.

"It is strange even to myself," said she in a hollow tone, "how I became what I now am. I feel miserably guilty. I have felt so for some time, and yet I could not withstand the intense desire which possessed me of rivalling every one at Carry's birthday party. I did not listen to your advice and hers to supply the place of jewels with flowers, but remembering that I had seen Mrs. Meredith with exquisite jewelry, I thought that I might borrow them for one night only. She seemed rejoiced to see me, embraced me, and told me it was one of the happiest days of her life for a daughter of the proud Mr. Manvers to ask a favor of her. Had she not come to-day with her insulting proffers of friendship, my fault *there* would have been forever unknown, for I knew there was no intercourse between our families. As to *these*," she said, in the same tone, and she drew the jewel box from her pocket, and opened it before her uncle, " the sin was blacker *here*. I went in your name as I knew that it could obtain anything in this city, and borrowed them for you as I said to see the new style of pearl setting, and that also would have remained undiscovered had not the *fortunate* or *unfortunate* event of the fire taken place. What I can do I know not, for the sum I am afraid is more than I can ever repay ; but so much for vanity, and pride and ambition." She smiled as she ended, and I thought her quite hardened. She asked nobody to pardon her, but putting her hand to her head, she said, " I feel strangely dizzy and I want to lie down."

Mr. Milward tore the note he had written into fragments, and mused for a moment gloomily ; then coming forward, he took her gently in his arms and bore her to her little white-curtained room, while I followed. We heard her uncle's receding steps, and he went down stairs, out of the street door, until the sound died away on the pavements. I helped to undress Lilly. Neither of us said one word ; but as she was stepping into bed, I said, " Lilly, let us pray." We both knelt down, and I repeated the Lord's prayer audibly. As she sank down upon the pillow, she said to me, softly, " I am cold and frightened! call mamma." Her mother came, and for a week she did not leave that bedside, for the life of her child was suspended on a mere thread, which was kept unbroken only by the grace of God and the kind attentions of those around her. I never saw such devotion as that poor uncle exhibited. He had witnessed the death of five loved ones; and when the physician said that there was hope for Lilly, he felt as if there was still some happiness in store for him. It was an exciting morning, that one on which she regained her consciousness. Her bright hair had all been shorn, and the marks of the blisters which had been applied to her forehead and temples gave a peculiar expression to her countenance. Her mother was kneeling by the bedside, her father looking from the window with an abstracted air. Her uncle, with her hand in his, was sitting upon the bed, watching every breath that she drew, and I, who had been so much with her in sickness as well as health, was weeping by her side. Each tick of the watch was distinctly heard, and the beating of our hearts was almost audible. And there lay this child of many hopes, as silent and motionless, almost, as death itself. Suddenly she opened her blue eyes and gazed at her uncle. She shuddered as she looked, and turned her head upon the pillow, as if she was fatigued; but she seemed to gather strength, and said, in a whisper, the word, "Mamma." Her mother took her hand, afraid, by a word, to break the blissful dream. "And papa," she said, raising her head upon the pillow. And he came forward and joined the group so softly that you could not hear his step. I could not help it, and I burst into a flood of tears. She looked at me and smiled. She tried to say something, but we shook our heads, afraid to trust her to speak, she was so weak and languid. But she persisted. "Only this," said she, in a whisper, while we bent forward to catch her slightest accent.

"I wish the forgiveness of each and all; and I will try, if I should recover, never to sin again."

This was more than enough for us. We kissed her pale cheek with many loving words, and then she slept sweetly.

After a while Lilly moved among us again, but changed in character and in actions. The events which had occasioned so much sad feeling in our little circle had been blessed indeed to her; and if there was a being on earth who practised strict rectitude of life, it was she. Many a wholesome lesson have I, who in times past had been the preacher, received from her. Her uncle defrayed without a murmur the bill at the jeweller's, and no one but her family and ours ever knew of the occurrence. The jewel case lies in a drawer, to which she daily repairs; and she rather courts than shuns the memory of the Untruth and the Broken Necklace.

TURN AWAY.

From companions bad and rude,
Who upon you will intrude,
   Turn away.

From profane and wicked word,
Which by your ears should not be heard,
   Turn away.

From any act you know is wrong,
And to the pure should not belong,
   Turn away.

From temptations each and all
Which from the right might make you fall
   Turn away.

From Sabbath breakers' sinful ways,
Who would profane those holy days,
   Turn away.

From deeds that God will not approve,
Nor sanction with his seal of love,
   Turn away.

THE FALL FROM THE SWING.

A TRUE STORY.

"I SHALL never, no, *never* forget it!" said the gentleman.

"Can you tell me about it?" said my mother, in her gentle, sympathizing tone.

"Yes; draw nearer."

I had been sewing very busily before these words were uttered, not interested in what my mother and her guest were conversing about. I merely heard the murmur of their voices, but that did not disturb my quiet, and I turned over in my mind my past, present, and future plans, scarcely conscious that any one was in the room but myself; but these words uttered by the gentleman were so emphatic that I almost thought that his invitation was for me to draw near too; and I laid aside my work, and listened to the following thrilling story.

"Francis Walpole and I were friends in our childhood, *friends* in the widest sense of a school-boy's interpretation of that sacred word, and we were neighbors in the broad and beautiful country where there were no bounds to our pleasures and no city restraints in our rambles. It seemed as if I could not love and prize him enough; and I sought for no other companionship, and cared for no other ear in which to whisper my triumphs, failures, or wrongs. His arm and his advice were always at my service; and many a hard blow did he gain for defending my cause, right or wrong. I love to dwell upon his refined and manly beauty, his strangely powerful strength of muscle, his determination when he felt that his cause was just; and few were the boys, even older than he, who feared not to feel a blow that he could give, either in jest or in earnest. I said that we were neighbors in the country; but besides our family and his, two others lived near us on terms of great intimacy. The grounds of each house met in a kind of court-yard, with no inhospitable fences to intervene; and we made a play-ground of this large space, and had ample room to indulge in the usual sports of boys, such as cricket, leap-frog, marbles, and kites; while the girls chose the more feminine diversions of battledoor, ball, and the skipping-rope. But whatever were our separate sports, we met on common ground in a swing, which Mr. Walpole, who was a kind and indulgent father, had erected for his son. Nothing was more fascinating. It consisted of two very high, upright posts, with a cross-piece on the top, from which the rope was suspended. The swing held two children easily, and we seldom paid a visit to the upper regions alone. Sometimes we rough boys mounted the air-car together, wild with joy and frolic; or at other times we would give the ropes a gentle impulse, while sweet Annie Morris floated to and fro, only wanting wings, in our imaginations, to resemble a flying angel; and sometimes, to our shame be it spoken, we twisted the rope while wild Bet Dayton was held prisoner, and released it on a concerted signal, while it carried the unfortunate girl whirling round and round, till she grew weary of asking mercy at our hands, or until we had obtained a promise from her, which she never afterwards kept, of playing upon us no more practical jokes. Oh, merry times did that old swing see; but, alas! it saw a sad scene too. One afternoon, a party of six girls and boys were gathered around it, ready to take their turn in our air-car, as we called it. Each selected his or her companion for the voyage. Annie Morris chose Dick White, for she knew that he, like herself, did not like to swing very high; and wild Bet Dayton found a corresponding spirit in Tom Stephens, who boasted that he could throw a ball so nicely upward that he could catch it in the next forward motion before it could fall to the ground. We had often heard of, but never seen, this wonderful feat; however, we did not for an instant doubt Tom's word. As usual, Frank and I, with arms interlaced, awaited our turn together. It was a delicious afternoon; the skies were glowing with the red rays of the departing sun, and the air was full of fragrance. From the open windows of the four neighbors' houses a friendly face was occasionally seen, or a mother or sister would smile upon our sport."

Here the gentleman paused suddenly, and covered his face with his hand, and sighed so deeply, that I thought that the action and the sigh were an earnest of something very sad that he was going to relate, and so it proved.

"At length our turn came. 'We can beat them all,' said Frank, with a loud, ringing laugh. 'Hallo! John, what do you say to trying to touch one of those low, white clouds which come so temptingly near us?' 'With all my heart,' replied I; 'nothing venture, nothing have; push, you lazy fellows! all's ready,—one, two, three; we're off!' and with the united efforts of the two other boys we soon attained a respectable height, and felt as happy as birds in the air. Higher and higher we swung, higher than we had ever ventured before. The boys below seemed like dwarfs to our eyes, and the girls' white dresses like fairy robes.

"'Is not this almost too high?' said I to Frank, tremblingly, for I felt a sensation of dizziness as I looked below.

"'Too high!' exclaimed Frank, who, I believe, never feared anything; 'too high, you coward! *No!* I tell you we could not be too near the skies, if we followed the flight of that swallow yonder.'

"Upward and upward, higher and higher, nearer the swallow we soared. We heard our companions below screaming to us to stop, and we saw from the windows of the neighbors' houses handkerchiefs waving, which we always understood as a signal to return home; and Frank, who was always thoughtful of the feelings of others, and obedient to his parents' slightest wish, stopped his exertions to keep the swing going, intending to let the motion 'die away' gradually.

"'Let us give the setting sun three cheers!' said he, 'before he leaves us'; and holding out both his hands, and waving them above his head (for he depended upon being balanced by his feet), he gave one ringing shout, gushing out from the very fulness of a happy heart, lost his equilibrium, and fell down, down, down, helpless to the earth."

The gentleman shivered here as if he were cold, and again covered up his eyes, and drew nearer to the fire. Mother made a motion for him to proceed, and at last he said, —

"There he remained, and there I beheld him, as each forward and backward motion of the swing brought me nearer to the ground. I was helpless myself, and I dared not spring out, for two reasons. One was, that I thought that I might crush him, for I could not calculate my distance; and the other was, that just after his fall the swing was too great a distance from the earth for me to have attempted it. The children screamed, and made several ineffectual attempts to draw him out; but the continued vibration of the pendulum-like swing prevented their touching him, as he was immediately under the path which it described. At length his mother came with a crowd of friends, and I, freed from my unhappy position, looked on frightened and with tearful eyes.

"His mother! Merciful heaven! shall I ever forget her strange expression, as she looked for some signs of blood, some bruise, to tell her where the injury was, and in vain? or will her idiotic stare, and her continued, ever-continued screams, forever come up to my mind, curdling my blood in my veins, and making a trembler of me even now?

"All was tried on the spot that kindness could suggest, to bring him back to life and to us, but with no effect. A messenger was instantly despatched to the nearest town, where his father pursued his business, and for a physician, although we felt that the aid of the latter would be useless.

"Mrs. Walpole was slight and delicate, but she took the body in her arms, and scarcely staggered beneath its heavy weight, and on she went, accepting no offers of assistance from the busy neighbors, until she laid him on a couch in her own room, and then sinking down by his side, with her strength overtasked, she fainted. Every one who wished came in to look at the lovely boy, beautiful beyond description. His long, dark eyelashes, the longest I ever saw, swept his pale cheeks; and his lips, so brilliant once, now, indeed, still smiling; but it was the smile of carved marble. Every restorative that we could think of was tried again and again, but the hand slid lifelessly from our loving grasp, and the heart-beats seemed hushed forever. The town of —— was several miles distant, and it would be some hours before we could hope for the arrival of Mr. Walpole and the physician. The ladies gathered round, and measured the white shroud which was to cover my beloved friend. Mrs. Walpole looked on unresisting, and saw them close his white eyelids more securely, and press together his smiling lips; but as they were about to clothe him in the accustomed robe of death, she stayed their hands, and whispered, hoarsely, —

"'Only let his father see him as he is, — so life-like, so beautiful! Array him not yet in the garments of the grave! A shroud! My Francis in a *shroud!* Oh, no! My God, it cannot be! Let *me* die, rather!'

"Her wish was granted; for her husband, many miles in advance of the physician, rushed into the room, and beheld the boy whom he had left in the early morning with a parting blessing on his beloved head, now stretched out, with no smile to greet him and no welcome in his voice. What cared he for the light of the sun, or the moon, or the stars, now that the light of his life had departed? He only felt that his boy was claimed by a new parent — Death!

"The physician came at last; but no encouraging smile was upon his benevolent countenance as he felt the boy's pulse, and while we all watched him, hopeful even in our despair, he pushed the thick curls from his white brow, and pressed his fingers upon the pulseless temples of our idol; he felt his heart, the seat of life, but at each action a greater cloud of disappointment shaded his face.

"'At any rate,' said he, with a mournful, sympathizing smile, 'we will leave no means untried, and we will see if the blood is entirely stagnated.'

"We all gathered round, wondering that the use of the lancet had not occurred to us before, and blamed each other for the omission; but as is often the case in great danger, we had neglected the only means that could have restored consciousness, had there been life there. We took a fresh gleam of hope from the proceeding. Each heart seemed beating with a redoubled impetus "

The gentleman stopped again here, and smiled as if communing with himself, but I did not like the interruption, for I felt as *I* were standing by the insensible child awaiting the issue, and I impatiently exclaimed, "Well?"

He recollected himself and continued. "The lancet did its work surely, nobly. No blood flowed for some time, but at length a drop slowly oozed from the puncture, and another, and another, until at last it came as freely as we could desire, and then a slight tinge of pink colored those silent lips, and a soft sigh came from his breast, as audible to us, though, as if it had been a trumpet's blast. There was life, there was hope. The physician motioned us to be quiet; the mother suppressed her screams of joy, while the father wept silently, bewildered by this sudden transition from agony to bliss; and we, who stood around, simultaneously bent our knees in silent prayer, each offering a petition to the Giver of all good, to continue the life which hung suspended there. And the prayer was granted. For three days my friend, who was the object of so many prayers, was unconscious of all that was passing around; but, on the fourth, his eyes opened calmly upon earth's scenes, and before long he was enabled to engage once more in the duties and pleasures that belong to earth. Whether in that long trance of unconsciousness his soul journeyed to the **land of pure spirits and there learned lessons of beauty and** goodness, I know not ; **nor can** he fathom that parting of **the** spirit from the body ; but this I do know, that since that awakening hour the steps **of my friend** have been onward and heavenward, trying to lead other souls into **the land of pure spirits and endeavoring to reach, by the holiness of his life** *here*, **the perfect rest hereafter."**

WHITHER.

WHITHER are you going, little birdie so bright,
Why fly you so fast from that tree ?
Said the bird, don't you know I am going **to my nest**
All my pretty young nestlings **to see** ?

Whither are you going, little fish in that stream,
'Neath yon smooth, shining, silvery **wave** ?
Said the fish, I am seeking a safe resting place
In some darksome and coral-lined cave.

Whither are you going, you brown autumn leaf,
Can't you stop and not hasten away ?
Said the leaf, I am seeking a still, sheltered nook,
Where in quiet my form I may lay.

Whither **are you** going, with your buzz and **your hum** ;
Say where **are** you going, little bee ?
Said the bee, some sweet honey I seek for my hive
In each pretty bright flower I see.

Whither are you going, little lamb in **that field,**
With your plaintive and tremulous bleat ?
Oh, I go, said the lamb, where the soft dew is fresh
And to crop the green herbage so sweet.

And where **are** *you* going, with your sleepy blue eyes,
Little girl, as you hasten along ?
Oh, mother waits for me to rock me, she said,
On her breast, fast to sleep, with a song.

DAY AND NIGHT.

THEIR QUARREL AND RECONCILIATION.

By my window I stood on a soft autumn even,
While the last blush of sunlight red tinted the heaven,
When the breeze, blowing softly, the restless leaves stirred,
And the faint pipe of birdlings around me was heard.

"How sweet," said I, gently, "this meeting of Day
And the first star of Night, with its tremulous ray,
While the sun calmly sinks from his throne in the skies,
As if leaving a blessing behind as he dies.

"Can any one tell which we ought to love best —
The Day when we labor, or Night when we rest?
The Day for glad meetings and pleasure and play,
The Night for the slumber which follows the Day?"

I started, for lo! from a crimson-fringed cloud,
A voice sounded sternly, impatient, and loud;
I looked, and a giant, whose face was the sun,
Outspoke as if I some great evil had done.

Oh, I do assure you, his eyes bright and bold
Were flashing all colors, from ebon to gold,
His arms seemed extended to crush my slight form,
And the frown on his brow was a menacing storm.

"How dare you, frail mortal, compare *me* with Night,
That babe, that mere insect with power and might?
I light man to labor, I give him his bread,
I quicken the seed in its cold, darksome bed.

"I color the flowers with delicate dyes,
With a brush that I dip in my own glowing skies,
The rainbow I paint and all rich fruitage send —
Oh! which of us, then, is of mortals the friend?

"I relieve the night watcher, all weary and worn,
I gladden the hearts of the cold and forlorn,
I give—" but he slowly sank down in the west,
And left **me all** trembling to finish the rest.

But, as **I was** thinking 'twas *really* the **sun**
Who all that was good on the wide earth had done,
Another voice came from the far-away east,
So sweet, that it frightened me not in the least.

A maiden I saw, oh, so pale and so fair,
That I thought her frail beauty would die in **the air**;
A silver light shone from her deep, **tender** eyes,
And she gracefully moved as a bird when it flies.*

"I come," said she, quickly, "as Queen of the **Night**,
Forever yon proud and bold upstart to blight;
Can you doubt, for one instant, *my* might and *my* **power**
To shed cooling dew on the sun-withered flower?

"**Who** brings quiet sleep **to** the work-tired frame,
When in anguish men call on my powerful name?
Who whispers blest dreams, gives sweet converse and rest,
If not I, who am ever a thrice-welcome guest?

"Rash being! **at** least, **when** the question you asked,
If your memory had for one instant been tasked,
I should think that your gratitude, small though it be,
Would have led **you to** choose, as the best of gifts, *me*."

"**I'm convinced,**" said I, frightened, "**that there is *no* choice**
'Twixt the Day and the Night,"—I assure you my voice
Issued hoarsely and trembling—"oh, *equal* are you,
Brilliant sun, lovely moon, in your power, 'tis true."

Then glad was **I** wisdom was lent me **that night**,
To lead me to answer these fearful foes right;
It was all that they wanted; I saw by her face,
As she drew her robe round her and quickened her pace.

"I am late," she said, softly, and went on her way,
"But see, there's once more that bold ruler of Day."
Sure enough, he peeped o'er the horizon once more,
And a smile lit his face far more bright than before.

And his voice, not now thunder but softened, uprose,
And his gaze flushed her face like a bud ere it blows.
"Peace," he said; "peace," she echoed;—all tumult was hushed,
And to tell the strange tale all the meteors rushed.

Then I, brooding solemnly over the same,
To my desk and my pen and ink, hastily came,
To tell this sky-news to earth's denizens, too,
And I hope, little reader, to interest you.

www.ingramcontent.com/pod-product-compliance
Lightning Source LLC
Chambersburg PA
CBHW030810230426
43667CB00008B/1153